Health Psychology

D1610534

The PsychologyExpress series

'All of the revision material I need in one place – a must for psychology undergrads.'
Andrea Franklin, Psychology student at Anglia Ruskin University

'Very useful, straight to the point and provides guidance to the student, while helping them to develop independent learning.'
Lindsay Pitcher, Psychology student at Anglia Ruskin University

'Engaging, interesting, comprehensive ... it helps to guide understanding and boosts confidence.'
Megan Munro, Forensic Psychology student at Leeds Trinity University College

'Very useful ... bridges the gap between Statistics textbooks and Statistics workbooks.'
Chris Lynch, Psychology student at the University of Chester

'The answer guidelines are brilliant, I wish I had had it last year.'
Tony Whalley, Psychology student at the University of Chester

'I definitely would (buy a revision guide) as I like the structure, the assessment advice and practice questions and would feel more confident knowing exactly what to revise and having something to refer to.'
Steff Copestake, Psychology student at the University of Chester

'The clarity is absolutely first rate ... These chapters will be an excellent revision guide for students as well as providing a good opportunity for novel forms of assessment in and out of class.'
Dr Deaglan Page, Queen's University, Belfast

'Do you think they will help students when revising/working towards assessment? Unreservedly, yes.'
Dr Mike Cox, Newcastle University

'The revision guide should be very helpful to students preparing for their exams.'
Dr Kun Guo, University of Lincoln

'A brilliant revision guide, very helpful for students of all levels.'
Svetoslav Georgiev, Psychology student at Anglia Ruskin University

'Brilliant! Easy to read and understand – I would recommend this revision guide to every sport psychology student.'
Thomas Platt, Psychology student at Leeds Metropolitan University

'Develops knowledge and understanding in an easy-to-read manner with details on how to structure the best answers for essays and practical problems – vital for university students.'
Emily Griffiths, Psychology student at Leeds Metropolitan University

Psychology Express

Health
Psychology

Angel Chater
University College London

Erica Cook
University of Bedfordshire

Series editor:
Dominic Upton
University of Worcester

PEARSON

Harlow, England • London • New York • Boston • San Francisco • Toronto • Sydney
Auckland • Singapore • Hong Kong • Tokyo • Seoul • Taipei • New Delhi
Cape Town • São Paulo • Mexico City • Madrid • Amsterdam • Munich • Paris • Milan

Pearson Education Limited
Edinburgh Gate
Harlow CM20 2JE
United Kingdom
Tel: +44 (0)1279 623623
Web: www.pearson.com/uk

First published 2014 (print and electronic)

ISBN: 978-1-4479-2165-3 (print)
      978-1-4479-3097-6 (PDF)
      978-1-4479-3098-3 (epub)
      978-1-4479-3096-9 (eText)

British Library Cataloguing-in-Publication Data
A catalogue record for the print edition is available from the British Library

Library of Congress Cataloging-in-Publication Data
Chater, Angel.
  Health psychology / Angel Chater, University College, London, Erica Cook, University of Bedfordshire.
      pages cm. – (Psychology express)
  Includes bibliographical references and index.
  ISBN 978-1-4479-2165-3
  1. Clinical health psychology. 2. Health behavior. I. Cook, Erica. II. Title.
  R726.7.C47 2014
  616.89–dc23

                              2013047250

10 9 8 7 6 5 4 3 2 1
18 17 16 15 14

Print edition typeset in 9.5 Avenir LT Std by 73
Print edition printed and bound in Malaysia, CTP-PJB

NOTE THAT ANY PAGE CROSS-REFERENCES REFER TO THE PRINT EDITION

Contents

Companion Website

For open-access **student resources** specifically written to complement this textbook and support your learning, please visit **www.pearsoned.co.uk/psychologyexpress**

Acknowledgements

Authors' acknowledgements

This book has been the biggest labour of love since our PhDs and has dominated many of our weekends and evenings to get to this end result. We truly hope you enjoy reading this book as much as we have enjoyed the journey of writing it.

We would like to thank all the many students we have taught over the years for their inspirational interest and passion in health psychology. They have been our motivation to get involved in this project and write this text to support them and others like them in learning about the discipline that we are so very passionate about. We thank Dominic Upton for inviting us to be involved in such a fulfilling project, and the editorial team at Pearson for all their time, patience, feedback and support in getting this text to the final stage.

On a more personal note, we would like to thank our families and friends for their support and encouragement, as without them, we may not have made it through to the other side! Their experiences will lie in-between the pages forever.

Angel: My warmest thanks go to my partner Ian and our beautiful children Tia and Kai. I thank you for the love and encouragement you always give me, and the never-ending cups of tea and Mississippi mud cakes you brought to my office (aka my bed) at all times of the day and night while I was working on this book. I cherish the pride you have for my work that you reflect to the outside world and I look forward to making up for all the 'family time' we have missed along the way! I would also like to thank my Godfather, Roger, for all the late night conversations around how I was getting on and his synopsis of what health psychology is all about. Finally, I thank my parents, Pinkie and Ian, who have always instilled a sense of determination in me that anything is possible and that I should aim for the stars. Mum and dad, I dedicate this book to you and hope you can look down on this accomplishment with pride.

Erica: I would firstly like to thank Angel and Dominic for allowing me to venture on this exciting project with them. I also want to personally thank my partner Drew for his continued love, support and encouragement. I feel deeply honoured to have you in my life! I am also indebted to my amazing family who have not only believed in me, but have gone out of their way to guide me, giving me the strength and motivation to keep going even through difficult times. Mum and dad you are my true inspiration and I dedicate this book to you.

To all who have inspired and motivated us, we thank you.

Publisher's acknowledgments

Our thanks go to all the reviewers who contributed to the development of this text, including students who participated in research and focus groups, which helped to shape the series format:

Dr Sandi Mann, University of Central Lancashire
Dr Ronald Roberts, Kingston University
Dr Imogen Tijou, Southampton Solent University

We are grateful to the following for permission to reproduce copyright material:

Figures

Figure 2.2 from A protection motivation theory of fear appeals and attitude change, *Journal of Psychology*, 91, 93–114 (Rogers R.W. 1975), reprinted by permission of the publisher (Taylor & Francis Ltd, http://www.tandf.co.uk/journals); Figure 2.3 from From intentions to action: A theory of planned behaviour. In J. Kuhl & J. Beckham (Eds.), *Action control: From cognitions to behaviors*, New York: Springer (Ajzen I. 1985) pp. 11–39, with kind permission from Springer Science and Business Media. Copyright © 1985, Springer-Verlag Berlin Heidelberg; Figure 3.1 from *Self-efficacy: Thought control of action*, Washington, DC: Hemisphere Publishing Corporation (Schwarzer, R. 1992), Republished with permission of Informa plc., permission conveyed through Copyright Clearance Center, Inc.; Figure 3.5 from Evaluating health promotion-progress, problems and solutions, *Health Promotion International*, 13(1), pp. 27–44 (Nutbeam D. 1998), by permission of Oxford University Press; Figure 3.6 from *Health promotion and planning: An educational and ecological approach*, 3rd ed., Mountain View, CA: Mayfield (Green L.W. and Kreuter M.W. 1999), © 1999 McGraw-Hill Education; Figure 4.3 from United States Department of Agriculture (1992). The Food Guide Pyramid. Washington DC: USDA, USDA Center for Nutrition Policy and Promotion (CNPP); Figure 4.4 from Development and validation of a new body-image assessment scale, *Journal of Personality Assessment*, 64(2), pp. 258–69 (Thompson M.A. and Gray J.J. 1995), reprinted by permission of the publisher (Taylor & Francis Ltd, http://www.tandf.co.uk/journals); Figure 8.1 from A syndrome produced by diverse nocuous agents, *Nature*, 138, pp. 32–3 (Seyle H. 1936), reprinted by permission from Macmillan Publishers Ltd, copyright (© 1936); Figure 8.3 from *Stress, appraisal, and coping*, New York: Springer (Lazarus R. and Folkman S. 1984), republished with permission of Springer, permission conveyed through Copyright Clearance Center, Inc.

Tables

Table 8.1 from The social readjustment rating scale. *Journal of Psychosomatic Research*, 11, pp. 213–8 (Holmes T.H. and Rahe R.H. 1967), reprinted with permission from Elsevier.

Text

Sample question on page 92 from Alcoholics Anonymous (http://www.alcoholics-anonymous.org.uk/About-AA/The-12-Steps-of-AA), The Twelve Steps are reprinted with permission of Alcoholics Anonymous World Services, Inc. ("AAWS"). Permission to reprint the Twelve Steps does not mean that AAWS has reviewed or approved the contents of this publication, or that AAWS necessarily agrees with the views expressed herein. A.A. is a program of recovery from alcoholism only - use of the Twelve Steps in connection with programs and activities which are patterned after A.A., but which address other problems, or in any other non-A.A. context, does not imply otherwise. Additionally, while A.A. is a spiritual program, A.A. is not a religious program. Thus, A.A. is not affiliated or allied with any sect, denomination, or specific religious belief.

In some instances we have been unable to trace the owners of copyright material, and we would appreciate any information that would enable us to do so.

Introduction

Not only is psychology one of the fastest-growing subjects to study at university worldwide, it is also one of the most exciting and relevant subjects. Over the past decade the scope, breadth and importance of psychology have developed considerably. Important research work from as far afield as the UK, Europe, USA and Australia has demonstrated the exacting research base of the topic and how this can be applied to all manner of everyday issues and concerns. Being a student of psychology is an exciting experience – the study of mind and behaviour is a fascinating journey of discovery. Studying psychology at degree level brings with it new experiences, new skills and knowledge. As the Quality Assurance Agency (QAA) has stressed:

> psychology is distinctive in the rich and diverse range of attributes it develops – skills which are associated with the humanities (e.g. critical thinking and essay writing) and the sciences (hypotheses-testing and numeracy). (QAA, 2010, p. 5)

Recent evidence suggests that employers appreciate the skills and knowledge of psychology graduates, but in order to reach this pinnacle you need to develop your skills, further your knowledge and most of all successfully complete your degree to your maximum ability. The skills, knowledge and opportunities that you gain during your psychology degree will give you an edge in the employment field. The QAA stresses the high level of employment skills developed during a psychology degree:

> due to the wide range of generic skills, and the rigour with which they are taught, training in psychology is widely accepted as providing an excellent preparation for many careers. In addition to subject skills and knowledge, graduates also develop skills in communication, numeracy, teamwork, critical thinking, computing, independent learning and many others, all of which are highly valued by employers. (QAA, 2010, p. 2)

In 2010, we produced a series of books under the Psychology Express title and we are proud to note that both students and tutors have found these books extremely valuable. We appreciated that these books, representing the foundation of the Psychology undergraduate course, covered only one part of a typical course (albeit one of the most important) and that there was a need to build on the success of these and produce a series that covered the application of psychology in applied settings often covered in the latter parts of the Psychology undergraduate programme. This book is part of this new series although written and designed with the positive attributes common to all in the Psychology Express series. It is not a replacement for every single text, journal article, presentation and abstract you will read and review during the course of your degree programme. It is in no way a replacement for your lectures, seminars or additional reading. A top-rated assessment answer is likely to include considerable additional information and wider reading – and you are directed to some of these in this text. This revision guide is a conductor: directing you through the maze of your degree by providing an overview of your course, helping you formulate your ideas, and directing your reading.

Each book within Psychology Express presents a summary coverage of the key concepts, theories and research in the field, within an explicit framework of revision. The focus throughout all of the books in the series will be on how you should approach and consider your topics in relation to assessment and exams. Various features have been included to help you build up your skills and knowledge, ready for your assessments. More detail of the features can be found in the guided tour for this book on page xii.

By reading and engaging with this book, you will develop your skills and knowledge base and in this way you should excel in your studies and your associated assessments.

Psychology Express: Health Psychology is divided into nine chapters and your course has probably been divided up into similar sections. However we, the series authors and editor, must stress a key point: do not let the purchase, reading and engagement with the material in this text restrict your reading or your thinking. In psychology, you need to be aware of the wider literature and how it interrelates and how authors and thinkers have criticised and developed the arguments of others. So even if an essay asks you about one particular topic, you need to draw on similar issues raised in other areas of psychology. There are, of course, some similar themes that run throughout the material covered in this text, but you can learn from the other areas of psychology covered in the other texts in this series as well as from material presented elsewhere.

We hope you enjoy this text and the others in the Psychology Express series, which cover the complete knowledge base of psychology:

- *Sport Psychology* (Paul McCarthy and Mark Allen);
- *Educational Psychology* (Penney Upton and Charlotte Taylor);
- *Occupational Psychology* (Catherine Steele, Kazia Solowiej, Anne Bicknell, Holly Sands);
- *Forensic Psychology* (Laura Caulfield and Dean Wilkinson);
- *Clinical Psychology* (Tim Jones and Phil Tyson).

This book, and the other companion volumes in this series, should cover all your study needs (there will also be further guidance on the website). It will, obviously, need to be supplemented with further reading and this text directs you towards suitable sources. Hopefully, quite a bit of what you read here you will already have come across and the text will act as a jolt to set your mind at rest – you do know the material in depth. Overall, we hope that you find this book useful and informative as a guide both for your study now and in your future as a successful psychology graduate.

Revision note

- *Use evidence based on your reading, not on anecdotes or your 'common sense'.*
- *Show the examiner you know your material in depth – use your additional reading wisely.*
- *Remember to draw on a number of different sources: there is rarely one 'correct' answer to any psychological problem.*
- *Base your conclusions on research-based evidence.*

Explore the accompanying website at www.pearsoned.co.uk/psychologyexpress
→ Prepare more effectively for exams and assignments using the answer guidelines for questions from this book.
→ Test your knowledge using multiple choice questions and flashcards.
→ Improve your essay skills.

Guided tour

→ Understand key concepts quickly

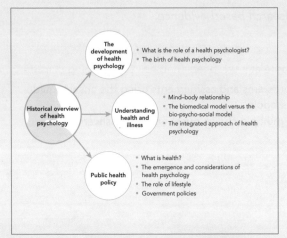

Start to plan your revision using the **Topic maps.**

Grasp **Key terms** quickly using the handy definitions. Use the flashcards online to test yourself.

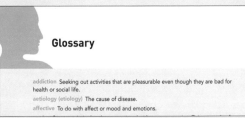

→ Revise effectively

Quickly remind yourself of the **Key studies** using the special boxes in the text.

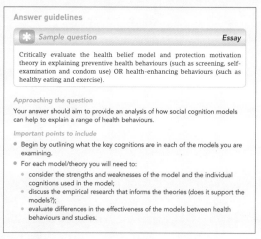

Test your knowledge

2.1 What are the cognitions of the health belief model?

2.2 What are the strengths and weaknesses of the health belief model?

Answers to these questions can be found on the companion website at:
www.pearsoned.co.uk/psychologyexpress.

Prepare for upcoming exams and tests using the **Test your knowledge** and **Sample question** features.

Compare your responses with the **Answer guidelines** in the text and on the website.

Answer guidelines

❋ *Sample question*   Essay

Critically evaluate the health belief model and protection motivation theory in explaining preventive health behaviours (such as screening, self-examination and condom use) OR health-enhancing behaviours (such as healthy eating and exercise).

Approaching the question

Your answer should aim to provide an analysis of how social cognition models can help to explain a range of health behaviours.

Important points to include

● Begin by outlining what the key cognitions are in each of the models you are examining.

● For each model/theory you will need to:

  ● consider the strengths and weaknesses of the model and the individual cognitions used in the model;

  ● discuss the empirical research that informs the theories (does it support the models?);

  ● evaluate differences in the effectiveness of the models between health behaviours and studies.

→ **Make your answers stand out**

Use the **Critical focus** boxes to impress your examiner with your deep and critical understanding.

CRITICAL FOCUS

Measuring hand washing

Critics argue there are methodological issues relating to the measurement of hand-washing behaviour. Let's say, for example, one hospital's statistics confirm 95% adherence compared to another which has a rate of 65%. You would think that the first hospital is better. However, is it that clear cut? Firstly, there is no standardised method for collecting and reporting rates of hand hygiene. Furthermore, organisations measure and report hand washing in many different ways, varying in sample group size, and hand hygiene pre-and post-interaction, thus the adherence rate is greatly influenced by what indications are chosen for measurement (CMHH, 2009).

Observation methods have been viewed as the gold standard, and although it is accepted that this has the advantage of linking the activity to the indication, there have also been many criticisms. There are potential biases such as the Hawthorne effect (Benson, 2001), in which people change behaviour because they know they are being observed. Furthermore, collecting reliable observation data requires a highly structured method of both observing care and documenting data. McAteer et al. (2008) propose a hand-hygiene observation tool (HHOT), which has been found to have good inter-rater

Make your answer stand out

Try not simply to describe different preventive health behaviours as this will not achieve a very high mark. A good answer will remember to take a critical stance and show a good engagement with a wide range of evidence to present an argument about to what extent preventive health behaviours impact on health status. For the highest marks you will need to present original insightful thinking, using well-balanced, evidence-based arguments.

Go into the exam with confidence using the handy tips to **make your answer stand out.**

1 Historical overview of health psychology: what is it and where has it come from?

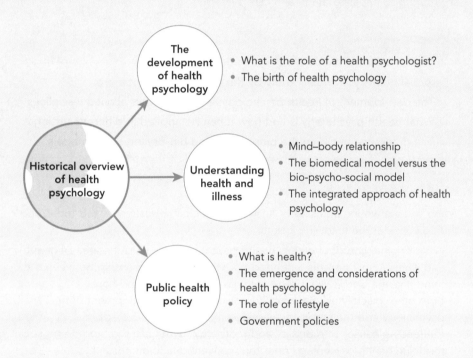

The development of health psychology
- What is the role of a health psychologist?
- The birth of health psychology

Historical overview of health psychology

Understanding health and illness
- Mind–body relationship
- The biomedical model versus the bio-psycho-social model
- The integrated approach of health psychology

Public health policy
- What is health?
- The emergence and considerations of health psychology
- The role of lifestyle
- Government policies

A printable version of this topic map is available from
www.pearsoned.co.uk/psychologyexpress

Introduction

Do you think psychology has anything to do with health? Can our mind influence whether we will suffer a heart attack or get cancer? Can exams really make us ill? How is health psychology different from clinical psychology?

Our 'easy' answer is this:

- 'Health psychology is the science of health, illness and health care.'
- 'Clinical psychology relates to mental health, while health psychology relates to physical health.'

Now, this is a very quick and simple answer, but although it is useful if you ever need to explain it to your grandmother, the reality is, of course, much more complex than this. Essentially, health psychology is a branch of psychology that aims to understand and assist people to manage health and illness, while also attempting to enhance the health care system.

 Revision checklist

Essential points you should know by the end of this chapter are:

❏ The development of health psychology as a field and its aligned disciplines
❏ What health psychology is and how it can be applied in different settings
❏ The difference between the biomedical and bio-psycho-social models.

Assessment advice

When you are writing an essay or answering an exam question on this topic, you should consider the following points:

- What *original contribution* has health psychology made to the area of health and illness? How has this extended our view of the relationship between the mind and the body? What can health psychology offer and how is it different from other disciplines? Be explicit in discussing the development of health psychology and the empirical evidence that supports the discipline. What are the leading causes of mortality and morbidity? What can the bio-psycho-social model in health psychology offer that conventional biomedical models cannot? How can health psychology be applied to the real world? Are there overlaps with other disciplines? How can they complement each other?

- *Evidence* is always required, so ensure you back up your argument with references to relevant research. Unsupported generalisations and statements based on your own opinion will not achieve a very high mark and might even fail.

- *Be critical of the evidence.* For example, are there gaps that may not have been addressed? Are there overlaps that create confusion between disciplines? Could this impact on practical settings?

- *Read widely* on the topics, and aim for primary sources (e.g. journal articles) where evidence is written by the author, rather than secondary sources (e.g. textbooks) which describe what someone else has done. If you wish to reference any of the studies we have reviewed in this book, you should find and read the primary sources yourself.

- *Do not include anecdotal details* about personal experiences (e.g. stating why you did or did not engage in a health behaviour), and for scientific reports write in the third person (not using 'I'). This allows you to stay objective (i.e. to create an argument from evidence that is not influenced by your own personal feelings and experiences) rather than being subjective (creating an argument based on how you feel and what you think). Therefore, if you cannot support your argument or point with a reference, you should consider where that argument came from. If it was just something that came to you, or that has been the case in your experience, you should consider the evidence and support the argument with that evidence. For example, it might be considered common knowledge that you are less likely to exercise when you are tired, but to put this into an essay, you need a source – someone who has researched the area and arrived at this conclusion. This way you can still get your point across but you are using the empirical evidence that supports or contests your argument.

Sample question

Could you answer this question? Below is a typical problem question that could rise on this topic.

 Sample question   *Essay*

Critically evaluate how health psychology challenges the assumptions of the biomedical model of health and illness.

Guidelines on answering this question are included at the end of this chapter, whilst guidance on tackling other exam questions can be found on the companion website at www.pearsoned.co.uk/psychologyexpress

The development of health psychology

What is the role of a health psychologist?

Health psychologists are trained to help people to deal with the challenges they may face in:

- keeping healthy (e.g. maintaining a good diet or engaging in physical activity);
- avoiding or stopping risk behaviours (e.g. smoking cigarettes, alcohol misuse or drug use);

- protecting their health (e.g. condom, seat belt or sunscreen use, brushing their teeth or getting an adequate night's sleep);
- preventing disease (e.g. screening behaviour, immunisation).

They are also trained to help people manage if they become ill in areas such as:

- stress management (and understanding its link with disease and the immune system);
- taking medication as prescribed (adherence).

The birth of health psychology

The roots of health psychology can be traced back to a meeting of the American Psychological Association (APA) in 1973 (Johnston, Weinman, & Chater, 2011). The agenda for this meeting included a question on how psychologists (who were mostly clinical) can support the maintenance of physical health, the management of people with physical health problems and the effectiveness of healthcare delivery. The Americans led the development of the discipline, creating a Division of Health Psychology in 1978 known as Division 38. In 1980, Matarazzo defined health psychology as:

> the aggregate of the specific educational, scientific, and professional contributions of the discipline of psychology to the promotion and maintenance of health, the prevention and treatment of illness, and the identification of etiologic and diagnostic correlates of health, illness, and related dysfunction. (Matarazzo, 1980, p. 815)

The British Psychological Society (BPS) followed this movement, developing a Health Psychology Section in 1986. As interest and research grew in the area, this section became a Special Interest Group in Health Psychology in 1993 and then a Division of Health Psychology (DHP) in 1997 (see Michie, Abraham and Johnston, 2004 for a full overview).

You will read in many places that Health Psychology is a growing discipline and this is certainly the case. Put simply (Ogden, 2012), health psychology aims to provide insight into the following questions:

- How can health be maintained?
- What causes illness?
- Who is responsible for health and illness?
- How should illness be treated?
- Who is responsible for treatment?
- What is the relationship between health and illness?
- What is the relationship between the mind and the body?
- What is the role of psychology in health and illness?

Mind–body relationship

To understand the development of health psychology we first need to go on a journey of our understanding of health, illness and medicine, and the relationship between the mind and the body. (For an overview of what follows, see Landrine and Klonoff (1994); Morrison and Bennett (2012); Ogden (2012).)

First, we take you right back to Stone Age times (1000–300 BC).

● It seems from archaeological studies and interpretation of Ancient Hebrew texts that illness and disease were seen as a result of some type of sorcery, possession of evil spirits or a punishment from God. Treatment was often received from a Shaman, who would perform a ritual known as trephination (Marino & Gonzales-Portillo, 2000), whereby a small hole was made in the skull to allow the evil spirits to leave the body.

The Ancient Greeks, however, had a different take on health and illness.

● Rather than focusing on the supernatural, Hippocrates (circa 460–377 BC), whose theory was later expanded by Galen (AD 129–199), believed that illness occurred due to a bodily imbalance of the four fluids – blood, black bile, yellow bile and phlegm. This humoral theory, which is still used in some cultures (Bastien, 1989), suggests that illness occurs when external pathogens, linked to the seasons of the year and to personality, cause one or more of the fluids to be out of balance (see Table 1.1).

Table 1.1 Specific bodily humours linked to personality and illness

Humour	Temperament	Season	Disease	Treatment
Phlegm	Phlegmatic (calm)	Winter (cold–wet)	Cold, headaches	Hot baths, warm food
Blood	Sanguine (optimistic)	Spring (wet–hot)	Angina, epilepsy	Bloodletting
Black bile	Melancholic (sadness)	Autumn (cold–dry)	Hepatitis, ulcers, breast cancer	Hot baths
Yellow bile	Choleric (angry)	Summer (hot–dry)	Stomach, jaundice	Bloodletting, liquid diet

However, this theory lost dominance in the early Middle Ages (fifth and sixth centuries), when the Church came to the forefront of medicine and we were back to beliefs in spirituality and illness being seen as God's punishment for sin.

● Individuals were not thought to be in control of their health at this time, and treatment was through hard work, self-punishment and confession.

● The functions of the physician were absorbed by the priest, who would release the body from evil through exorcism.

Fast forward now to the early seventeenth century. Descartes (1596–1650) continued with the view that the mind and the body were separate.

● He proposed that the mind was 'non-material' (i.e. not visible, as with a thought), while the body was 'material' (i.e. made of real stuff, like your organs). He termed this situation dualism; however, he did acknowledge that interaction between the two domains was possible.

- The body was seen as a 'machine'. As the discipline of medicine grew, illness was seen as a malfunction of this machine, leading to the early development of the *biomedical model.*

The eighteenth (tissue pathology), nineteenth (germ theory) and twentieth centuries (pathogens and virus) moved this concept forward, acknowledging:

- molecular, biological, biochemical and genetic influence on cellular and physiological processes;
- the medical profession's responsibility for treatment, often with a 'magic bullet' (medicine), with the individual becoming a passive observer.

In short, the biomedical model assumes a dualistic stance, the mind and body disconnected, ill health caused by a malfunction of bodily parts, and psychological and social factors largely independent of the disease process.

Test your knowledge

1.1 What is dualism?

1.2 How has our view of health and illness evolved over time?

Answers to these questions can be found on the companion website at: **www.pearsoned.co.uk/psychologyexpress**

The biomedical model versus the bio-psycho-social model

Think back to the last time you went to your doctor. What treatment did you receive? Were you given a pill or medical technique to restore you back to health, or were you also given advice about changing your lifestyle or environment, or reducing your level of stress?

The answer you give will depend on whether your physician comes from a purely biomedical background or encompasses something more. Unlike the biomedical model that still dominates much of the field of health care, health psychology does not draw solely on the biological sciences to provide explanations for health and illness. It challenges this somewhat simplistic view of the diagnosis and treatment of illness, aiming to identify and examine the dynamic relationships between psychological, biological and social factors that determine health status. It explores the ways by which a bio-psycho-social perspective (Engel, 1977; Engel, 1980; see Figure 1.1) can be applied to manage health and prevent disease in a contemporary, multicultural society. It therefore draws very much on a view that the mind and the body are part of the same system, and can interact and work together. This concept is known as monism.

Health psychology critically evaluates methods utilised in the discipline, adopting a scientist-practitioner model. It draws on empirical evidence and considers how this may be applied in health-care settings and community practice.

But how did we get to this? Well, while the biomedical mechanistic scientists were diagnosing and treating illness in terms of the physiological state,

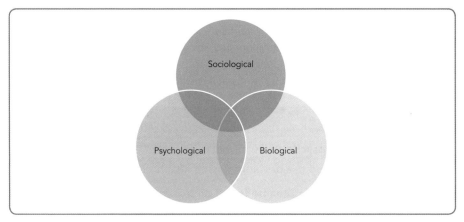

Figure 1.1 A visual representation of the domains of the bio-psycho-social model

psychologists were, perhaps unintentionally, challenging the dualism perspective. The first key psychologist to do this was Sigmund Freud (1856–1939), who suggested that the interface between the mind and the body was consciousness. He initiated the development of psychosomatic medicine, and postulated that personality and illness may be related to repressed unconscious desires, offering the explanation that bodily disorders are caused by emotional conflict.

This development, along with the understanding of the link between behaviour and health (e.g. between smoking and cancer), and the understanding of societal adaptation to health and illness through medical anthropology and epidemiology (which examines the frequency and distribution of disease and illness), has led to the development of health psychology as a discipline.

The integrated approach of health psychology

Health psychology aims to unravel the role of the mind (thoughts, emotions) and behaviour in promoting and maintaining health, preventing illness, and aiding recovery and quality of life. From this perspective, health, illness and longevity, far from being the sole preserve of our genetic predisposition and biology, are thought to be intrinsically linked to many aspects of everyday life. In the field of health psychology, therefore, it is necessary to adopt an integrated approach to research and practice, which draws upon a diverse range of psychological models, theories and approaches that you may cover while studying traditional psychology.

To provide an example of this integrated approach:

- We may utilise knowledge from the fields of social and cognitive psychology to understand the role of classical and operant conditioning and vicarious learning (reinforcement and modelling) in the uptake of behaviours such as healthy eating and cigarette smoking.
- Similarly, in the field of psychoneuroimmunology (PNI), the impact of cognitions, beliefs, lifestyle and life events on health may be more readily understood if we draw on biopsychology and examine pathways between the nervous and immune systems.

- Finally, it should be acknowledged that any study (whether cross-sectional, prospective or longitudinal) which seeks to describe or explain relations among mind, behaviour, social influences, immunity and disease will always be open to criticism. This critical debate is essential to keep the discipline growing strongly and you should embrace it with open arms.

Test your knowledge

1.3 Describe the bio-psycho-social model.

1.4 What has influenced the development of health psychology?

Answers to these questions can be found on the companion website at: **www.pearsoned.co.uk/psychologyexpress**

Further reading Development of health psychology

Topic	Key reading
Background to the development of health psychology and the bio-psycho-social model	Morrison, V., & Bennett, P. (2012). *An introduction to health psychology* (3rd ed.). Harlow: Pearson Education.
	Ogden, J. (2012). *Health psychology: A textbook* (5th ed.). Maidenhead: Open University Press.

 Sample question   *Essay*

Discuss in detail the influence of biological, psychological and sociological factors in the maintenance of health and prevention of illness.

The biology of health and illness

One thing that is essential for any health psychologist to understand is how the body works. Imagine a dancer who didn't understand rhythm, or a painter who had no knowledge of how to create colour. Both may be able to dance or paint, but to do it well, they would need to know and understand these basic foundations of their discipline. For those who wish to work in health and illness, it is important to know how the body works from a biological perspective.

The human body has many 'systems' that have different roles in maintaining health status and managing illness, and many of these work together. These are also important when trying to determine symptoms.

- *The endocrine system* – where hormones are produced. Hormones can influence hunger, thirst, sexual drive and growth, to name but a few.
- *The digestive and excretory systems* – which work from the moment we eat to the time the waste is released from our body. These systems are important when we try to understand obesity or diabetes.

- *The nervous system* – the most complex system, consisting of the brain, spinal cord and nerves, split into two: the *central nervous system (CNS)* and the *peripheral nervous system (PNS)*.
  - The PNS is further divided into the *somatic nervous system* and the *autonomic nervous system*.
  - The autonomic nervous system is split into the *sympathetic nervous system* (where the 'fight or flight' response occurs, e.g. in response to a stressor) and the *parasympathetic nervous system* (which works with the sympathetic to help in recovery).
- *The respiratory system* – involved in breathing, including the mouth, nose, windpipe (trachea) and lungs, which help move air into and out of the body. Asthma and panic attacks (involving hyperventilation – breathing too much too quickly) are linked here.
- *The cardiovascular system* – focusing on the heart, veins and arteries, which are responsible for heart rate and blood pressure, and transporting oxygen, nutrients, waste products and toxins. Knowledge of this system is important when trying to understand coronary heart disease and hypertension.
- *Biological rhythms* – such as the circadian (daily) rhythm that operates our wake–sleep cycle. Insomnia is linked to this system.

Test your knowledge

1.5 What system is linked to the fight or flight response?

1.6 What health concerns are linked to the cardiovascular system?

Answers to these questions can be found on the companion website at:
www.pearsoned.co.uk/psychologyexpress

Further reading Biological systems and health status

Topic	Key reading
Overview of the biological systems	Forshaw, M. (2002). *Essential health psychology.* London: Oxford University Press.
Chapter on bodily experience	Lyons, A. C., & Chamberlain, K. (2006). *Health psychology: A critical introduction.* Cambridge: Cambridge University Press.

Public health policy

What is health?

One thing that is important to consider when working in health psychology is the definition of health itself. Health should not been seen as just an absence of illness or disease. And our field is health psychology, not illness psychology. The World Health Organisation (WHO, 1948) describes health as 'a complete state of physical, mental and social well-being and not merely the absence of disease and infirmity'. So we need to ensure that we are not just nurturing people back to health when they are ill, or preventing illness, we are also promoting the enhancement of health and well-being, which may often go unnoticed until it has been taken away.

The emergence and considerations of health psychology

So why has health psychology grown so rapidly in the last 25 years? There has been an epidemiological shift in the leading causes of mortality and morbidity over the last few centuries, from infectious diseases that required medical/societal intervention in the seventeenth to nineteenth centuries (e.g. cholera, smallpox, plague), to illnesses that are now more controllable through psychosocial action (e.g. cancer, coronary heart disease) (McKeown, 1979). The field of epidemiology has contributed to our understanding of mortality and morbidity and the role that health behaviours play in illness. Epidemiology is a science founded by John Snow, whose mapping of cases of cholera and household use of water sources led to the hypothesis that one water pump was responsible for the transmission of the disease. Disabling the water pump by removing the handle brought the outbreak of cholera to a close (Snow, 2002) and showed that illness can be traced back to a cause, identifying incidence and prevalence.

The effect of lifestyle and behaviour on health status and longevity has become more salient, and the extent to which behaviour can be predicted, regulated and even controlled by health beliefs is now much better understood. The study of health behaviours is based on two assumptions (Stroebe & Stroebe, 1995):

1 that in industrialised countries a high proportion of the mortality from the leading causes of death is due to particular behaviour patterns;

2 that these behaviour patterns are modifiable.

Matarazzo (1984) proposed that behaviours can be either:

- *health-protective* (behavioural immunogens), having a positive effect on health (e.g. a healthy diet or adequate sleep), or

- health-impairing (behavioural pathogens), having a negative effect on health (e.g. smoking or drug use).

In a correlational analysis of almost 7,000 people (Belloc & Breslow, 1972) it was found that there is a significant relationship between lifestyle and health. The following behaviours were seen to be important for maintaining health:

1 sleeping seven to eight hours per day;

2 having breakfast almost every day;

3 never smoking cigarettes;

4 rarely eating between meals;

5 being near or at appropriate weight;

6 having moderate or no use of alcohol;

7 regular vigorous physical activity.

Just under ten years later, Breslow and Enstrom (1980) followed up the people in the study and found that those who did not engage in these behaviours had higher mortality rates, showing quite clearly how health behaviours are linked to both health status and survival.

Based on epidemiological data, Figures 1.2 and 1.3 show the UK mortality rates by cause of death for men and women in 2002, while Figures 1.4 and 1.5 show mortality rates by cause in 2007.

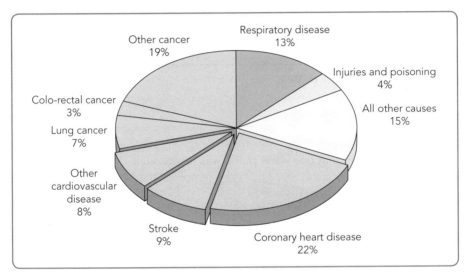

Figure 1.2 Death by cause in 2002, men
Source: British Heart Foundation, 2004.

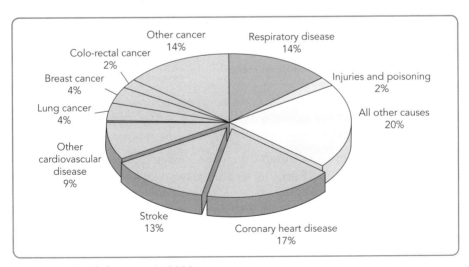

Figure 1.3 Death by cause in 2002, women
Source: British Heart Foundation, 2004.

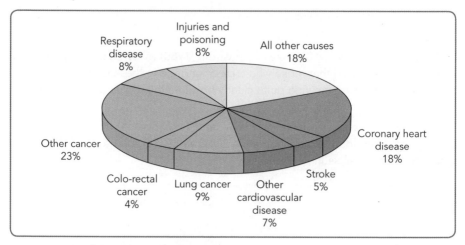

Figure 1.4 Death by cause in 2007, men
Source: British Heart Foundation, 2010.

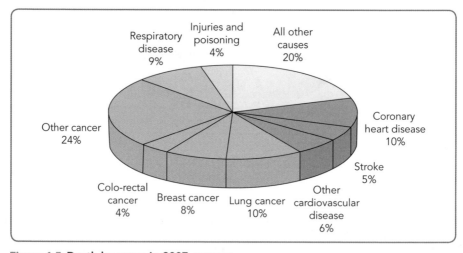

Figure 1.5 Death by cause in 2007, women
Source: British Heart Foundation, 2010.

The role of lifestyle

As you can see from these figures, deaths from illnesses such as cancer and coronary heart disease (CHD) account for around two-thirds of all deaths in England. Many of these deaths are preventable through psycho-social intervention. Individuals can improve their health and prevent premature death through a good diet, regular physical activity, avoiding smoking cigarettes, and drinking alcohol in moderation (Department of Health: DH, 2004a). Taking into account both the biomedical and bio-psycho-social models, it would seem that while nature may load the gun, lifestyle often pulls the trigger.

The World Health Organisation (WHO) is considered by many to be the leading authority on health and illness. In a stark opening message to a 2002 report the Director-General stated:

> … in many ways, the world is a safer place today. Safer from what were once deadly or incurable diseases. Safer from daily hazards of waterborne and food-related illnesses. Safer from dangerous consumer goods, from accidents at home, at work, or in hospitals. But in many other ways the world is becoming more dangerous. Too many of us are living dangerously – whether we are aware of that or not. (WHO, 2002, p. 3)

This is where health psychology can make a real impact. By understanding and intervening in people's lifestyles, we can change behaviours that we know are detrimental to health. But this still leaves a central concern: where lies the element of free choice?

KEY STUDY

UK mortality and morbidity (Murray et al., 2013)

Background

This study aimed to understand the leading causes of mortality and morbidity in the UK, using data from the Global Burden of Diseases, Injuries, and Risk Factors Study (2010). UK statistics were compared with other countries in 1990 and 2010.

Method

Data were gathered from the original 15 members of the European Union, along with Australia, Canada, Norway and the USA (named as EU15+). Outcomes assessed included mortality, cause of death, years of life lost (YLLs), years lived with disability (YLDs), disability-adjusted life-years (DALYs), and healthy life expectancy (HALE).

Findings

Results confirmed that there had been an overall improvement of health in the UK from 1990 to 2010, with life expectancy increasing by 4.2 years. However, compared to the other countries, age-standardised death rates and age-standardised YLL rates had worsened. The age range that had the worst rankings for premature death was 20–54 years. Compared with the other countries, the UK had higher rates of age-standardised YLLs for ischemic heart disease, chronic obstructive pulmonary disease, lower respiratory infections, breast cancer, other cardiovascular disorders, oesophageal cancer, preterm birth complications, congenital anomalies and aortic aneurysm. Yet it showed a significantly lower rate for road injury, diabetes, liver cancer and chronic kidney disease. Premature mortality rose during the time period for Alzheimer's disease (up 137%), cirrhosis (up 65%) and drug use disorders (up 577%). In 2010, diet and physical inactivity accounted for 14.3% of UK DALYs.

Conclusion

There is great concern over the health of the UK population, and more work is needed in terms of prevention and treatment of the leading causes of death: namely, cardiovascular diseases and cancers.

Sample question *Problem-based learning*

Think of the last time you were ill. Consider the factors that may have contributed to your illness using the bio-psycho-social model. Which factor do you feel was the strongest contributor to your condition?

Government policies

Is the government becoming too paternalistic? Don't we as human beings have a choice to smoke or drink too much if we want to? Or should the government be doing more to help us? Or perhaps we should be doing more to help ourselves?

The effectiveness of health promotion lies both at a micro level with the individual, and at a macro level with the government and society. In response to growing concern among health professionals, organisations and the general public, the need for a formulated set of policies for improving health was established. The UK government launched a white paper in July 1992 titled *The Health of the Nation* (HOTN), which was devised to reduce high-risk behaviours as a strategy for national health gain. The HOTN set targets in five keys areas: coronary heart disease and stroke, cancers, mental illness, HIV/AIDS and sexual health, and accidents. Each key area had an objective that related to the aims of the HOTN.

The objective for the key area coronary heart disease (CHD) and stroke was to reduce the level of ill health and death caused by the two, and the risk factors associated with them. CHD accounted for about 26% of deaths in England in 1991. It was both the single largest cause of death, and the main cause of premature death. Strokes were responsible for approximately 12% of all deaths in 1991 (DH, 1992). Risk factors associated with these diseases include: smoking, which accounted for up to 18% of CHD deaths and 11% of stroke deaths; eating and drinking habits, which are the most important risk factor for CHD; plasma cholesterol; and lack of physical exercise. Success in achieving all the targets within this area would not only reduce the number of CHD and stroke fatalities; it would also lead to improvements in many other conditions. For example, a reduction in smoking prevalence and excessive alcohol consumption would lower the risk of certain cancers (DH, 2004a), and a reduction in obesity would reduce the risk of non-insulin-dependent diabetes (WHO, 1990).

The key area targeting cancers aimed to reduce ill-health and death caused by breast, cervical, skin and lung cancer. Cancers were and still are the second most common cause of death (DH, 2004a), accounting for 25% of deaths in 1991 (DH, 1992).

HOTN forecast significant changes in the prevalence of smoking, high-fat diets and alcohol consumption in an attempt to reach these targets, yet the research literature suggests that subsequent health education programmes designed to promote 'healthy choices' failed to deliver the changes that are recognised as desirable (Marks, 1994).

In 1998 the UK government launched a green paper on public health, *Our Healthier Nation*, which proposed a 'Contract for health'. In addition to past initiatives that emphasised empowering people to live healthy lives by changing their lifestyle, this paper focused attention on structural inequalities, such as poverty, and aimed to improve people's living conditions and health. This paper moved away from previous victim blaming, stating that *'Good health is no longer about blame, but about opportunity and responsibility'* (DH, 1998a). It promised that information given to the public would be accurate, comprehensible and credible.

In 1999, the subsequent white paper, *Saving Lives: Our Healthier Nation* (DH, 1999) was introduced, which confirmed the aims of the previous green paper: to save lives, promote healthier living and reduce inequality in health. It set targets to reduce the death rate of people under 75 years of age from cancer, accidents, mental illness, coronary heart disease and stroke by 2010. Figures from the 1998 green paper, *Our Healthier Nation*, show that these five areas accounted for more than 75% of all deaths before the age of 75 years. If these targets were achieved, it was estimated that up to 300,000 premature and unnecessary deaths would be prevented. The government at this point stated that it was *'re-activating a dormant duty of the NHS – to promote good health, not just treat people when they fall sick'* (DH, 1999). However, looking at the graphs presented in Figures 1.2–1.5, there is little difference in these figures a decade on, suggesting that the efforts at prevention are not working as had been hoped.

Conclusion

It is clear from these government health policies (see Key Readings below for full details) that their aim is to improve the population's health. However, it is also clear that information alone is not sufficient to motivate individuals to take the best care of their health, and that human behaviour is much more complex. The biomedical model is still widely used in health care at the present time; however, it does not offer a full explanation of health and illness. The bio-psycho-social model of health psychology goes a long way in offering a fuller explanation.

Test your knowledge

1.7 What are the leading causes of death in the UK?

1.8 How has mortality and morbidity changed over the last decade?

Answers to these questions can be found on the companion website at: **www.pearsoned.co.uk/psychologyexpress**

Further reading UK public health policies

Topic	Key reading
Public health policies and key health targets	Department of Health (1992). *The health of the nation.* London: HMSO.
	Department of Health (1998). *Our healthier nation: A contract for health.* London: HMSO.
	Department of Health (1999). *Saving lives: Our healthier nation.* London: HMSO.
	Department of Health (2004). *Choosing health: Making healthy choices easier.* London: HMSO.

CASE STUDY

Asthma

The client

Gillian is a 32-year-old woman who has recently been suffering with breathing difficulties and was diagnosed with asthma six months ago. She has been prescribed both a preventer steroid inhaler to reduce inflammation, and a reliever inhaler to open her airways when needed. However, she re-visits her physician as her symptoms have not improved. What things would you need to consider as a health psychologist working on Gillian's team?

Background – the problem

Asthma is characterised by an obstruction of air exchange in the lungs. The bronchial tubes are narrowed by swelling (inflammation) and muscle spasms, making it difficult to breathe. It is most commonly known to be triggered by allergens (such as dust mites or mould), and irritants (e.g. cigarette smoke), although emotional factors such as anxiety can also cause symptoms to occur (Lehrer, Isenberg, & Hochron, 1993).

Advice

What things would you consider? The medication is not right for her? Maybe. But what if she is just not taking her medication? There may then be a case for looking at her adherence (her level of taking her medication as prescribed). Research has confirmed that one-third of asthma patients are concerned about their medication, which has an impact on whether they take it or not (Horne, 2006) and there is evidence of non-adherence in this population (Heaney & Horne, 2012).

How about her lifestyle? She may not be engaging in physical activity, which is important for a healthy respiratory system. There may be many reasons for this, including lack of motivation, weather and time constraints, although some research suggests that asthma sufferers think exercise will make their condition worse (Mancuso et al., 2006).

She may smoke, which of course would have a negative effect (Stapleton et al., 2011). What about her living conditions? She may be living in a city that has high pollution in the air, or live in a damp housing environment. She may dry her clothes indoors on the radiator. All of these things are environmental allergens that are known to increase the risk of or to exacerbate asthma (Pongracic et al., 2010).

But not all of these things would be considered under a traditional biomedical model. The bio-psycho-social model in health psychology would, therefore, be more suitable for trying to understand and support Gillian's health condition.

Chapter summary – pulling it all together

→ Can you tick all of the points from the revision checklist at the beginning of this chapter?

→ Attempt the sample question from the beginning of this chapter using the answer guidelines below.

→ Go to the companion website at www.pearsoned.co.uk/psychologyexpress to access more revision support online, including interactive quizzes, flashcards, You be the marker exercises as well as answer guidelines for the Test your knowledge and Sample questions from this chapter.

Further reading Health Psychology

Abraham, C., Conner, M., Jones, F., & O'Connor, D. (2008). *Health psychology: Topics in applied psychology.* London: Hodder Education.

Albery, I. P., & Munafò, M. (2008). *Key concepts in health psychology. London: Sage Publications.*

French, D., Vedhara, K., Kaptein, A. A., & Weinman, J. (Eds.) (2010). *Health psychology* (2nd ed.). Oxford: BPS Blackwell.

Marks, D. F., Murray, M. P., Evans, B., & Estacio, E. V. (2011). *Health psychology: Theory, research and practice* (3rd ed.). London: Sage.

Taylor, S. E. (2006). *Health psychology* (6th ed.). New York: McGraw-Hill.

Answer guidelines

 Sample question   ***Essay***

Critically evaluate how health psychology challenges the assumptions of the biomedical model of health and illness.

Approaching the question

Your answer should aim to provide an analysis of how health psychology has developed, the disciplines that align it and its contribution to the field of health and illness.

Important points to include

● Begin by outlining the definition of health psychology, and contextualise it in a real-world setting.

● Then critically discuss its development and evolution from the biomedical model, linking to other disciplines such as mainstream psychology, sociology, medical anthropology, biology, epidemiology and so on.

- Discuss the empirical research that informs this.
- Evaluate differences in the use of the biomedical and the bio-psycho-social models.
- You should then consider the usefulness of using health psychology in an applied setting. Link to health behaviours, mortality and morbidity.
- Conclude by making suggestions about how the field of health psychology can be improved and directions for future research.

Make your answer stand out

Try to avoid simply describing the above information. A good answer will remember to take a critical stance, evaluating the strengths and limitations of the disciplines, models and research that support it. A good student will also show original thinking by considering the overlaps between the disciplines and research that supports them, their differences and future considerations, in order to challenge the current empirical evidence and advance the development of the discipline.

Explore the accompanying website at www.pearsoned.co.uk/psychologyexpress

→ Prepare more effectively for exams and assignments using the answer guidelines for questions from this chapter.
→ Test your knowledge using multiple choice questions and flashcards.
→ Improve your essay skills by exploring the You be the marker exercises.

Notes

Health cognitions and beliefs: predicting health behaviour

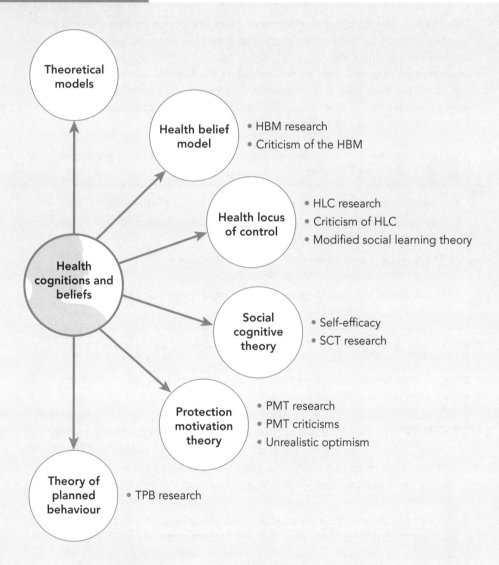

- **Theoretical models**

- **Health belief model**
  - HBM research
  - Criticism of the HBM

- **Health locus of control**
  - HLC research
  - Criticism of HLC
  - Modified social learning theory

- **Health cognitions and beliefs**

- **Social cognitive theory**
  - Self-efficacy
  - SCT research

- **Protection motivation theory**
  - PMT research
  - PMT criticisms
  - Unrealistic optimism

- **Theory of planned behaviour**
  - TPB research

A printable version of this topic map is available from
www.pearsoned.co.uk/psychologyexpress

Introduction

Think of how useful it would be to be able to predict who will follow medical advice, go for screening, be physically active, eat well or misuse substances.

Health psychologists don't have a crystal ball. However, they do have a selection of validated and scientifically challenged theories that can assist in understanding the psychological predictors of health behaviour. They go further than the biomedical model, which sees illness as a malfunction of a biological system, to truly embrace the bio-psycho-social model.

This chapter describes the components of key theoretical models that have been developed to explain why people engage in health-risk, health-protective or health-enhancing behaviours. Research that has tested the performance of these models in predicting health behaviours will be examined. Focus will be placed on the strengths and limitations of models such as the health belief model, health locus of control, social cognitive theory, protection motivation theory and the theory of planned behaviour.

 Revision checklist

Essential points you should know by the end of this chapter are:
- ❏ The structure of key theories, including the cognitions that are influential in predicting health behaviour
- ❏ The strengths and weaknesses of these theories and how some components overlap between theories
- ❏ Examples of how health psychology theories have been influential in explaining a variety of health behaviours.

Assessment advice

When you are writing an essay or answering an exam question on this topic, you should consider the following points:

- *Content.* Be explicit in relating health psychology theory to the topic. What can health psychology theories offer that conventional biomedical models cannot? Which ones are the most successful, and why? Are there differences in the effectiveness of each model depending on the behaviour that you are trying to explain? Are there overlaps between the models that you can evaluate critically?

- *Evidence* is always required, so ensure you *back up your argument with references* to relevant research. You will find research using the models we discuss in this chapter for many health behaviours. However, as you will see during this chapter, in the case of the classic studies that drove the development of the theory, some of the research will be rather dated, so be mindful of this.

- *Be critical* of theories and the nature of evidence. For example, has longitudinal or prospective research been conducted to establish cause and effect or is research limited to correlational and cross-sectional studies?

Sample question

Could you answer this question? Below is a typical problem question that could rise on this topic.

 Sample question   Essay

Critically evaluate the health belief model and protection motivation theory in explaining preventive health behaviours (such as screening, self-examination and condom use) OR health-enhancing behaviours (such as healthy eating and exercise).

Guidelines on answering this question are included at the end of this chapter, whilst guidance on tackling other exam questions can be found on the companion website at **www.pearsoned.co.uk/psychologyexpress**

Theoretical models

Theoretical frameworks provide key assumptions about factors that need to be taken into account when trying to understand how to achieve desired outcomes. A theory may explain:

- factors influencing a phenomenon (e.g. why some people do not go for screening);
- the relationship between these factors (e.g. whether this decision is related to levels of knowledge and risk perceptions, attitudes, beliefs about disease, influence of other people (social norms) and so on);
- the conditions under which these relationships occur (e.g. do screening rates fall when there is media attention highlighting risk?).

A better understanding of such factors and how they interact could aid the understanding of why people perform or avoid certain health behaviours, and in turn the effectiveness of health interventions, such as those that will be discussed in Chapter 3.

The task of changing unhealthy practices to healthier alternatives is notoriously problematic and complex. Simply to expect an individual to change their behaviour when presented with information or a threat of disease or illness is naïve. Theoretical models have greatly influenced the direction of health behaviour research and have provided a wider framework to base interventions on than mere education.

Health belief model

The health belief model (HBM) is one of the oldest cognition models. It was first proposed by Rosenstock (1966) and was further developed by Becker, Haefner and Maiman (1977).

The HBM (Figure 2.1) suggests that behaviour is a result of a set of beliefs which are the individual's perceptions of:

- their *susceptibility* to illness (e.g. '*My chances of getting breast cancer are high*');
- the *severity* of the illness (e.g. '*Breast cancer is a serious illness*');
- *costs versus benefits* involved in carrying out behaviour (e.g. '*The benefits of knowing whether I am at risk of breast cancer outweigh the embarrassment/ discomfort of the procedure*').

Two other variables are commonly included in this model: *cues to action* (added by Becker and Maiman in 1975) and *health motivation* (added by Becker et al. in

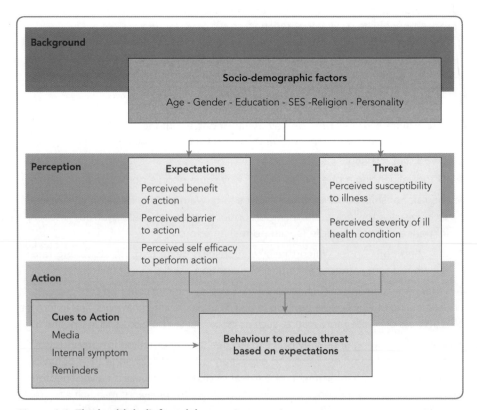

Figure 2.1 **The health belief model**

Source: Based on Rosenstock (1966, 2005); Becker & Maiman (1975); Becker et al. (1977).

1977). Cues to action include a wide range of triggers to take up an action, and can be internal (e.g. a physical symptom such as pain) or external (e.g. a public health campaign or media attention). Becker (1974) argues that certain individuals may be predisposed to respond to such cues because of the value they place on their health. Health motivation suggested that if a person was motivated and ready to act then they were more likely to adopt the behaviour (Rosenstock, 2005).

Demographics (age, gender, ethnicity) are also seen as modifying factors within the HBM, along with *socio-psychological* (personality, social economic status, peer and group pressure) and *structural* (knowledge about disease, prior contact with disease) influences. However, Rosenstock (2005) suggests that few attempts have been made to show the mechanisms that link behaviour with fixed personal characteristics. There is also no clear identification of the way the HBM variables work and interact to produce behaviour change.

HBM research

The HBM has been widely used (Glanz, Rimmer, & Lewis, 2002) to predict a range of health behaviours, including:

- smoking behaviour (Li et al., 2003);
- contraceptive use (Drayton, Montgomery, Modeste, & Frye-Anderson, 2002);
- diet and exercise (Wallace, 2002);
- seat belt use (Tayafian, Aghamolaei, Gregory, & Madani, 2011);
- breast screening behaviour (Yarbrough & Braden, 2001);
- breast self-examination (Luszczynska & Schwarzer, 2003);
- health service use (Rosenstock, 2005).

Becker and Rosenstock (1984) reviewed 19 studies and through a meta-analysis (which is when you statistically test all the studies together) confirmed that costs, benefits and perceived severity were the most significant cognitions. However, in a review of 13 studies investigating breast screening behaviour, Curry and Emmons (1994) found that uptake was explained by susceptibility, low perceived barriers and cues to action. A more recent meta-analysis (of 18 studies) by Carpenter (2010) confirmed that perceived benefits and barriers were consistently the most significant predictors of health behaviour. In contrast, however, there are studies that have found no support of the HBM at all once other variables, such as past behaviour, are taken into consideration, such as that by Abraham, Sheeran, Abrams and Spears (1996), who were seeking to predict condom use in adolescents.

Criticism of the HBM

The HBM has come under criticism as being a weak or insignificant model in explaining health behaviour. It fails to include:

- intentions to perform behaviour;
- social factors;
- coping appraisal.

Furthermore, there is no distinction between a motivational (cognitive) stage and a volitional (planning) phase (Schwarzer, 1992). Thus, the model is viewed as static (Conner & Norman, 1995).

KEY STUDY

Predicting TB screening (Hochbaum, 1956)

Background

A key study that led to the development of the HBM, this research investigated the uptake of tuberculosis (TB) screening in a mobile chest x-ray unit.

Method

In total 1,200 adults were examined, investigating their readiness to obtain an x-ray based on their beliefs of susceptibility to TB and the perceived benefits of early detection.

Findings

Those who believed they were susceptible to TB and that detection would be beneficial were more likely to have a voluntary x-ray, with 82% of those holding these views taking up the screening. Only 21% of those who did not hold these beliefs had an x-ray.

Conclusion

Both susceptibility and benefits of action were key determinants in the screening behaviour.

Test your knowledge

2.1 What are the cognitions of the health belief model?

2.2 What are the strengths and weaknesses of the health belief model?

Answers to these questions can be found on the companion website at:
www.pearsoned.co.uk/psychologyexpress

Further reading Health belief model

Topic	Key reading
An easy-to-read chapter on the HBM	Abraham, C., & Sheeran, P. (2005). Health belief model. In M. Conner & P. Norman (Eds.), *Predicting health behaviour* (2nd ed.). Buckingham: Open University Press.
A meta-analysis of HBM studies – a good overview	Carpenter, C. J. (2010). A meta-analysis of the effectiveness of health belief model variables in predicting behaviour. *Health Communication, 25,* 661–669.

Health locus of control

The 1950s was an era of theory development. Around the same time that the research leading to the HBM was conducted, Rotter (1954) was introducing a concept he termed 'locus of control'. Its origins lie in the social learning tradition, which focuses on expectancies, incentives and reinforcement. If a behaviour has an incentive (e.g. a healthier body) or is reinforced (e.g. makes you feel good), you are more likely to want to engage in the behaviour.

Rotter (1954) distinguished between those with an internal and an external locus of control:

- *Internal locus of control.* Individuals are more likely to believe that outcomes (i.e. their health) are a consequence of their own efforts.
- *External locus of control.* Individuals are more likely to believe that outcomes are determined by factors beyond their control.

Wallston (1978) developed Rotter's theory and constructed a Multidimensional Health Locus of Control (MHLC) Scale. This scale measures health expectancy beliefs along three dimensions: *internal, powerful others* and *chance.*

- *Internal* – the belief that health is under the influence of your own actions: '*I am directly responsible for my health.*'
- *Powerful others* – the belief that your health is determined by powerful others (i.e. health professionals): '*I can only do what my doctor tells me to do.*'
- *Chance* – the belief that health is uncontrollable and is in fact in the hands of fate or destiny: '*Whether I am well or not is a matter of luck or fate.*'

HLC research

An internal health locus of control (HLC) has been associated with:

- greater knowledge of illness and disease, such as asthma (Meyer, Sternfels, Fagan, Copeland, & Ford, 2001);
- physical activity, tooth brushing, consuming fruit and vegetables and seat belt use (Steptoe & Wardle, 2001).

In contrast, external HLC beliefs and 'chance health outcomes' are related to:

- early and repeated experience of illness and injury (Tolar, 1978);
- experience of family illness (Lau, 1982).

However, research findings in this area are mixed, with some reporting a positive relationship (Weiss & Larson, 1990) between HLC and health behaviours such as adherence to asthma medication (Burkhart & Rayens, 2005) and others showing a weak (Norman, Bennett, Smith, & Murphy, 1997) or inconsistent relationship in areas such as healthy eating (Bennett, Moore, Smith, Murphy, & Smith, 1994), alcohol consumption (Bennett, Norman, Murphy, Moore, & Tudor-Smith, 1998) and exercise (Rabinowitz, Melamed, Weisberg, Tal, & Ribak, 1992).

Criticism of HLC

The criticism of health locus of control continues, by questioning whether HLC is a state or a trait.

- Is an internal HLC stable?
- Could it change over time, or with respect to different behaviours and situations?
- Is it possible to have both high external and high internal HLC beliefs at the same time?
- Is it always beneficial to have an internal HLC? Think about a life-threatening, uncontrollable situation: it could be argued that an individual with an external HLC would possess the more desirable belief (i.e. 'Fate will decide if I live or die'), whereas those with internal beliefs may become more anxious due to their perceived lack of control over the potential outcome of the situation.

Beliefs in fate may also provide comfort for those who are terminally ill. Burish, Carey, Wallston, Stein, Jamison and Lyles (1984) found that in 62 chemotherapy patients, those who had an external HLC had lower levels of negative affect and physiological arousal. In contrast, Langer and Rodin (1976) found that giving hospitalised patients some control over their day-to-day lives (e.g. meal choice) led to a significant difference in mortality rates compared to a ward where patients were given no control.

There is further uncertainty as to whether certain actions should be considered as external or internal. For example, is the act of going to the doctor drawing on external HLC beliefs ('The doctor is a powerful other who can make me well'), or internal HLC beliefs ('I am determining my health status by seeking help') (Ogden, 2000)?

Modified social learning theory

Wallston (1992) suggested that failure to include the role of health value may deem the HLC concept inadequate. He developed a 'modified social learning theory' (MSLT), which suggests that HLC beliefs are necessary but not sufficient to perform health behaviour. It is argued that health value and self-efficacy (personal control) beliefs must also be present. Therefore, to perform a health behaviour an individual must value their health, believe that it is owing to their own health-related actions and concurrently believe that they are capable of performing the health behaviour in question. However, there seems to be little evidence in support of the MSLT in the literature and it is thought to have seen little application in the health behaviour field (Conner & Norman, 2005).

Test your knowledge

2.3 What is health locus of control?

2.4 What are the strengths and weaknesses of the health locus of control model?

Answers to these questions can be found on the companion website at:
www.pearsoned.co.uk/psychologyexpress

Further reading Health locus of control

Topic	Key reading
Background to the development of the MHLC scale	Wallston, K. A., Wallston, B. S., & DeVellis, R. (1978). Development of multidimensional health locus of control (MHLC) scales. *Health Education Monographs, 6*, 160–170.
The paper that introduced the MSLT	Wallston, K. A. (1992). Hocus-pocus, the focus isn't strictly on locus: Rotter's social learning theory modified for health. *Cognitive Therapy and Research, 16*, 183–199.

Social cognitive theory

Social cognitive theory (SCT; Bandura, 1982), which evolved from the social learning tradition, moves from a focus merely on cognition, to one that encompasses social influences on cognition and behaviour. It is predominantly a theory of human motivation based on three types of expectancy (Conner & Norman, 2005):

- *Situation–outcome expectancies* – beliefs about what outcome will occur without personal action (e.g. *'My smoking behaviour may lead to lung cancer'*); the belief in susceptibility to a health threat.

- *Action–outcome expectancies* – beliefs that outcomes occur as a result of personal action (e.g. *'Quitting smoking will lead to a reduced risk of lung cancer'*).

- *Perceived self-efficacy* – beliefs in personal capability to perform a specific action required to attain a desired outcome (e.g. *'I can stop smoking to reduce my risk of lung cancer'*).

While situation–outcome expectancies represent the belief that things happen in the world without personal action, action–outcome expectancies and self-efficacy expectancies allow the option to change the world and to cope actively with health threats by taking action (Schwarzer, 1992).

Schwarzer (1992) suggests that there is a clear causal ordering among these three types of expectancy. It is assumed that situation–outcome expectancies influence behaviour by the impact they have on action–outcome expectancies. For example, imagine you develop a risk perception (situation–outcome expectancy) from a health threat that makes you feel susceptible to an illness. This is thought to motivate you to consider relevant action that may reduce this risk. You would then evaluate an action–outcome expectancy (i.e. what you need to do to reduce your risk), and this is thought to be a precursors of self-efficacy (e.g. how confident you are that you can do what you need to do to reduce your risk), as individuals predominantly make assumptions about the consequences of behaviours before contemplating their ability to take action.

Self-efficacy

Self-efficacy expectancies are thought to be the most significant of the three beliefs, having a direct impact on behaviour and an indirect impact on the ability to influence intention. This first impact is derived from the fact that optimistic self-beliefs predict actual behavioural performance (Bandura, 1992; Schwarzer, 1992). The second impact reflects the fact that individuals typically intend to perform behaviours that they perceive to be within their control (Bandura, 1992; Schwarzer, 1992). If an individual believes that they can take action to solve a problem instrumentally, they become more inclined to do so, and feel more committed to this decision. Furthermore, people with high self-efficacy beliefs pursue more challenging and ambitious goals (Luszczynska, Scholz, & Schwarzer, 2005) and often picture themselves succeeding. This is strongly related to better health, higher achievement and more social interaction (Schwarzer & Fuchs, 1995).

This theory suggests that the likelihood that you will adopt a health-enhancing behaviour or refrain from a health-impairing behaviour is based on (a) the expectancy that you are at risk, (b) the expectancy that behaviour change would reduce this risk, and finally (c) the expectancy that you are capable of adopting or refraining from the behaviour in question.

SCT research

When measured as part of SCT or as a stand-alone cognition, self-efficacy is frequently reported as a strong predictor for health behaviours and behavioural intentions towards:

- exercise (Luszczynska et al., 2005);
- fruit intake (Wind et al., 2006);
- eating behaviours (Povey, Conner, Sparks, James, & Shepherd, 2000);
- the avoidance of smoking cigarettes (Fagan et al., 2003);
- alcohol consumption (Engels, Wiers, Lemmers, & Overbeek, 2005);
- breast self-examination (Luszczynska & Schwarzer, 2003).

Based on social cognitive theory, self-efficacy and outcome expectancy beliefs are often the more significant predictors of both behavioural intentions and health behaviours. So in essence, in performing a health-related behaviour, feeling at risk may motivate you to think about the behaviour, but you are more likely to do it if you feel it will improve your health and that you are capable of doing it.

Test your knowledge

2.5 Describe the three expectancies of SCT.

2.6 What are the strengths and weaknesses of SCT?

Answers to these questions can be found on the companion website at:
www.pearsoned.co.uk/psychologyexpress

Protection motivation theory

Making you feel like your health is at risk is a common strategy for many health campaigns. But as we have seen from the health belief model, inducing feelings of susceptibility and severity and conducting a cost–benefit analysis only goes some of the way to explaining why we engage in health behaviours. Social cognitive theory provides a further set of cognitions to consider, focusing more on our expectancies of health behaviours and our belief in our ability to do them. We know from the literature that this second theory provides a higher level of variance in explaining health behaviour. So it makes sense that someone has developed a theory that encapsulates the key parts of these two theories.

A common theory used in the investigation of the use of fear-arousing messages within health promotion is the protection motivation theory (PMT) (Figure 2.2), developed by Rogers (1975). The model focuses on two cognitive factors:

- *threat appraisal* – a function of both perceived *vulnerability* to illness and its *severity*;

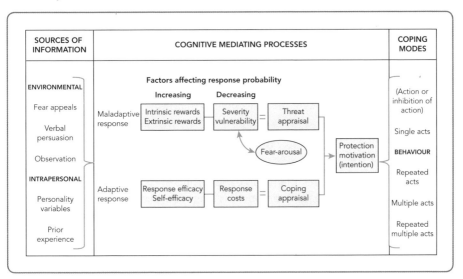

Figure 2.2 Protection motivation theory
Source: A protection motivation theory of fear appeals and attitude change, Rogers, R. W., *Journal of Psychology*, 1975, Taylor & Francis Ltd, reprinted by permission of the publisher (Taylor & Francis Ltd, http://www.tandf.co.uk/journals).

- *coping appraisal* – a function of both *response efficacy* (which is like an outcome-expectancy) and *self-efficacy* beliefs, leading to an evaluation of *response costs*.

The outcome of these appraisals is an *intention* (protection motivation), the strength of which reflects the degree of motivation to protect health, which in turn is thought to predict behaviour.

An individual is, therefore, more likely to intend to change their behaviour in response to a fear-arousing health message (Bennett & Murphy, 1997) if they believe:

- they are vulnerable to disease ('*My chances of getting bowel cancer are high*');
- the disease will have severe consequences ('*Bowel cancer is a serious illness*');
- there is a link between protective behaviours and reduced risk for disease ('*Eating more fruit and vegetables will reduce my risk of getting bowel cancer*'); and
- they are capable of engaging in them ('*I am confident I am able to eat more fruit and vegetables*').

PMT research

Findings from meta-analyses examining the use of the PMT (Floyd, Prentice-Dunn, & Rogers, 2000; Milne, Sheeran, & Orbell, 2000) show that components of the coping appraisal (response efficacy and self-efficacy) are stronger predictors of the protection motivation (intention) than components of threat appraisals (perceived vulnerability and severity). Plotnikoff and Higginbotham (2002) further found that intentions to exercise were best explained by self-efficacy beliefs, with weak effects reported for the elements within threat appraisal. Norman, Boer and Seydel (2005) confirm that self-efficacy is the strongest cognition in the model, emerging as the only significant predictor of exercise intentions and explaining 53% of the variance. However, when past exercise behaviour was added to the model, as in the case of Abraham et al. (1996), the effects of self-efficacy were diminished, resulting in past behaviour becoming the sole significant predictor of exercise intention, explaining 59% of the variance. This again suggests that past behaviour is a significant factor to bear in mind when trying to predict future behaviour.

PMT criticisms

The assumption that the recipients of fear-arousing messages are rational thinkers when it comes to their health is an obvious limitation of theoretical constructs incorporating the emotional element of fear. We, as humans, are not always rational thinkers. We may know all the risks linked to a behaviour that we do or do not do, but this may not influence our performance of it. Fear has been found to be associated with the prediction of a negative outcome (Walker, 2001) and a meta-analysis (Witte & Allen, 2000) shows that although fear appeals are effective in increasing levels of susceptibility and severity, they can lead to resistance towards messages, and consequently denial of a health threat, unless they are also able to enhance self-efficacy (Soames-Job, 1988).

The *dual process model* (Leventhal, 1984) suggests that fear-arousing messages point to two sets of cognitive processing:

- *Danger control* – threat is evaluated and ways of dealing with it considered.
- *Fear control* – which leaves the individual considering how to cope with any emotional reaction to the threat. The emotion is short-lived, but the cognitive representation and coping plan remain in the long-term memory.

The *elaboration likelihood model* (Petty & Cacioppo, 1986) suggests that persuasive communication will work only if people are interested in the health relevant message, it has relevance to them and they are cognitively able to process it.

Therefore, we need to be careful when inducing fear to motivate individuals to protect their health and ensure that they are cognitively able to receive the message and then facilitated to produce effective, positive coping strategies to minimise the threat.

In sum, the protection motivation theory is a good model when predicting health behaviours. However, the evaluation of the outcome (response efficacy) and personal control beliefs (self-efficacy) are the cognitions most likely to influence health behaviour.

 Sample question   *Problem-based learning*

Think of two of your own behaviours: one that enhances your health and one that impairs your health. Evaluate which cognitions motivate these behaviours.

Unrealistic optimism

The reason why fear appeals may not have their desired effect could be explained by *unrealistic optimism*. This concept, proposed by Weinstein (1982), suggests that the reason people are not motivated to protect their health is because they have an inaccurate, or unrealistically optimistic, perception of their risk: '*It won't happen to me*'.

Weinstein (1987) proposed that this egocentric, selective and irrational perception of health risk, also known as *optimistic bias*, is due to four cognitive factors:

- lack of personal experience with the problem;
- the belief that the problem is preventable by individual action;
- the belief that, if the problem has not yet appeared, it will not appear in the future;
- the belief that the problem is infrequent.

Weinstein (1984) suggests that individuals tend to ignore their risk-increasing behaviours (such as unsafe sex) and focus on their risk-decreasing behaviours (such as avoiding drugs). They also tend to ignore other people's risk-reducing behaviours (such as their friends practising safe sex). Unrealistic optimism has been shown in those who:

● smoke (Weinstein, Marcus, & Moser, 2005);
● use sun beds (Sjöberg, Holm, Ullén, & Brandberg, 2004);
● do not use condoms (Chapin, 2001).

Therefore, if people hold unrealistically optimistic views of their health risk, they may not even evaluate a potential threat to their health status, and would, in turn, not consider how they would cope, leading to no change in their health behaviour.

Test your knowledge

2.7 What are the two key cognitive dimensions in the protection motivation theory?

2.8 List the four cognitive factors of unrealistic optimism.

Answers to these questions can be found on the companion website at:
www.pearsoned.co.uk/psychologyexpress

Further reading Protection motivation theory

Topic	Key reading
Protection motivation theory meta-analysis	Milne, S., Sheeran, P., & Orbell, S. (2000). Prediction and intervention in health-related behaviour: A meta-analytic review of protection motivation theory. *Journal of Applied Social Psychology, 30*, 106–143.
Unrealistic optimism	Weinstein, N. D. (1982). Unrealistic optimism about susceptibility to health problems. *Journal of Behavioral Medicine, 5*, 441–460.

? Sample question   Essay

Compare and contrast the contribution of any two social cognition models to the understanding of exercise behaviour OR healthy eating.

Theory of planned behaviour

The theory of planned behaviour (TPB; Ajzen, 1985) is an extension of the theory of reasoned action (TRA; Fishbein & Ajzen, 1975). The TRA examines the individual within their social context and emphasises the importance of social cognitions in the form of attitudes (behavioural beliefs and evaluations of outcomes) and subjective norms (normative beliefs about the attitudes of important others towards a behaviour and motivation to comply). The TPB expanded the TRA by incorporating the measure of perceived behavioural control (PBC) (see Figure 2.3).

The theory of planned behaviour suggests that behaviour is predicted by intentions, which are in turn predicted by attitudes, subjective norms and perceived behavioural control:

- *Attitudes* – an evaluation of the behaviour (Conner & Sparks, 2005) made up of a set of beliefs in the likelihood of an outcome occurring as a result of performing a behaviour (*behavioural belief*) and the evaluation of that outcome (*outcome evaluation*).

- *Subjective norms* – a function of *normative beliefs* encapsulating the perception of how *significant others* (e.g. parents, friends) would view the behaviour, and how much the person is *motivated to comply* with these significant others.

- *Perceived behavioural control* – the belief that the individual can access the resources and opportunities necessary to perform the behaviour successfully. These factors are both *internal* (knowledge, skills, emotions) and *external* (opportunities, dependence on others, barriers).

The determinant of behaviour is intention, reflecting the hypothesis that people engage in behaviours they intend to perform (Conner & Sparks, 2005):

- *Intention* – represents a conscious decision, reflecting a person's motivation to put effort into the performance of behaviour.

The TPB states that any particular behaviour comprises:

a   an action (or behaviour);

b   performed on or towards a target;

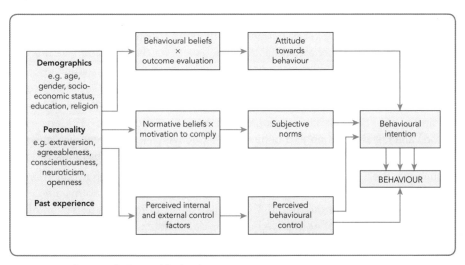

Figure 2.3 Theory of planned behaviour

Source: *From intentions to action: A theory of planned behaviour*. In J. Kuhl & J. Beckham (Eds.), Action control: From cognitions to behaviors, New York: Springer (Ajzen I. 1985) pp. 11–39, with kind permission from Springer Science and Business Media. Copyright © 1985, Springer-Verlag Berlin Heidelberg.

c in a context;

d at a time or occasion.

An example of this has been provided by Conner and Norman (1995) in relation to oral hygiene. In this instance, a person (a) brushes, (b) their teeth, (c) in the bathroom, (d) every morning after breakfast. A combination of these elements is important for the model, with the statement of an action and time-frame constituting the minimum elements.

TPB research

The theory of planned behaviour has been applied to a range of behaviours (Armitage & Conner, 2001) and has been successful in explaining:

- adolescent smoking (McMillan, Higgins, & Conner, 2005);
- alcohol and drug use (McMillan & Conner, 2003);
- blood donation (Giles & Cairns, 1995);
- healthy eating (Povey et al., 2000);
- physical activity (Hagger, Chatzisarantis, & Biddle, 2002).

When applying the TPB to physical activity, reporting on a meta-analysis of 72 studies using the theory for both adults and young people, Hagger, Chatzisarantis and Biddle (2002) found that the strongest influences on intentions were perceived behavioural control, self-efficacy and past behaviour. Subjective norms were found to be a small but significant predictor. Overall, the TPB explained 45% of the variance in intentions.

In contrast, in a meta-analysis of 206 prospective studies using the TPB to examine a range of health behaviours, McEachan, Conner, Taylor and Lawton (2011) report that attitude, subjective norms and perceived behavioural control contribute to 44.3% of the variance in behavioural intention. Attitude was revealed as the strongest predictor of behavioural intentions, except for detection behaviours, where PBC explained the largest amount of the variance. However, subjective norms were found to be the most important predictor for safe-sex behaviours.

Earlier work (Armitage & Conner, 2001) using a meta-analytic review (of 185 studies) of a range of behaviours found that the TPB accounted for 39% and 27% of the variance in intention and behaviour, respectively. Across all studies, the subjective norm construct was found to be a weak predictor of intentions.

In summary the TPB is a successful model at explaining health behaviour. There is, however, a common indication which suggests that subjective norms are the weakest element of the model. Explanations for this include a reflection of the lesser importance of normative beliefs as determinants of intentions and methodological differences across studies, such as the use of single versus multiple item measures (Conner & Norman, 1995). However, there seems to be more influence of subjective norms when the behaviours in question involve others (e.g. safe sex). Further research is needed to see if these findings differ in terms of different cultures and populations (e.g. children).

Practical application Theory of planned behaviour

Background

Wong and Mullan (2009) tested the TPB's ability to predict breakfast consumption in a one-week prospective study.

Method

Attitude, subjective norm, perceived behavioural control, intentions and past behaviour in relation to breakfast consumption were examined in 96 participants (mean age 19.46 years; [SD = 2.17]) at baseline and one week later.

TPB questionnaire

The authors provided wordings of the questions they used to measure the TPB, which you will find often differs between studies. Not all authors do this, which makes it difficult to replicate studies. You can find guidelines on how to format questions for the TPB in Conner and Norman's book *Predicting Health Behaviour* (2005).

Findings

Results confirmed that the TPB was a significant model in predicting breakfast consumption intentions (R^2 = 0.53). However, it was only attitude and perceived behavioural control that were significantly contributing to explaining intention, with no contribution from subjective norm. Past behaviour was the most significant predictor of behavioural intention (23%) and actual behaviour (74%). Intention predicted behaviour one week on (by 64%). However, the other cognitions were unable to explain actual behaviour over and above that of intention.

Conclusion

The TPB was a good model at explaining breakfast consumption, with more strength in its ability to predict intention than behaviour. Findings confirm that subjective norm is a weak component in the model and highlights the need to take past behaviour into consideration.

Test your knowledge

2.9 What are the key cognitions of the TPB?

2.10 What are the strengths and weaknesses of the TPB?

Answers to these questions can be found on the companion website at:
www.pearsoned.co.uk/psychologyexpress

Further reading Theory of planned behaviour

Topic	Key reading
Meta-analysis looking at many health behaviours	Armitage, C. J., & Conner, M. (2001). Efficacy of the theory of planned behaviour: A meta-analytic review. *British Journal of Social Psychology*, 40, 471–499.
A well-written chapter on TPB	Conner, M., & Sparks, P. (2005). The theory of planned behaviour and health behaviours. In M. Conner & P. Norman (Eds.), *Predicting health behaviour* (2nd ed.). Buckingham: Open University Press.

CASE STUDY

Exercise

The client

Gemma is a 32-year-old woman, who works in the City of London, travelling three hours a day with little time or motivation for exercise. Gemma recently went to see her GP after experiencing symptoms of dizziness and headaches, and after a thorough investigation her GP informed her that her blood pressure had increased. Meta-analysis has provided evidence to suggest that aerobic exercise can reduce blood pressure (Whelton, Chin, Xin, & He, 2002), and consequently the GP suggested that she should aim to become more active. But how as a health psychologist can you support her to do this?

Background – the problem

Government guidance suggests that 30 minutes of moderate to vigorous activities five times a week can lead to a 20–30% reduced risk of premature death and up to 50% reduced risk of major diseases such as coronary heart disease (for which high blood pressure is a risk factor) and cancer (Department of Health, 2004b).

Advice

Let's relate this to the theory of planned behaviour. Gemma may evaluate this behaviour negatively (*attitude*), and may believe that exercising will not help her to reduce her blood pressure (*behavioural belief*). She may not believe that reducing her blood pressure will make her feel any better (*outcome evaluation*).

Her social support network may be influential. What if none of Gemma's friends exercise? She may hold low *normative beliefs* of how *significant others* (e.g. parents, friends) view this behaviour. What if they do exercise but Gemma has no *motivation to comply* with these significant others?

Gemma may also feel that she has low levels of *perceived behavioural control* (i.e. she may feel she does not have access to the resources and opportunities necessary to exercise). Perhaps Gemma used to be active before holding her present job and needs to work on time management and her belief in her ability to factor exercise into her daily routine.

So, how can we help her to be more physically active? As health psychologists we should aim to increase cognitions such as confidence (self-efficacy), attitude (by providing information on the benefits) and social norms (increasing her awareness of others of her age who work in the City and are physically active), while also moderating optimistic bias of health risk, evaluating vulnerability and severity, and ensuring that Gemma has the cognitive ability to cope with such threats.

Further reading Social Cognition Models

Topic	Key reading
Overview of the models	Conner, M., & Norman, P. (Eds.) (1998). Special issue: Social cognition models in health psychology. *Psychology and Health, 13,* 179–185.
Excellent, easy-to-read book that discusses each model chapter by chapter	Conner, M., & Norman, P. (2005). *Predicting health behaviour* (2nd ed.). Buckingham: Open University Press.

▶

Topic	Key reading
Good critique of social cognition models	Ogden, J. (2003). Some problems with social cognition models: A pragmatic and conceptual analysis. *Health Psychology, 22*, 424–428.

Chapter summary – pulling it all together

→ Can you tick all of the points from the revision checklist at the beginning of this chapter?

→ Attempt the sample question from the beginning of this chapter using the answer guidelines below.

→ Go to the companion website at www.pearsoned.co.uk/psychologyexpress to access more revision support online, including interactive quizzes, flashcards, You be the marker exercises as well as answer guidance for the Test your knowledge and Sample questions from this chapter.

Answer guidelines

 Sample question   *Essay*

Critically evaluate the health belief model and protection motivation theory in explaining preventive health behaviours (such as screening, self-examination and condom use) OR health-enhancing behaviours (such as healthy eating and exercise).

Approaching the question

Your answer should aim to provide an analysis of how social cognition models can help to explain a range of health behaviours.

Important points to include

● Begin by outlining what the key cognitions are in each of the models you are examining.

● For each model/theory you will need to:

   ● consider the strengths and weaknesses of the model and the individual cognitions used in the model;

   ● discuss the empirical research that informs the theories (does it support the models?);

   ● evaluate differences in the effectiveness of the models between health behaviours and studies.

- You should then consider the usefulness of using social cognition models to be able to predict health behaviour.
- Conclude by making suggestions about how the models could be improved and directions for future research.

Make your answer stand out

It is easy to fall into the trap of simply describing different types of social cognition models in relation to health behaviour. However, a good answer will remember to take a critical stance, evaluating the strengths and limitations of the model/theory and research that has used it. A good student would also show original thinking by considering the overlaps of cognitions between the models, the differences in the effectiveness of the models for different health behaviours, and future considerations in order to challenge the current empirical evidence and advance theoretical development.

Explore the accompanying website at www.pearsoned.co.uk/psychologyexpress

→ Prepare more effectively for exams and assignments using the answer guidelines for questions from this chapter.
→ Test your knowledge using multiple choice questions and flashcards.
→ Improve your essay skills by exploring the You be the marker exercises.

Notes

3

Intervention design: changing health behaviour

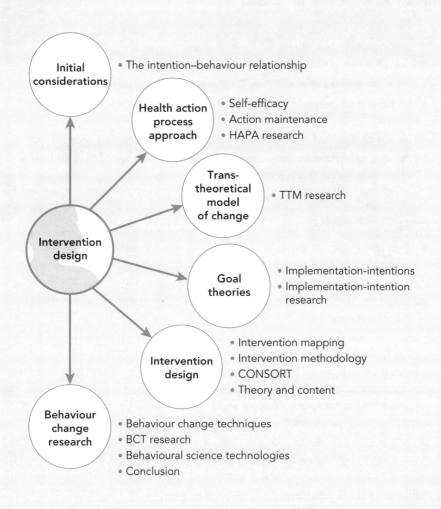

- **Initial considerations** — • The intention–behaviour relationship

- **Health action process approach** — • Self-efficacy
  • Action maintenance
  • HAPA research

- **Trans-theoretical model of change** — • TTM research

- **Intervention design**

- **Goal theories** — • Implementation-intentions
  • Implementation-intention research

- **Intervention design** — • Intervention mapping
  • Intervention methodology
  • CONSORT
  • Theory and content

- **Behaviour change research** — • Behaviour change techniques
  • BCT research
  • Behavioural science technologies
  • Conclusion

A printable version of this topic map is available from
www.pearsoned.co.uk/psychologyexpress

Introduction

How do you change health behaviour? Is an intention to be more physically active enough to increase the uptake of physical activity? Is wanting to stop smoking enough to change?

This chapter focuses on the theoretical and practical considerations of health intervention research. Constructs such as the *health action process approach*, the *transtheoretical model of change* and *implementation-intentions* will be discussed. Intervention design and the taxonomies that should be considered when conducting evidence-based, theoretically driven behaviour-change research will be considered critically.

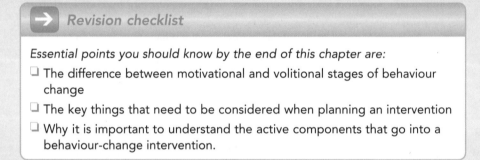

Revision checklist

Essential points you should know by the end of this chapter are:

❑ The difference between motivational and volitional stages of behaviour change

❑ The key things that need to be considered when planning an intervention

❑ Why it is important to understand the active components that go into a behaviour-change intervention.

Assessment advice

When you are writing an essay or answering an exam question on this topic, you should consider the following points:

● *Content.* What is the difference between motivating behaviour change and making it happen? What do you need to consider in designing an effective health intervention?

● *Evidence* is always required, so ensure you *back up your argument with references*. You will find lots of experiments in this area that use an intervention design, so be sure to draw from that body of research and look out for any additional follow-up studies from the authors of interventions. You may also find published protocols which give you a little more detail of what went into the intervention.

● *Be critical* of the evidence. For example, if an intervention was being tested, did it use a within- or between-subjects design? Was there a control group? And if so, was it active (i.e. the control group has some type of contact or intervention not based on the one under investigation) or passive (i.e. no contact or intervention, such as those on a waiting list)? Was the sample big enough to give adequate power? Were pre- and post-test measures taken? What was the effect size? Was the intervention effect followed up to see if it was sustained over time?

If so, for how long? Were there any fidelity issues? Is there enough information for the intervention to be replicated? What are the strengths and weaknesses of the intervention? What are the recommendations for future research?

Sample question

Could you answer this question? Below is a typical essay question that could rise on this topic.

 Sample question   *Essay*

What motivates behaviour change? Discuss in detail, with reference to at least one health behaviour.

Guidelines on answering this question are included at the end of this chapter, whilst guidance on tackling other exam questions can be found on the companion website at **www.pearsoned.co.uk/psychologyexpress**

Initial considerations

When designing an intervention, you should first consider its need. This would often come from an epidemiological view of a health problem – the behaviours that are linked to the problem and the cognitions linked to the behaviours. For example, will changing health behaviour X result in a substantial reduction in disease outcome Y? Or, will changing cognition X result in a substantial reduction/increase in health behaviour Y and thus disease outcome Z?

The intention–behaviour relationship

An intention is the instruction an individual gives themselves to perform a particular behaviour or achieve a certain goal, and is often used as a measure of subsequent action. However, some people may develop an intention towards a behaviour, then not take any action (Sheeran, 2002). This discrepancy has been labelled the *intention–behaviour gap* and has been a focal challenge for research (Sniehotta, Scholz, & Schwarzer, 2005).

Given the reliance on 'intention' in cognition models, it seems plausible to question how well they predict behaviour. Sheeran (2002) concluded from a meta-analysis of studies that intentions do predict behaviour, although they are found to be able to explain only 28% of behavioural outcomes from a sample of 82,107 participants (422 studies).

There are, therefore, substantial 'gaps' between intention and behaviour. Across a number of studies investigating exercise, condom use and cancer screening, just under half (47%) of the participants did not see their intention through to action (Sheeran, Milne, Webb, & Gollwitzer, 2005).

Health action process approach

One model that attempts to understand the link between intention and behaviour is the *health action process approach* (HAPA: Schwarzer, 1992). The HAPA suggests that the adoption, initiation and maintenance of a health behaviour involves two phases (see Figure 3.1): a motivation phase and a volition (action) phase.

● During the *motivation phase*, an intention is formed, based on three cognitions: *self-efficacy*, *outcome expectancies* and *risk perceptions*.

● The *volition phase* focuses on cognitions that instigate and control the action and can be subdivided into a further three phases: *planning*, *action* and *maintenance*. The volition phase consists of three levels: cognitive, behavioural and situational. It is suggested that it is the cognitions that control the action, which is subdivided into action plans and action control. This second phase describes how hard people try and how long they persist.

Self-efficacy

Schwarzer (1992) suggests that self-efficacy plays a vital role at all stages, while other cognitions have a limited scope. For example, risk perceptions are important for thinking about changing your behaviour, but are not significant after you have decided to change. Moreover, outcome expectancies are

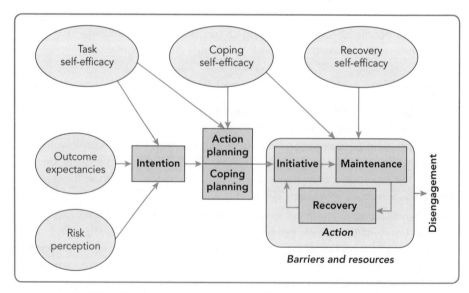

Figure 3.1 Health action process approach (HAPA)

Source: Self-efficacy: Thought control of action, Washington, DC: Hemisphere Publishing Corporation (Schwarzer, R. 1992), republished with permission of Informa plc., permission conveyed through Copyright Clearance Center, Inc.

important when you may weigh up the pros and cons of a behaviour, but they lose their influence after a decision has been made.

Action maintenance

When an action has been initiated, it must be maintained. The action could be at risk from opposing cognitions, therefore a meta-cognitive strategy is needed. For example, you may intend to go running after college (your goal is to be more active) but other cognitions, such as 'It's cold outside', 'I'm tired' or 'It will make me miss Hollyoaks', may compete with your intention to act. Self-efficacy determines the amount of effort and perseverance given. Once an action has been initiated, it is self-efficacy which determines how hard you try to maintain the action. Coping and recovery self-efficacy are matched to specific risk situations. People with high levels of self-efficacy are less likely to foresee failure and will visualise success and persevere more when faced with obstacles (Schwarzer, 2011).

HAPA research

The HAPA has been applied to many health behaviours, such as physical activity, breast self-examination, seat belt use, smoking cigarettes, dietary behaviours and dental flossing (Abraham, Conner, Jones, & O'Connor, 2008; Schwarzer, 2008; Schwarzer & Luszczynska, 2008; Schwarzer et al., 2003; Sutton, 2008).

Test your knowledge

3.1 What are the cognitions of the HAPA and how do they work?

3.2 What are the strengths and weaknesses of the HAPA?

Answers to these questions can be found on the companion website at: www.pearsoned.co.uk/psychologyexpress

---

Further reading Health action process approach

Topic	Key reading
Overview and discussion of the HAPA	Leventhal, H., & Mora, P. A. (2008). Predicting outcomes or modelling process? Commentary on the health action process approach. *Applied Psychology, 57*(1), 51–65.
Intention–behaviour gap	Sutton, S. (2008). How does the health action process approach (HAPA) bridge the intention–behaviour gap? An examination of the model's causal structure. *Applied Psychology, 57*(1), 66–74.

 Sample question　　　　　　　　　　　　　　　　　*Essay*

Evaluate the mechanisms and effectiveness of the transtheoretical model of change in the understanding of smoking cessation.

Transtheoretical model of change

Theories of behaviour change suggest that people progress through stages that involve an individual contemplating a new behaviour and preparing for change. One of the best-known stage theories is the *transtheoretical model (TTM) of change* (Prochaska & DiClemente, 1983). Also referred to as the 'stages of change', this model suggests that a person could be in one of five key stages (see Figure 3.2). This is not a linear model, where an individual moves from one stage to the next, but more like a revolving door, where they can go in at one stage, and go out at another. Let's use smoking as an example:

- *Precontemplation.* The person has no intention of stopping behaviour. They may be unaware of the risk to health, uninterested or unwilling to make a change: '*I am happy being a smoker and have no intention to stop.*'

- *Contemplation.* The person intends to take action in the next six months. They are aware that smoking is a problem and are thinking about action. But they are often struggling with ambivalence (the pros and cons of the behaviour) and so are not quite committed to action: '*I want to stop, but it's so difficult*'; '*I have been coughing a lot lately, perhaps I should stop smoking*'.

- *Preparation.* The person intends to change in the next 30 days and has begun to take steps towards it. They are committed to stopping and have made plans: '*I will stop by the end of the month*'; '*This is the last pack of cigarettes that I will buy*'.

- *Action.* The person has changed their behaviour (but for less than six months): '*I've stopped smoking!*'.

- *Maintenance.* Behaviour has changed for over six months: '*I haven't smoked for six months now*'. Many go through the stages of change several times (relapsing) before maintenance is established.

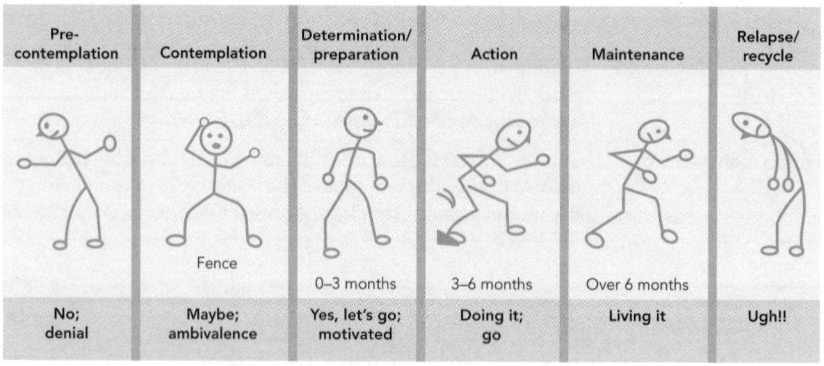

Figure 3.2 **Transtheoretical model of change**

The model also has a further two stages in relation to:

- *Relapse.* This is where the person goes back to a former stage. It is acknowledged (DiClemente, 1997) as common and can occur at any stage. Relapse prevention can help to avoid this stage and it is important to distinguish between a 'lapse' and a 'relapse'.
- *Termination.* This is where behaviour change has occurred for long enough for the individual to feel completely free from their previous behaviour and strong enough to maintain the change.

However, the TTM is not just about the stages of change; it also includes other constructs that are each used to support the transition between these stages:

- *Decisional balance.* The benefits and costs (pros/cons) of changing behaviour are weighed up. This is often helpful in the contemplation phase when an individual is struggling with *ambivalence* (feeling two ways about something), but would not be used if they were precontemplating, and may be redundant once preparation and action have occurred.
- *Confidence.* Similar to self-efficacy, this refers to how confident an individual feels that they are to be able to change their behaviour, especially in the face of challenges.
- *Temptation.* This is the desire to perform the unhealthy behaviour in challenging situations.
- *The processes of change* (Prochaska, Velicer, DiClemente, & Fava, 1988). This is separated into two processes with five differing activities in each:
  - *Cognitive-affective/experiential processes* through which individuals gain relevant information on the basis of their own actions/experiences, including:
    - *Consciousness raising* – such as enhancing knowledge and tips to support the behaviour change.
    - *Dramatic relief* – relating to the experience of negative emotions evoked by the health risks of the unhealthy behaviour.
    - *Self-re-evaluation* – which refers to a realisation that behaviour change is important to self-identity.
    - *Environmental re-evaluation* – realising the negative impact of the old behaviour or the positive impact of the behaviour change on the individual's social and physical environment.
    - *Self-liberation* – making a firm commitment to change.
  - *Behavioural processes* in which the information is generated by environmental events and behaviours, including:
    - *Helping relationships* – linked to the use of social support.
    - *Counterconditioning* – referring to the substitution of the unwanted behaviour with something more positive.
    - *Reinforcement management* – rewarding positive behaviour change and reducing any reward for the unwanted behaviour.

- *Stimulus control* – removing cues to the unhealthy behaviour, and adding reminders to support behaviour change.
- *Social liberation* – allowing the belief that social norms are changing in favour of behaviour change.

TTM research

The TTM has most widely been used to understand smoking cessation (DiClemente et al., 1991; Guo, Aveyard, Fielding, & Sutton, 2009; Hoeppner et al., 2012; Prochaska & DiClemente, 1983) but has also been applied to:

- poly-drug use (Evers et al., 2012);
- physical activity (Spencer, Adams, Malone, Roy, & Yost, 2006) and sedentary behaviour (Woods, Mutrie, & Scott, 2002);
- fruit and vegetable intake (Di Noia, Schinke, Prochaska, & Contento, 2006);
- weight management (Johnson et al., 2008);
- condom use (Arden & Armitage, 2008);
- sun protection (Weinstock, Rossi, Redding, & Maddock, 2002).

However, although still a popular model, the TTM has received some criticism. A systematic review suggests that there is little evidence for its effectiveness in intervention programmes for a range of health behaviours (Bridle et al., 2005). Others claim there is a need to rethink the model (Sutton, 2001) or abandon it altogether in addiction research (West, 2005). Some, however, maintain that the model has some promise (Armitage, 2009).

Test your knowledge

3.3 What are the five key stages of change in the TTM?

3.4 Identify the two processes of change in the TTM and the ten activities within them.

Answers to these questions can be found on the companion website at: **www.pearsoned.co.uk/psychologyexpress**

Further reading Transtheoretical model

Topic	Key reading
Classic paper in the development of the TTM	Prochaska, J. O., & DiClemente, C. C. (1983). Stages and processes of self-change of smoking: Toward an integrative model of change. *Journal of Consulting and Clinical Psychology, 51*, 390–395.
Article looking at decisional balance and temptation	Guo, B., Aveyard, P., Fielding, A., & Sutton, S. (2009). Do the transtheoretical model processes of change, decisional balance and temptation predict stage movement? Evidence from smoking cessation in adolescents. *Addiction, 104*(5), 828–838.

Goal theories

From the principles of self-regulation (Carver & Scheier, 2001), behaviours are thought to be goal-driven, controlled by feedback and outcome expectancies, which may lead to disengagement of a goal if it is viewed as unattainable (Wrosch, Scheier, Miller, Schulz, & Carver, 2003). It is, therefore, important for goals to be SMART (specific, measurable, achievable, relevant and timely), although there are many variations to this acronym (Rubin, 2002). A goal needs to be clear and specific: 'being healthier' is not a specific goal, but 'exercising for 30 minutes each day' is. In making the goal specific, it is more likely to be measureable, and this way, the person can see when they have reached it. It also needs to be within their grasp and achievable; if not, they will probably fail, and that failure may prevent them from trying again. It needs to be relevant to them – not a goal someone else has imposed on them – and it needs to be the right goal for them at that moment in time, making it timely. A good place to look at how to develop SMART goals is the *NHS Health Trainer Handbook* (Michie et al., 2004).

Holding a strong intention does not necessarily mean goal achievement (Gollwitzer & Sheeran, 2006). Therefore, it is suggested that an action plan (stating when, where and how) has a positive effect on goal attainment. Gollwitzer (1993) developed the concept of *implementation-intentions* based on previous work on the *model of action phases* (MAP: Heckhausen & Gollwitzer, 1987; Gollwitzer, 1990). MAP suggested that goal achievement consisted of two phases: a motivational phase of goal setting (intention formation) and the volitional phase of goal striving (intention realisation).

Implementation-intentions

While goal setting describes what will be done, an implementation-intention also includes when, where and how it will be achieved. It takes the form of an *'if–then'* planning tool (Gollwitzer, 1999; Gollwitzer & Sheeran, 2006). The 'if' relates to the anticipated situation, and the 'then' is in reference to the response (Sheeran et al., 2005). For example: *if* situation Y occurs, *then* I will initiate goal-directed behaviour Z (or: *if* 'it is 8 a.m.', *then* 'I will take my medicine with a cup of tea'). The creation of this plan implies that the person creates a commitment to the goal-directed behaviour in a given situation (i.e. to adhere to medication at a certain time (8 a.m.) with a cue (tea) to action), which can then become habitual, illuminating possible barriers before they have occurred.

Implementation-intention research

Gollwitzer and Sheeran (2006) identified 94 independent studies ($n = 8,461$), showing that implementation-intentions significantly increase goal achievement compared to other contemporary models (such as the theory of planned behaviour and protection motivation theory). Further support of this technique shows it is a powerful predictor of:

- healthy eating (Kellar & Abraham, 2005);
- physical activity (Prestwich, Lawton, & Conner, 2003);
- condom use (Abraham et al., 1999);
- testicular self-examination (Steadman & Quine, 2004);
- flu vaccinations (Milkman, Beshears, Choi, Laibson, & Madrian, 2011);
- a change in smoking behaviour (Webb, Sheeran, & Luszczynska, 2009).

The technique has also been found to improve the ability of other theories, such as protection motivation theory, to promote physical activity (Milne, Orbell, & Sheeran, 2002). However, the technique is not always found to be effective, such as when used in a study to increase breast-screening behaviour (Steadman & Quine, 2006).

Bagozzi and Edwards (2000) argue that implementation-intentions will be strengthened with added appraisals, such as affect. Cook, Gaitán and Chater (2010) support this, identifying the effectiveness of implementation-intentions in a weight loss trial drawing on response outcomes that increased positive affect (happiness: i.e. *If* I am bored, *then* I will do something that makes me happy). It may be the case, therefore, that while implementation-intentions obtain strong goal achievement, they may be strengthened by other constructs.

Test your knowledge

3.5 What are implementation-intentions?

3.6 Try to write an implementation-intention to increase physical activity.

Answers to these questions can be found on the companion website at:
www.pearsoned.co.uk/psychologyexpress

Practical application Implementation-intentions

Background

Luszczynska (2006) assessed physical activity implementation-intentions after a heart attack (myocardial infarction: MI).

Method

Data were collected from 114 patients at three time points: one week after an MI, eight weeks after an MI (where they were assigned to an intervention or control group) and eight months after an MI.

Findings

Level of physical activity engagement was significantly lower in the control group as compared to the intervention group, who received the implementation intervention eight months after randomisation.

Conclusion

This research supports the use of implementation-intentions in a real-world setting and confirms that they were effective in supporting physical activity to aid rehabilitation.

Further reading **Implementation-intentions**

Topic	Key reading
Good meta-analysis that reviews many studies in the area	Gollwitzer, P. M., & Sheeran, P. (2006). Implementation intentions and goal achievement: A meta-analysis of effects and processes. *Advances in Experimental Social Psychology, 38*, 69–119.
Easy-to-read chapter on the background of implementation-intentions	Sheeran, P., Milne, S., Webb, T. L., & Gollwitzer, P. M. (2005). Implementation intentions and health behaviour. In M. Conner & P. Norman (Eds.), *Predicting health behaviour* (2nd ed., pp. 276–323). Maidenhead: Open University Press.

 Sample question   *Problem-based learning*

Develop a behaviour change intervention with specific reference to at least one health behaviour, with the aim of improving public health.

Intervention design

Any intervention that aims to change behaviour needs careful consideration. When developing an intervention, it is useful to follow the six steps of the *generalised model for programme development* (see Figure 3.3) proposed by McKenzie and Smeltzer (2000):

1 First, there must be an engagement with and understanding of the target audience. This could be achieved through an extensive literature review, or focus groups.

2 You then need to assess the needs of the target audience, to develop an understanding of their issues and/or constraints.

3 From here, goals and objectives of the intervention need to be formalised; what can realistically be achieved from the intervention and how will this be accomplished?

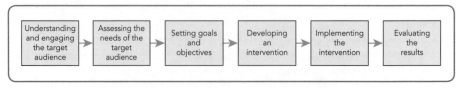

Figure 3.3 **Generalised model for programme development (McKenzie & Smeltzer, 2000)**

4 Then format the design of the intervention. It must be relevant to the audience, who should be receptive to it. This is known in social marketing as audience segmentation (Evans, 2006).

5 When the intervention is implemented, consideration must be given to how, where, when and for how long the intervention will run.

6 Finally, the effectiveness of the intervention must be evaluated. Fidelity (how accurately the intervention was delivered, as specified in the protocol/manual) of the intervention should also be considered (Borrelli et al., 2005).

Intervention mapping

What we describe above is a type of intervention map. *Intervention mapping* (Kok, Schaalma, Ruiter, Van Empelen, & Brug, 2004) provides a protocol for considerations that may improve our understanding of behaviour change when planning interventions. Figure 3.4 represents the six stages that Bartholomew, Parcel, Kok, Gottlieb and Fernandez (2011) suggest should be considered:

1 *Needs assessment.* Establish the problem and specify goals.

2 *Matrices.* State measureable outcome and create change objectives.

3 *Theory-based methods and practical strategies.* Develop methodology, drawing on theoretical frameworks.

4 *Programme.* Develop intervention and create a protocol.

5 *Adoption and implementation plan.* Implement intervention.

6 *Evaluation plan.* Evaluate intervention.

Other popular intervention design models include the *six-stage model for health promotion* (Nutbeam, 1998), as seen in Figure 3.5, and the PRECEDE/PROCEED model (PRECEDE: **P**redisposing, **R**einforcing and **E**nabling **C**onstructs in **E**ducational/**E**nvironmental **D**iagnosis and **E**valuation; PROCEED: **P**olicy, **R**egulatory,

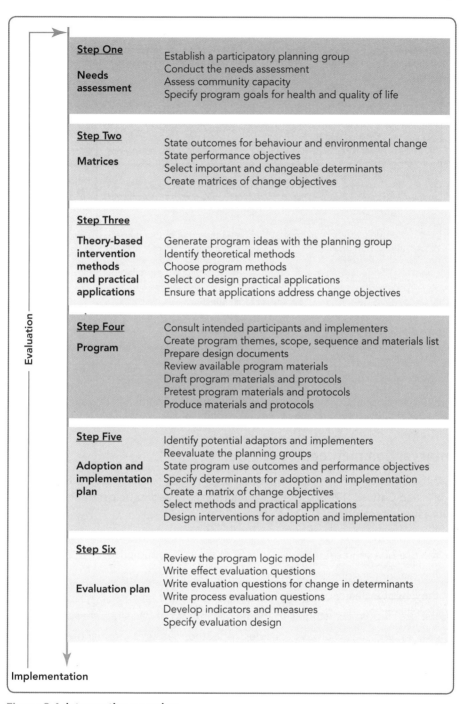

Figure 3.4 Intervention mapping

Source: Based on Kok et al. (2004) and Bartholomew et al., 2011.

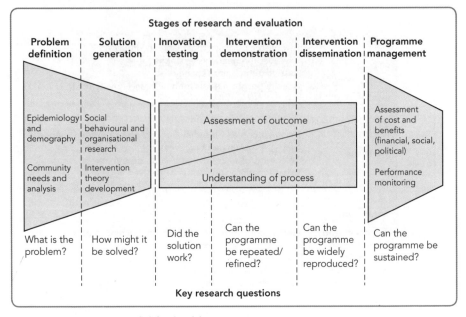

Figure 3.5 Six-stage model for health promotion

Source: Evaluating health promotion-progress, problems and solutions, *Health Promotion International*, 13(1), pp. 27–44 (Nutbeam D. 1998), by permission of Oxford University Press.

and **O**rganisational **C**onstructs in **E**ducational and **E**nvironmental **D**evelopment), first introduced in the 1970s (Green & Kreuter, 1999), as seen in Figure 3.6.

Intervention methodology

The methodology of an intervention is a key thing to consider. Nutbeam, Smith and Catford (1990) suggest five factors that need to be established for a successful intervention:

- the use of pre-test studies to determine baseline measurements;
- the use of a representative sample from the target audience;
- the random assignment to intervention and control groups;
- the use of a clearly designed intervention;
- the use of post-test studies to identify change from baseline measurements.

Therefore, you should always consider: repeated measures, normal distribution, randomisation, intervention mapping and follow-up procedures.

Randomised controlled trials (RCT) are gold standard. However, there are drawbacks to interventions that use a RCT design in some settings (e.g. individuals randomised from a whole school or department setting), as there is a risk of cross-contamination of the intervention (whereby the content is shared socially). In these cases, a clustered randomised controlled trial may be more appropriate (Campbell, Elbourne, & Altman, 2004).

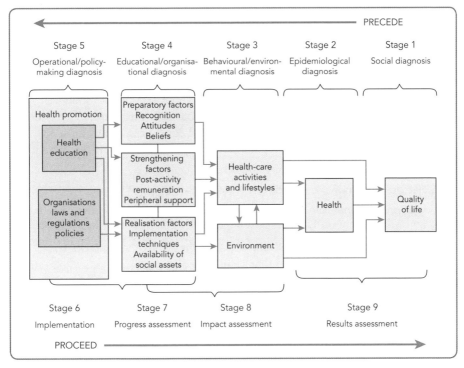

Figure 3.6 **PRECEDE/PROCEED model**

Source: Health promotion and planning: An educational and ecological approach, 3rd ed., Mountain View, CA: Mayfield (Green L.W. and Kreuter M.W. 1999), © 1999 McGraw-Hill Education.

CONSORT

There are some studies in the published literature that are poorly written in terms of the content of an intervention, which makes it difficult to know the methodology used (e.g. a lack of clarity on randomisation or the use of control groups). This is a problem in behaviour change research (Michie, Fixen, Grimshaw, & Eccles, 2009). Intervention testing should abide by the CONSORT (CONsolidated Standards Of Reporting Trials) guidelines (Moher et al., 2010) (see www.consort-statement.org for full details). There is also TREND (Transparent Reporting of Evaluations of Nonrandomised Designs: Des Jarlais et al., 2004) for studies that do not meet CONSORT.

Theory and content

Just as a drug trial needs to know the ingredients of its medicines, so too should a psycho-behavioural trial know the components of its intervention. If you are advised by your GP to take some Paracetamol, and go into either a supermarket or a pharmacy to buy some, no matter where you buy it, it should give the same effects, and these effects are well known (i.e. to reduce pain and fever). However, if your GP advises you to get some 'behavioural counselling' and you go to see Psychologist A and Psychologist B, there is no clear way of telling (a) what techniques they will use and (b) what effect they will have. It is like saying 'go and buy a small, white, round pill' (instead of Paracetamol). There is a need for a clearer understanding of psychological interventions to understand how they work and whether they can be replicated.

Although interventions with psychological content are effective, there is often no way of knowing *how* they work (Michie & Abraham, 2004). Therefore, there became a need to understand behaviour change techniques and the theoretical domains that they fall into. In light of this, Michie et al. (2005) published a paper, linking psychological theory to evidence-based practice and intervention design. Twelve domains were identified from 128 constructs, drawn from 33 psychological theories, to explain factors that may influence behaviour change:

1 *Knowledge* (do they know they should do x?)

2 *Skills* (do they know how to do x?)

3 *Social/professional role and identity* (will doing x change who they feel they are?)

4 *Beliefs about capabilities* (self-efficacy – do they think they can do x?)

5 *Beliefs about consequences* (do they think doing x will give a positive outcome?)

6 *Motivation and goals* (have they an intention to do x?)

7 *Memory, attention and decision processes* (will they remember to do x?)

8 *Environmental contexts and resources* (are there barriers to x?)

9 *Social influences* (norms – do others do x?)

10 *Emotion* (does x evoke an emotional response?)

11 *Behavioural-regulation* (what steps are needed to do x?)

12 *Nature of behaviours* (how long will change take if they do x?)

These 12 domains all represent psychological areas. However, from an intervention perspective, some can be addressed more *practically* (e.g. forgetting, which could be intervened with reminders), while others are more *perceptually driven* (e.g. feeling they cannot do something, which would need a cognitive shift).

Behaviour change research

A great deal of research has occurred over the last decade to understand how to assist people to change their behaviour, which has resulted in NICE guidance on behaviour change interventions (NICE, 2007) and a House of Lords (2011) inquiry into behaviour change.

Behaviour change techniques

Michie et al.'s (2005) research, along with later work by Michie, Johnston, Abraham, Francis and Eccles (2013), paved the way for an understanding of an overview of many theoretical models and how they map onto behaviour change constructs. Abraham and Michie (2008) developed a taxonomy that identified 26 behaviour change techniques (BCTs: see Table 3.1) from a systematic review of behavioural interventions.

Table 3.1 Abraham and Michie's (2008) 26-item behaviour change techniques (BCTs)

Behaviour change techniques	
1 General information	14 Provide feedback
2 Information on consequences	15 General encouragement
3 Information about approval	16 Contingent rewards
4 Prompt intention formation	17 Teach to use cues
5 Specific goal setting	18 Follow up prompts
6 Graded tasks	19 Social comparison
7 Barrier identification	20 Social support/change
8 Behavioural contract	21 Role model
9 Review goals	22 Prompt self-talk
10 Provide instruction	23 Relapse prevention
11 Model/demonstrate	24 Stress management
12 Prompt practice	25 Motivational interviewing
13 Prompt monitoring	26 Time management

A BCT is described as something that aims to change behaviour and is proposed to be an 'active ingredient' of interventions (like the different elements such as carbon, hydrogen, oxygen and nitrogen that go into making a drug such as Paracetamol). Like the periodic table, which presents all the elements, a taxonomy presents all the BCTs relevant to support health behaviour change. In a true scientific form, BCTs should be observable and replicable and have a measurable effect on behaviour.

BCT research

Guidance from the Medical Research Council (MRC) now confirms the need to consider theory when designing complex interventions (Craig et al., 2008) and evidence from the Workgroup for Intervention Development and Evaluation Research (WIDER: Abraham & Michie, 2008; http://interventiondesign.co.uk) suggests a need to systematically report intervention content and component BCTs, with the ultimate aim of advancing the science of behaviour change intervention research (Michie, Rothman, & Sheeran, 2007).

One way of developing the knowledge base in this area is to begin by identifying BCTs that have been used in existing interventions. Research has aimed to reduce these active ingredients down to the smallest active component, which in the right circumstances is able to induce behavioural change, creating bigger taxonomies.

In an attempt to test the 26-item taxonomy, Michie, Abraham, Whittington, McAteer and Gupta (2009) published a meta-regression in healthy eating and physical activity interventions, concluding that the BCT 'self-monitoring' used with any other technique derived from control theory was the most effective.

Later research has confirmed taxonomies for:

- *Physical activity and healthy eating* (Michie, Ashford, et al., 2011). Aiming to improve the 26-item taxonomy, the CALO-RE taxonomy has 40 BCTs, leading to less overlap between items and clearer definitions.
- *Smoking cessation* (Michie, Hyder, Walia, & West, 2011). In this study, 43 BCTs were found from treatment manuals, reduced to four functions:
  - directly addressing motivation (e.g. providing rewards contingent on abstinence);
  - maximising self-regulatory capacity or skills (e.g. facilitating barrier identification and problem solving);
  - promoting adjuvant activities (e.g. advising on stop-smoking medication);
  - supporting other BCTs (e.g. building general rapport).
- *Reducing excessive alcohol use* (Michie et al., 2012). Of the 42 BCTs identified in this area, 'prompt self-recording' was most effective.
- *Weight management* (Dombrowski et al., 2012). Coding from a systematic review using the original 26-item taxonomy, the BCTs 'provision of instructions', 'self-monitoring', 'relapse prevention' and 'prompting practice' were most successful.

Behavioural science technologies

There currently seem to be four key behavioural science technologies that are assisting our understanding and development of behaviour change interventions (Atkins & Michie, 2013). These are the *COM-B* (Michie, van Stralen, & West, 2011) and the *theoretical domains framework* (TDF: Cane, O'Connor, & Michie, 2012; Francis, O'Connor, & Curran, 2012; Michie, Johnston, Abraham et al., 2005) to guide understanding of behaviour, and the *behaviour change wheel* (BCW: Michie, van Stralen, & West, 2011) and the *behaviour change techniques taxonomy* (v1) (Michie, Abraham, et al., 2011) to guide the development and create the content of interventions.

COM-B

Michie, van Stralen, and West (2011) proposed the COM-B model of behaviour, which suggests that for any behaviour to occur, the individual must have:

- *Capability* – the physical and psychological capability to enact the behaviour;
- *Opportunity* – the physical and social opportunity for the behaviour; and
- *Motivation* – be motivated to engage in/refrain from the behaviour over and above competing sources.

Theoretical domains framework

Based on Michie, Johnston, Abraham et al.'s (2005) work on theoretical domains, the theoretical domains framework (TDF) was validated and refined by Cane, O'Connor and Michie (2012). Through a series of sorting tasks, 14 domains (with

84 component constructs) were agreed upon in the TDF: 1) Knowledge, 2) Skills, 3) Social/professional role and identity, 4) Beliefs about capabilities, 5) Optimism, 6) Beliefs about consequences, 7) Reinforcement, 8) Intentions, 9) Goals, 10) Memory, attention and decision processes, 11) Environmental context and resources, 12) Social influences, 13) Emotions and 14) Behavioural regulation.

The TDF in its original guise has been used to guide intervention development in a number of areas (Francis, O'Connor, & Curran, 2012), including:

- hand hygiene (Dyson, Lawton, Jackson, & Cheater, 2010);
- compliance with diagnostic imaging guidelines for spine disorders (Bussières, Patey, Francis, Sales & Grimshaw, 2012);
- improving lower back pain (French et al., 2012).

Behaviour change wheel

While presenting the concept of COM-B, Michie, van Stralan and West (2011) further propose the *behaviour change wheel* (BCW: see Figure 3.7), which has three parts:

- At the centre of the BCW is the COM-B, which is thought of as a 'behaviour system' with three *essential conditions* (capability, opportunity and motivation) that are needed for behaviour (change) to occur.
- Positioned around the COM-B hub are nine *intervention functions* thought to be able to bring about the changes needed in the conditions to elicit behaviour (change).

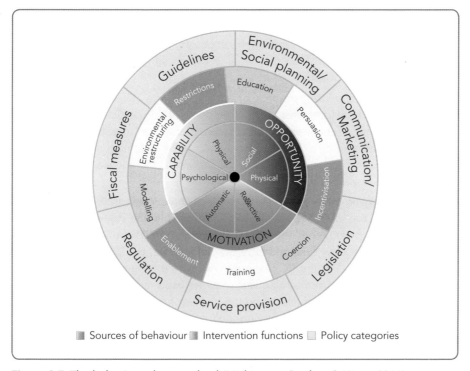

Figure 3.7 **The behaviour change wheel (Michie, van Stralan, & West, 2011)**

- Surrounding these are seven *categories of policy* that could enable interventions to occur.

Behaviour change techniques taxonomy (v1)

The final thing to consider is what the intervention will actually be made up of. While there are now several taxonomies in the literature for differing behaviours, the BCT taxonomy v1 is a general taxonomy system with 93 BCTs, collated into 16 groups (Michie et al., 2013).

Conclusion

It is clear that there is more to behaviour change then just having a behavioural intention. Taking what we have covered in this chapter into account, Atkins and Michie (2013) suggest a six-step approach to behaviour change intervention design:

- *Step 1: Selecting the target behaviour.* Decide what the target behaviour is and who it is aimed at (e.g. 'healthy eating' could include advertising, food promotions, meal planning, portion control, food choice).

- *Step 2: Specifying the target behaviour.* Make the target behaviour specific (SMART goal). This will help with measurement (e.g. 'healthy eating' is difficult to measure, but eating 2,000 calories or five pieces of fruit and vegetables per day are quantifiable targets).

- *Step 3: Understanding the target behaviour.* Analyse why the behaviours are a problem and how changing them can improve health (e.g. the links between diet and cancer or obesity).

- *Step 4: Building the intervention.* Consult COM-B, the TDF and the BCW to identify which factors need to be addressed for this particular target and which intervention functions can be created. In the case of eating five pieces of fruit and vegetables a day, capability and opportunity may need to be addressed due to social economic status, by enhancing knowledge, social influences or environmental resources.

- *Step 5: Specifying intervention content.* Once the constructs that need to be addressed are identified as intervention functions, the BCTs that aim to change these components need to be decided upon. These would come from the relevant taxonomy system. In the example above, the CALO-RE taxonomy would be suitable, but the BCT taxonomy v1 would have more BCTs to consider. The BCT 'information giving' may be used to increase knowledge and belief in capability to overcome the barrier of cost. 'Rewards' may enhance motivation, and 'self-monitoring' may aid behaviour attainment.

- *Step 6: Delivering the intervention.* Finally, the mode of delivery should be considered and the methodology appropriate to it applied. Evaluation of the intervention should also be well thought out.

Test your knowledge

3.7 What are the six stages that Kok et al. (2004) state should be considered when planning interventions?

3.8 What is a BCT?

Answers to these questions can be found on the companion website at:
www.pearsoned.co.uk/psychologyexpress

Further reading BCT taxonomies and intervention design

Topic	Key reading
Key paper that identified the 12 theoretical domain constructs	Michie, S., Johnston, M., Abraham, C., Lawton, R., Parker, D., & Walker, A. (2005). Making psychological theory useful for implementing evidence based practice: A consensus approach. *Quality and Safety in Health Care*, *14*(1), 26–33.
Nice overview of the current position in behaviour change research	Atkins, L., & Michie, S. (2013). Changing eating behaviour: What can we learn from behavioural science? *Nutrition Bulletin*, *38*(1), 30–35.

CASE STUDY

Binge drinking

The client

Shanice is an 18-year-old girl, who studies hard at college through the week and works at the weekend. She eats well, is active and does not smoke; however, she likes to go out drinking after work and often exceeds the recommended daily allowance. Drinking on average seven mixers, four jager bombs and five shots a night, her alcohol intake would be considered as binge drinking. However, she is not concerned about her behaviour and has no plans to change as it has had no detrimental consequences to her health … yet.

Background – the problem

Around a quarter of young people (22% male; 17% female) admit to binge drinking (NHS Health and Social Care Information Centre, 2012a). There is no international definition of binge drinking, but the NHS suggests that it is the consumption of double or more of the daily recommended allowance (which is four to five units for a man and three to four for a woman, so at least eight or six units respectively). Shanice would have drunk 16 units on her night out.

Binge drinking has been linked to poor performance at school and other health risk behaviours, such as being a passenger in a car with a drunk-driver, smoking cigarettes, unprotected sexual activity, being a victim of dating violence, attempting suicide and using illicit drugs (Miller, Naimi, Brewer, & Jones, 2007). Binge drinkers are also more at risk of alcohol dependency in later life (Jennison, 2004).

Advice

The college that Shanice attends has asked a health psychologist to develop an intervention to reduce binge drinking. What things do you think should be considered in an intervention for students like Shanice?

> **Further reading** Changing health behaviour
>
> | Topic | Key reading |
> |---|---|
> | Overview and samples of tools discussed in this chapter | Michie, S., Rumsey, N., Fussell, A., Hardeman, W., Johnston, M., Newman, S., & Yardley, L. (2004). *Improving health: changing behaviour. NHS health trainer handbook.* London: Department of Health/BPS. |

Chapter summary – pulling it all together

→ Can you tick all of the points from the revision checklist at the beginning of this chapter?

→ Attempt the sample question from the beginning of this chapter using the answer guidelines below.

→ Go to the companion website at **www.pearsoned.co.uk/psychologyexpress** to access more revision support online, including interactive quizzes, flashcards, You be the marker exercises as well as answer guidance for the Test your knowledge and Sample questions from this chapter.

Answer guidelines

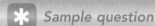 *Sample question*   *Essay*

> What motivates behaviour change? Discuss in detail, with reference to at least one health behaviour.

Approaching the question

Your answer should aim to provide an analysis of how intentions can be translated into action and what needs to be considered when developing a behaviour change intervention.

Important points to include

● Begin by outlining what the key considerations are for the intention–behaviour relationship and/or behaviour change interventions and discuss the key models in this area. For each model/theory you will need to:

  ● Consider the strengths and weaknesses of the models and the individual cognitions used within.

  ● Discuss the empirical research that informs the theories (does it support their efficacy?).

  ● Evaluate differences in the effectiveness of the models between health behaviours.

● You should then consider the usefulness of an overarching theoretical domain framework and conclude with future considerations in this area.

Make your answer stand out

This type of question is testing to see whether you can apply your knowledge of what motivates behaviour yet also what motivates behaviour change and apply this to a real-world setting for a particular health behaviour. A good student would show original thinking by considering how the research, theories and models to date have addressed this question, where there are overlaps, and where there are gaps for future considerations to challenge the current empirical evidence and advance behaviour change intervention development.

Explore the accompanying website at www.pearsoned.co.uk/psychologyexpress
→ Prepare more effectively for exams and assignments using the answer guidelines for questions from this chapter.
→ Test your knowledge using multiple choice questions and flashcards.
→ Improve your essay skills by exploring the You be the marker exercises.

Notes

Notes

4

Health promotion: health-enhancing behaviours

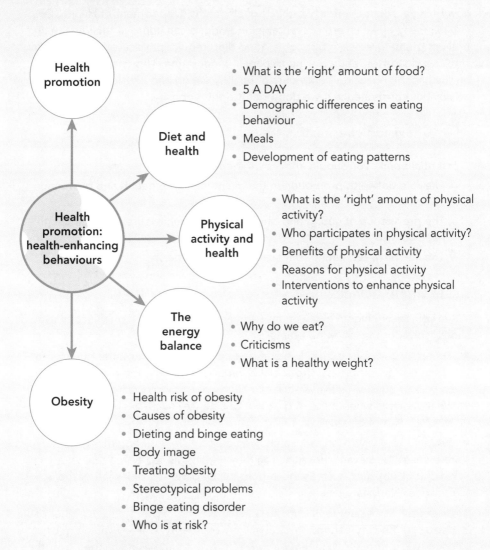

- **Health promotion**

- **Diet and health**
  - What is the 'right' amount of food?
  - 5 A DAY
  - Demographic differences in eating behaviour
  - Meals
  - Development of eating patterns

- **Health promotion: health-enhancing behaviours**

- **Physical activity and health**
  - What is the 'right' amount of physical activity?
  - Who participates in physical activity?
  - Benefits of physical activity
  - Reasons for physical activity
  - Interventions to enhance physical activity

- **The energy balance**
  - Why do we eat?
  - Criticisms
  - What is a healthy weight?

- **Obesity**
  - Health risk of obesity
  - Causes of obesity
  - Dieting and binge eating
  - Body image
  - Treating obesity
  - Stereotypical problems
  - Binge eating disorder
  - Who is at risk?

A printable version of this topic map is available from
www.pearsoned.co.uk/psychologyexpress

Introduction

Who is responsible for our health? Us? The government? Our significant others?

Health-enhancing behaviours such as healthy eating and physical activity are essential in order to maintain a good health status. Brownell (1991) argues that good health has become a symbol of self-control, hard work, ambition and success, and a means to the achievement of personal goals such as physical attractiveness and a long life.

Illnesses such as cancer and coronary heart disease (CHD) continue to rise, now being accountable for two-thirds of all deaths (Department of Health: DH, 2004a), many of which are preventable. Individuals can improve their health and prevent premature death through a good diet, regular physical activity, avoiding smoking cigarettes, and drinking alcohol in moderation. This chapter will focus on the health-enhancing behaviours of healthy eating and physical activity, and an obvious consequence if we don't get it right – obesity.

 Revision checklist

Essential points you should know by the end of this chapter are:

❑ The role of health promotion in the maintenance of health and prevention of illness

❑ The prevalence of eating and physical activity behaviours and their link to health status

❑ The link between eating, physical activity and obesity.

Assessment advice

When you are writing an essay or answering an exam question on this topic, you should consider the following points:

- *Content.* How does our understanding of eating behaviour differ between a biomedical and bio-psycho-social approach? What are the psychological barriers to physical activity? How can health psychology address these issues? What happens when our energy is out of balance? What is our understanding of the causes of obesity?

- *Evidence* is always required: so ensure you *back up your argument with references* to relevant research. You may find in this topic area that you draw on official statistics, such as those from the Department of Health or the Office for National Statistics.

- *Be critical.* For example, if data are presented on the prevalence (number of people) of healthy eating, physical activity or obesity, is it *relevant* (e.g. what country is it from? Is it generalisable?) is it *recent* and has it changed over the course of time? Are there demographic differences (age, gender, social and economic status)?

Sample question

Could you answer this question? Below is a typical problem question that could rise on this topic.

✳ *Sample question*	*Essay*

Discuss the considerations that need to be taken into account when attempting to promote a healthy diet.

Guidelines on answering this question are included at the end of this chapter, whilst guidance on tackling other exam questions can be found on the companion website at **www.pearsoned.co.uk/psychologyexpress**

Health promotion

'It is not enough to treat people when they fall ill, more must be done to prevent them from falling ill in the first place' (DH, 1999). The process of enabling people to increase control over and improve their health is known as health promotion (World Health Organisation: WHO, 1984).

Applying biomedical models to health has been referred to as a *'downstream approach'*, where medical intervention pulls drowning individuals from the river's current. In contrast, health promotion is viewed as an *'upstream approach'*, intervening early to reduce the risk of people falling into dangerous rivers in the first place. This is represented in Figure 4.1, based on Crosby, Salazar, DiClemente and Wingwood's visual representation (2005).

Figure 4.1 Graphic representation of the upstream approach of health promotion

The protective nature of health promotion strategies may reduce medical costs while also improving health. However, unlike the biomedical model, which can show a clear rate of people 'cured' through treatment, health promotion initiatives are far less tangible.

Diet and health

Our diet (what we eat) has both direct and indirect effects on our health. An estimated one in three deaths from the leading causes of mortality is attributable to a poor diet (DH, 2004a). Good nutrition will help protect against coronary heart disease, stroke, diabetes, obesity and cancer (Kumanyika et al., 2000; WHO, 1990) and can have an effect on cognitive and physical performance, mood, energy levels and attractiveness (O'Dea, 2003).

The food we eat can be divided into five groups:

- fruit and vegetables;
- starchy foods (such as rice, pasta, bread – ideally wholegrain – and potatoes);
- meat, fish, eggs and beans;
- milk and dairy foods;
- foods containing fat and sugar.

What is the 'right' amount of food?

Figure 4.2 represents the UK recommendations for a healthy diet, displayed on the Eatwell Plate from NHS Choices (DH, 2011). In contrast, Figure 4.3 represents

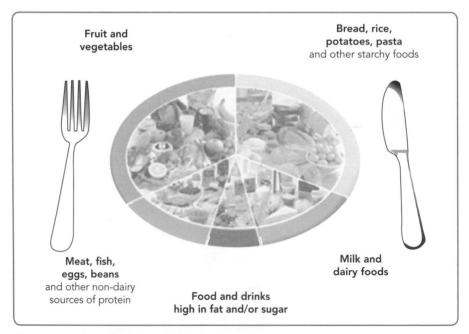

Figure 4.2 Eatwell Plate from NHS Choices

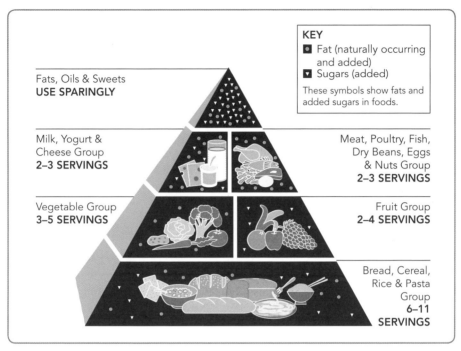

Figure 4.3 Food Pyramid from USDA

the United States Department of Agriculture's (USDA, 1992) Food Pyramid. This was replaced with MyPyramid based on 2005 recommendations, which was then replaced by MyPlate in 2010.

5 A DAY

The '5 A DAY' campaign recommends the consumption of five portions of fruit and vegetables a day (DH, 2003; WHO, 1990). One portion is a piece of fruit, a bowl of salad, two spoonfuls of vegetables or a glass of fruit juice, and these can be fresh, frozen or tinned (DH, 2003). Figures (NHS Health and Social Care Information Centre: HSCIC, 2013) confirm that:

- 24% of men and 29% of women (27% of adults) consume the recommended 5 a day;
- 16% of boys (aged 5–15 years) and 20% of girls are meeting the guidelines.

Demographic differences in eating behaviour

Eating behaviours are reported to differ significantly by gender, age and socio-economic status:

- Females, both adults (NHS HSCIC, 2013) and children (Glynn, Emmett, & Rogers, 2005; Todd, Currie & Smith, 2000), report higher levels of healthy eating.
- Young people perceive too many barriers to eating healthily, which results in the consumption of unhealthy foods (Croll, Neumark-Sztainer, & Story, 2001).

- On average, children's consumption is under half (two out of five) of the recommended daily amount, with those from the lowest socioeconomic status groups eating 50% less than those from a high group (DH, 2005; Gregory, Lowe, Bates, & Britain, 2000).
- The consumption of fruit and vegetables decreases with social class, and from higher to lower income households, while the proportion consuming sweet foods, soft drinks and crisps increases (DH, 2005; Gregory et al., 2000; Kurtz & Thornes, 2000; NHS HSCIC, 2013). These observed differences may be related to a number of interacting factors, including education, social norms (Lamerz et al., 2005) and availability of fresh produce.

Meals

- A higher proportion of boys than girls eat breakfast everyday (Pearson, Atkin, Biddle, Gorely, & Edwardson, 2009).
- Skipping breakfast is significantly related to levels of obesity in both adults (Ma et al., 2005) and children (Mota et al., 2008), and to other health-compromising behaviours such as physical inactivity and smoking (Keski-Rahkonen, Kaprio, Rissanen, Virkkunen, & Rose, 2003).
- Parental breakfast eating significantly influences adolescent breakfast consumption (Keski-Rahkonen et al., 2003).
- Meal frequency has a negative relationship with obesity: that is, the more frequent the meals, the lower the risk of obesity (Toschke, Küchenhoff, Koletzko, & Kries, 2005).

Development of eating patterns

A developmental approach to eating behaviour emphasises the importance of learning and experience in childhood, explained by:

- *Exposure.* A neophobic response (fear of new foods) is described as a developmental phase, believed to be innately ingrained as a protective function to reduce the likelihood of unintentionally eating a harmful toxin (Martins, 2002). The selective eating linked to neophobia is more common in boys, and is thought to be related to autistic spectrum disorders (Chater, Stein, & Chowdhury, 2012). When trying to enhance food range, particularly to increase fruit and vegetable intake, exposure alone is insufficient (Moore, Paisley, & Dennehy, 2000). However, exposure to vegetables over time (14 days) has been found to increase acceptability in 2–6-year-olds (Wardle et al., 2003), and if parents buy vegetables, children are more knowing about and willing to try them (Busick, Brooks, Pernecky, Dawson, & Petzoldt, 2008).
- *Social learning.* Behaviour is thought to be learned through observing others (Bandura, 1986). Children with food refusal, who are encouraged to eat by watching 'food dudes' (enthusiastically eating refused food), increase food range (Lowe, Horne, Tapper, Bowdery, & Egerton, 2004). Parents also influence eating attitudes and behaviours, with strong correlations found between mother's and child's food intakes (Brown & Ogden, 2004).

- *Associative learning.* Rewarding eating behaviour (through operant conditioning) improves food preferences (Birch, Zimmerman, & Hind, 1980). However, this approach should be used cautiously, as using food as a reward for comfort could lead to emotional eating and subsequent weight gain (Rodgers et al., 2013) in later years.

Test your knowledge

4.1 Why is healthy eating important for health status?

4.2 What demographic differences are there in eating behaviour?

Answers to these questions can be found on the companion website at: **www.pearsoned.co.uk/psychologyexpress**

Further reading Eating behaviour

Topic	Key reading
Two good textbooks on eating behaviour, full of relevant research	Dovey, T. M. (2010). *Eating behaviour.* Maidenhead: Open University Press.
	Ogden, J. (2010). *The psychology of eating: From healthy to disordered behaviour* (2nd ed.). Oxford: Blackwell.

? Sample question   Essay

To what extent do demographic differences impact on the uptake of physical activity and how can a bio-psycho-social model improve engagement?

Physical activity and health

Physically active children are more likely to be physically active adults (Telama et al., 2005). Physically active adults have:

- a significantly lower age-adjusted mortality rate from coronary heart disease and cancer (Hardman, 2001; Hu et al., 2005);
- a 20–30% reduced risk of premature death and up to 50% reduced risk of major diseases (DH, 2004b);
- more control over weight, blood pressure and diabetes, and protection against osteoporosis (Warburton, Nicol, & Bredin, 2006).

Similar benefits are true for children (Biddle, Cavill, & Sallis, 1998):

- physical activity improves self-esteem, mood and cognitive functioning (Biddle, Gorely, & Stensel, 2004).

What is the 'right' amount of physical activity?

A physically active lifestyle can come from a number of activities, including walking, cycling, participating in sports and even housework. It has been recommended that for general health benefit, adults should achieve at least 150 minutes (formally 30 minutes, five times a week; DH, 2004b) of moderate to vigorous physical activity (MVPA) per week, with children aiming for 60 minutes on all seven days (NHS HSCIC, 2013). These levels can be achieved during one session, or a number of short bouts of activity of 10 minutes or more.

Who participates in physical activity?

National statistics from England (NHS HSCIC, 2013) show age and gender differences when it comes to physical activity participation. In 2008:

● 39% of men and 29% of women aged 16 and over met the recommendations – an increase from 32% and 21% respectively in 1997.

● In young people, more boys (32%) met the recommendations than girls (24%). This is supported in the literature (Todd et al., 2000, Kimm et al., 2005).

● The proportion of girls meeting the recommendations decreased with age, ranging from 35% in girls aged 2 to 12% among girls aged 14.

● 88% of teenage girls are not meeting the government recommendations.

Low levels of physical activity are associated with:

● lack of confidence, embarrassment at an unfit body and lacking the skills to engage (Allender, Peto, Scarborough, Boxer, & Rayner, 2006);

● lack of time, money and company, disliking exercise and feeling too tired (Reichert, Barros, Domingues, & Hallal, 2007);

● greater perceived barriers to exercise (Biddle et al., 2004), especially during the transition to secondary school.

Physical activity has been shown to increase with:

● the intention to perform exercise and preferences towards it (Biddle et al., 2004);

● perceptions of enjoyment, self-efficacy, competence, control and autonomy, positive attitudes towards activity, and a perception of fewer barriers and many benefits (Cavill, Biddle, & Sallis, 2001).

There is also evidence that level of physical activity is negatively correlated with smoking in adolescent girls (Biddle, Whitehead, O'Donovan, & Nevill, 2005), and this is also true for women (Trost, Owen, Bauman, Sallis, & Brown, 2002).

Benefits of physical activity

There are many benefits to a physically active life:

● It has a positive impact on mood. However, if the intensity is too severe, it can lead to negative affect (Biddle & Ekkekakis, 2005).

- It can have a protective function towards being unhappy (Wang et al., 2012) and is effective at treating depression (Ströhle, 2009).
- This link is life long, with low levels of physical activity in childhood showing as a risk factor for depression in later life (Jacka et al., 2011).
- Biological reasons for this may be due to the increase in monoamines, which are thought to act in a similar way to antidepressant drugs, and the release of endorphins (our natural opiates) producing a natural high and a sense of calm when we are physically active (La-Forge, 1995).
- Physical activity has been found to improve self-esteem (Ekeland, Heian, Hagen, & Coren, 2005).
- It may also help to maintain cognitive functioning, and protect against the risk of dementia (Rovio et al., 2005).

Reasons for physical activity

Different types of physical activity have been linked to different reasons for engagement. In women, cardio-based workouts have been linked to appearance and body esteem, while yoga-style fitness is more linked to general health benefits (Prichard & Tiggeman, 2008). This could in turn lead to a negative use of physical activity in those suffering from an eating disorder. Research has found the excessive use of exercise to maintain body weight and shape in a sample of anorexia and bulimia nervosa patients (Mond & Calogero, 2009), with feelings of intense guilt exhibited when physical activity is missed. Using physical activity as a way of maintaining a low body weight and slim shape seems to be a motivator from early in life (Allender, Cowburn, & Foster, 2006), with young girls reporting this as a reason for engagement. However, this study also confirmed more positive reasons for physical activity, such as social interaction and enjoyment, with older people citing the benefits of the social network that exercise provides and an attempt to ward off old age.

Interventions to enhance physical activity

- It was previously thought that interventions that encouraged home-based activity were most effective (Hillsdon & Thorogood, 1996).
- Advising individuals to take more activity was seen as ineffective (Hillsdon, Thorogood, White, & Foster, 2002).
- However, it is now suggested (Foster, Hillsdon, Thorogood, Kaur, & Wedatilake, 2005) that interventions should provide professional guidance and ongoing support.
- Implementation intentions have been found to significantly increase physical activity (Armitage & Arden, 2010).
- Intervention effects may differ depending on the demographics of the recipient (van Sluijs, McMinn, & Griffin, 2007) and these need to be taken into consideration when developing an intervention in this area, while it is argued that more randomised controlled trials are needed.

Test your knowledge

4.3 What is the recommended level of physical activity?

4.4 What are the benefits of physical activity?

Answers to these questions can be found on the companion website at:
www.pearsoned.co.uk/psychologyexpress

Further reading Physical activity

Topic	Key reading
Cochrane reviews are systematic overviews of an area	Foster, C., Hillsdon, M., Thorogood, M., Kaur, A., & Wedatilake, T. (2005). Interventions for promoting physical activity. *Cochrane Database of Systematic Reviews, 1*, CD003180.
Current recommendation and links to health status	O'Donovan, G., Blazevich, A. J., Boreham, et al. (2010). The ABC of physical activity for health: A consensus statement from the British Association of Sport and Exercise Sciences. *Journal of Sports Sciences, 28*(6), 573–591.

 Sample question   *Problem-based learning*

Kai is an 11-year-old boy who is mad about his Xbox, spending at least three to four hours a day in game play with his friends. Although he is active at school and goes out on his bike at the weekends, his mum is worried that his sedentary behaviour will have a negative effect on his health. Kai doesn't like going out when it's cold and has little motivation for exercise.

If you were a health psychologist designing an intervention to decrease the sedentary behaviour of children like Kai, what would you consider and why?

The energy balance

A healthy weight is all about energy balance. If calories consumed are the same as calories expended (through exercise and bodily functioning), weight will remain stable. The NHS recommends a daily calorie consumption of:

- men = 2,500;
- women = 2,000;
- children (5–10 years) = 1,800.

Why do we eat?

There are both biological and physiological explanations of appetite regulation:

- The *gastric theory* suggests that appetite is a direct response to stomach motions (Cannon & Washburn, 1912). When your stomach grumbles, you feel hungry and you eat. However, this theory does not explain food choice or satiety.

- A *nutrient approach* links appetite control with food types:
  - fat (lipids) in the *lipostatic approach* (Kennedy, 1953);
  - carbohydrate (glucose) in the *glucostatic approach* (Mayer, 1953);
  - amino acids in the *aminostatic approach* (Mellinkoff, Frankland, Boyle, & Greipel, 1956).

These theories suggest that the body and not the brain controls our eating behaviour. In the glucostatic theory, for example, low blood glucose would lead to high hunger, with high blood glucose creating short-term hunger control. However, an alternative theory suggests that the hypothalamus (a part of the brain) is key to appetite regulation, suggesting the link between neurotransmitters and hormones (Brobeck, Tepperman, & Long, 1943). The key neurotransmitter linked to our motivation to eat is neuropeptide Y (NPY). When a dip in blood glucose occurs, NPY is released and this makes us search for food.

Dovey (2010) describes the different organs and hormones responsible for hunger (stomach: ghrelin) and fullness (intestines: cholecystokinin-CCK, GLP-1 and peptide YY), along with those that signal to the brain how much reserve energy it has (adipose tissue: leptin). Foods high in carbohydrate and lipids (which create sugar and fat) can enhance levels of serotonin and opioids. This can lead to both an elevated mood and a sense of calm, and is an important influence in connection with emotional eaters.

Criticisms

As with the biomedical model of health and illness, the key criticism of this biological approach to appetite is its assumption that eating only occurs when physiological mechanisms detect a drop in nutrients or changes in hormones or neurotransmitters. But what about individual differences? We have seen that our eating behaviours are influenced by age, gender and socioeconomic status, alongside psychological and affective influences. We may condition our eating behaviour to occur when we watch TV. Research has found an increase in calories and fatty food consumption while screen viewing (Gore, Foster, DiLillo, Kirk, & Smith West, 2003); however, this is not always the case (Martin, Coulon, Markward, Greenway, & Anton, 2009). We may also eat when we are sad, bored, lonely or even happy (Arnow, Kenardy, & Agras, 1995; Geliebter & Aversa, 2003), conditions that are not directly regulated by biological influences.

Furthermore, can psychological factors override our feelings of hunger? Consider the influence of body image, for example, leading to a cognitive restriction of

 Sample question   **Essay**

Critically discuss the causes and consequences of obesity.

eating (dieting) (Polivy & Herman, 1985). A biological approach to eating also does not explain obesity, which is not evolutionarily beneficial.

What is a healthy weight?

In the UK, body mass index (BMI: measured by dividing your weight in kilograms (kg) by your height in metres (m), then dividing the answer by your height again – squared) is most often the measure used to diagnose obesity (see Table 4.1). However, there is some debate over the sensitivity of this measure, particularly as it does not distinguish fat from fat-free mass (Burkhauser & Cawley, 2008), such as muscle or bone. Other techniques can be used, such as skin fold thickness, waist circumference, hip to waist ratio and neck circumference, and some suggest (Janssen, Katzmarzyk, & Ross, 2004) that measures such as waist circumference are more effective at identifying obesity-related health risk than BMI.

Table 4.1 World Health Organisation BMI classification for adults

$BMI = kg/m^2$	Classification
<18.5	Underweight
18.5–24.9	Normal weight
25–29.9	Overweight
30–34.9	Obese I
35–39.9	Obese II
>40	Obese III (morbidly obese)

Obesity

The prevalence of obesity has trebled since the 1980s (DH, 2004a) and over half (60%) of all adults are now either overweight or obese (24%) (NHS HSCIC, 2008). Reporting on the epidemiological trends of obesity (BMI), the NHS HSCIC (2013) found that:

- adults with a normal BMI decreased between 1993 (men = 41%; women = 50%) and 2011 (men = 34%; women = 39%);
- overweight adults (including obese) increased from 58% to 65% in men and from 49% to 58% in women between 1993 and 2011;
- obesity increased over the years in both men (1993 = 13%; 2011 = 24%) and women (1993 = 16%; 2011 = 26%);
- in 2011, three in ten children (aged 2–15) were classed as either overweight or obese (boys = 31%; girls = 28%), similar to in 2010 (boys = 31%; girls = 29%).

Health risk of obesity

Obese and underweight individuals have a higher risk of premature death (Kopelman, 2000). It has been reported (NHS HHSCIC, 2013) that:

- There were 11,740 hospital admissions with a primary diagnosis of obesity in 2011–12. This is triple the number recorded in 2006–07 (3,860).
- Female admissions were almost three times the number of male admissions (8,740 compared to 2,990).

Obesity is strongly linked to:

- coronary heart disease (Allender, Peto, Scarborough, Boxer, & Rayner, 2006);
- hypertension (high blood pressure) and type 2 diabetes (NHS HSCIC, 2006);
- a higher level of triglycerides (fats in the blood) and cholesterol increasing the risk of arthritis (Soltani-Arabshahi et al., 2010), fatty liver and gallbladder disease (Liew et al., 2008);
- sleep apnoea, breathlessness and asthma, infertility, osteoarthritis and increased risk of many cancers (Finer, 2006);
- low mood, depression, poor self-esteem and anxiety (Dragan & Akhtar-Danesh, 2007; Tuthill, Slawik, O'Rahilly, & Finer, 2006);
- social isolation (Simon et al., 2006).

Causes of obesity

Research examining the causes of obesity is often contradictory, perhaps as a result of the vast amount of individual differences. There is some agreement, however, that obesity may be related to a genetic predisposition, over-consumption of food and under-activity (Ogden, 2004; Vögele, 2005). Causes of obesity include:

- *Genetics.* Obese parents are more likely to have obese children (Danielzik, Czerwinski-Mast, & Langnäse, 2004), and this is supported by twin/adoptee research (Stunkard, Harris, Pedersen, & McClearn, 1990). A significantly higher proportion of obese children (19.8%) come from a family where both parents are overweight or obese, compared to those (8.4%) with only one parent overweight or obese, and those (6.7%) with neither parent overweight or obese (Jotangia, Moody, Stamakakis, & Wardle, 2005).
- *Metabolic rate.* A low resting metabolic rate is thought to be a risk factor for weight gain (Tataranni et al., 2003). However, there is no evidence to suggest that the metabolic rate of obese people is lower than those with a healthy weight (Ogden, 2012), and this theory is unsupported in the literature.
- *Appetite regulation.* From a biological perspective, there is evidence of the 'ob gene'. This gene produces leptin, which is responsible for telling us when we are full. Research giving daily leptin injections to a child who had a defect in the ob gene showed a reduction in food intake and weight (Farooqi et al., 1999), suggesting that a lack of leptin may be linked to overeating and obesity.
- *The obesogenic environment.* Egger and Swinburn (1997) coined this term to highlight the influence of the environment on eating behaviour, such as

food advertising, labelling, packaging, availability (e.g. fast food), and factors that reduce the likelihood of physical activity, such as the use of cars, lifts and escalators, lack of street lights and so on (for a full review see Kirk, Penney, & McHugh, 2010).

- *Physical inactivity.* Sedentary behaviour and inactivity are obvious risk factors. Adolescents who spend five hours or more a day watching television are 4.6 times more likely to be obese than those who watch two hours or less per day (Chaput, Brunet, & Tremblay, 2006). And even if you meet physical activity recommendations, long periods of sedentary behaviour (such as sitting at a desk) can still increase your health risk (Sugiyama, Healy, Dunstan, Salmon, & Owen, 2008).

- *Eating behaviour.* Conditioned (classical and operant) eating behaviour could be linked to obesity. If a child is rewarded with food (Puhl & Schwartz, 2003) or given food to soothe (Baughcum et al., 2001), it could lead to weight gain.

- *Affect – emotional eating.* Some people eat in response to emotions, particularly negative affect (Byrne, Cooper, & Fairburn, 2003). The *masking hypothesis* suggests that individuals attempt to mask negative emotions by eating to increase mood, comfort and distraction (Polivy & Herman, 1999) and the *escape theory* (Heatherton & Baumeister, 1991) suggests that eating is a form of escapism.

- *Dieting and body image.* There is a volume of research which suggests that overeating is caused by dieting behaviour guided by the *restraint theory* (Herman & Mack, 1975; Polivy & Herman, 1985), and this is often linked to appearance as suggested in the *dual-process model* (Stice, 2001).

Dieting and binge eating

People who are overweight or obese will often 'diet' to try to lose weight. However, one possible hypothesis that may explain fluctuations in weight and energy intake is the *restraint theory* (Herman & Mack, 1975; Polivy & Herman, 1985). Normal eating is generally under the control of appetite (Kendall & Hammen, 1998): people often stop eating when they feel full. However, this theory suggests that when an individual attempts to regulate their weight through deliberate control of their eating behaviours (dietary restraint), they begin to 'unlearn' internal signals of hunger and satiety. This restraint may be 'disinhibited' – eating more as a result of the loosening of restraints in response to emotional distress, intoxication, preloading or the availability of appetising foods. This 'all or nothing' perspective is thought to lead to a 'What the hell …' effect (Polivy & Herman, 1985). This, in turn, may explain why individuals attempting to restrict their eating (dieting), frequently overeat (Williamson et al., 1995), shedding some light on 'yo-yo' dieting.

The evidence to suggest a link between dieting and binge eating goes back to the 1950s. Keys, Brozek, Henschel, Mickelson and Taylor (1950) in the Minnesota study investigated the effects of starvation due to rations during the Second World War. A sample of young, normal-weight male volunteers were starved down to 74% of their initial body weight using a very low calorie diet (VLCD), which we now know can reduce the leptin levels that tell us when we are full (Morel et al., 2011). Findings highlighted that when re-fed to their initial weight, participants became preoccupied with food, developing binge eating tendencies. Literature in the eating disorder field also suggests that binge eating occurs after a period of restraint. Both normal-weight women with bulimia nervosa and low-weight women with anorexia nervosa who engage in binge eating almost invariably report that dietary restriction preceded their binge eating (Yanovski, 1995).

Body image

Dieting often occurs due to body dissatisfaction. To measure body image, whole body silhouettes (Thompson & Gray, 1995: see Figure 4.4) are used and a score is derived from the discrepancy between the body size that the individual believes they are, and their ideal size. The higher the score, the more the body dissatisfaction.

Children as young as nine years old have been found to have concerns over their weight, reporting dietary restriction as a means to control their body shape (Hill, Draper, & Stack, 1994; Vögele & Woodward, 2005). The desire to be thinner is frequently reported in overweight children (Rolland, Farnhill, & Griffiths, 1996). Pre-adolescent girls (aged nine years) have been found to confuse healthy eating with dieting (Hill & Silver, 1995), and with reported links between adolescent dieting and the onset of eating disorders (Hill, 1993) this is an area of great concern. A clear distinction needs to be made with children between healthy eating and dietary restriction, and caution must be exerted when teaching young people the importance of a healthy diet.

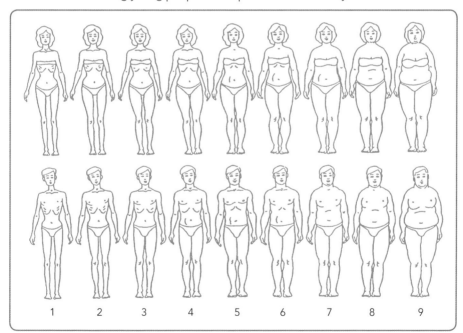

Figure 4.4 **Contour Drawing Rating Scale (Thompson & Gray, 1995)**

Source: Development and validation of a new body-image assessment scale, Thompson, M. A., & Gray, J. J., *Journal of Personality Assessment*, 1995, Taylor & Francis Ltd, reprinted by permission of the publisher (Taylor & Francis Ltd, http://www.tandf.co.uk/journals).

Practical application Treating obesity

Psychological and behavioural intervention

Treating obesity depends on the many individual differences that account for its onset in the first place. Psychological and behaviourally based strategies are commonly used within weight loss interventions (Lang & Froelicher, 2006) and NICE (National Institute for Clinical Excellence, 2006) recommends that they are person-centred. Lang and Froelicher (2006) and Avenell, Sattar and Lean (2006) outline strategies to support overweight individuals in learning skills to facilitate a change in eating behaviour and increase exercise uptake. Strategies used within this approach have included self-monitoring (keeping a diary), goal setting and action planning, stress management (relaxation techniques), stimulus control (identifying high-risk situations), problem solving (identifying, planning and evaluation), contingency management (rewarding), cognitive restructuring (modifying unrealistic goals and beliefs), social support (inclusion of important others) and relapse prevention (skills to overcome setbacks).

Understanding what works in an intervention to enhance healthy eating and physical activity is important for weight management. Michie, Ashford, et al. (2011) investigated two systematic reviews of interventions in these areas and coded for the behaviour change techniques (BCT) that were used within them. This resulted in a 40-item BCT taxonomy (CALO-RE), which identified techniques such as goal setting and self-monitoring as effective strategies. Martin, Chater and Lorencatto (2013) later applied this to childhood obesity interventions, while Dombrowski et al. (2012) used a 26-item BCT taxonomy (see Chapter 3), and found that the BCTs 'providing instruction', 'self-monitoring', 'relapse prevention' and 'prompt practice' were most often linked with successful interventions for weight management in an obese sample.

Drug therapy

Prescribed drug therapies are only available to those with a BMI over 30, although there are lower doses available over the counter (OTC) with a pharmacist consultation. There has been a 90% increase in the use of anti-obesity drugs since 2001, with 0.9 million prescription items logged in 2011 (NHS HSCIC, 2013). There are two types of drug therapy: one suppresses appetite through the central nervous system, the most common type being Sibutramine (Reductil), whilst the other acts on the gastrointestinal system to reduce fat absorption, the most common type being Orlistat (Xenical). Both types of drug have shown some effective results (Rucker, Padwal, Li, Curioni, & Lau, 2007); however, Sibutramine has recently been suspended due to a European review. Along with pharmacological support, Ogden and Sidhu (2006) have found that Orlistat can assist in behaviour change based on the motivation to reduce the effects of the drug when fat is eaten (such as liquid stools and anal leakage). These highly visual side-effects were seen as an education tool to those who linked their eating (fat) with the unpleasant outcome.

Bariatric surgery

A surgical procedure is recommended by NICE if all other weight reduction options have been tried. To be considered for bariatric surgery (Royal College of Physicians: RCP, 2013), individuals will usually have a BMI of over 40, or 35 with co-morbidities (e.g. diabetes, sleep apnoea). The number of people undergoing bariatric surgery has increased considerably over the last decade from 261 cases in 2000/01, to 1,038 cases in 2005/06 and 8,794 cases in 2011/12. Females continue to account for the majority of such procedures; with recent figures showing 6,711 procedures for females and

2,081 procedures for males (NHS HSCIC, 2013). There are several different surgical options available, but the most common are the gastric band (which works by making the stomach smaller) and the Roux-en-Y gastric bypass (which reduces the size of the stomach and the ability to absorb food), both of which are found to be effective in terms of weight loss (Torgerson & Sjöström, 2001) and improving quality of life (Ogden, 2005), although the bypass leads to greater weight loss due to its dual mechanisms.

Stereotypical problems

Obese people may unknowingly come across another problem in their weight loss process, as many health professionals hold negative stereotypes towards those who are obese, labelling them as lazy, stupid and worthless (Schwartz, Chamblis, Brownell, Blair, & Billington, 2003). This discrimination is also seen in employment and educational settings, with bias against overweight and obese individuals (Puhl & Brownell, 2001). The relationship between the health professional and patient is essential for optimal adherence to medical advice (including diet and physical activity), so if this relationship is influenced by such stereotypes, this could have an impact on the success of treatment. With physicians believing that obese individuals are non-compliant and that obesity treatment is less effective than treatment for nine other chronic health conditions (Foster et al., 2003), there is more work to be done in the attitudes of those supporting weight loss as well as those undergoing weight loss treatment themselves.

Binge eating disorder

One final thing to consider if you ever work in the obesity setting is whether the person you are working with is suffering with an eating disorder. While anorexia nervosa (AN) and bulimia nervosa (BN) are well known, binge eating disorder (BED) is currently classified in the DSM-IV (American Psychiatric Association, 1994) as an Eating Disorder Not Otherwise Specified (EDNOS). BED is indicated when someone engages in recurrent binge eating, eating a large amount of food in a short period of time, with a lack of control and marked distress, for at least two days a week for six months.

Who is at risk?

Epidemiological studies have shown BED to be the most common of the eating disorders, affecting 3.5% of women and 2% of men in the general population (Hudson, Hiripi, Pope, & Kessler, 2007), with a mean age of 43 years (Grilo, Masheb, & Salan, 2005). This is substantially higher in an obese treatment-seeking population, with around 20–40% reporting BED (Hsu et al., 2002; Spitzer et al., 1992). In those seeking bariatric surgery, approximately 27% of individuals are found to meet the criteria (Dymek-Valentine, Rienecke-Hoste, & Engelberg, 2005). As those with BED show significantly more eating disturbances than those without (Hsu et al., 2002), caution should be taken if you come across someone with the above characteristics. This will help you to understand the full extent of influences on their eating behaviour, which may assist the weight loss treatment approach.

Test your knowledge

4.5 Evaluate the causes of obesity.

4.6 What health risks do those who are obese face?

Answers to these questions can be found on the companion website at:
www.pearsoned.co.uk/psychologyexpress

Further reading Obesity

Topic	Key reading
Two reports from the medical professions providing recommendations to tackle obesity	Royal College of Physicians (2013). *Action on obesity: Comprehensive care for all. Report of a working party.* London: RCP.
	Academy of Medical Royal Colleges (2013). *Measuring up: The medical profession's prescription for the nation's obesity crisis.* London: AMRC.

CASE STUDY

Obesity

The client

Louis had never really considered himself to be overweight, until he began to feel tired all of the time, lacked energy during the day and was at times delirious with blurry vision. He used to have a physically active job, but after a change in occupation he became more sedentary. After concerns expressed by his wife, Louis visited his doctor and at 5ft 11inches and 16st 4lbs his BMI was calculated as 31.8, classifying him as obese. Blood tests concluded that he had type 2 diabetes, and when he was asked about his daily food intake, he confirmed it was high in fat and sugar, reporting cake for breakfast, snack food for lunch and fast food on his way home, although he did eat a good quantity of fruit, so he thought his eating habits were satisfactory.

Background – the problem

Known as an autoimmune condition, type 2 diabetes occurs when the cells that take up glucose–insulin molecules become resistant and are unable to be absorbed. This condition, thought to be caused in part by a poor diet and lack of exercise (Marx, 2002), leads to high levels of sugar in the blood and a failure to transfer it to the organs that need it due to insulin resistance.

Advice

Louis was advised to monitor his diet and modify it in terms of the Eatwell Plate, and to increase his level of physical activity. Louis returned in six weeks, with little change in his weight, reporting that he had tried but had not been able to change his lifestyle due to a number of barriers and lack of motivation, which are common issues (Vermeire et al., 2007).

If Louis were referred to you for support to change his diet and physical activity, and ultimately to manage his diabetes and lose weight, what things would you consider?

There are many variables to evaluate, but a good place to start is the COM-B model (Michie, van Stralen, & West, 2011) that we discussed in Chapter 3, which suggests that for a behaviour to occur, the individual must have both the physical and psychological *capability*, and the physical and social *opportunity*, to enact it and be *motivated* to do it more than any competing behaviour.

Further reading Healthy eating

Topic	*Key reading*
Techniques in healthy eating and physical activity interventions	Michie, S., Abraham, C., Whittington, C., McAteer, J., & Gupta, S. (2009). Effective techniques in healthy eating and physical activity interventions: A meta-regression. *Health Psychology, 28*(6), 690–701.

Chapter summary – pulling it all together

→ Can you tick all of the points from the revision checklist at the beginning of this chapter?

→ Attempt the sample question from the beginning of this chapter using the answer guidelines below.

→ Go to the companion website at www.pearsoned.co.uk/psychologyexpress to access more revision support online, including interactive quizzes, flashcards, You be the marker exercises as well as answer guidance for the Test your knowledge and Sample questions from this chapter.

Answer guidelines

 Sample question   *Essay*

Discuss the considerations that need to be taken into account when attempting to promote a healthy diet.

Approaching the question

Your answer should aim to provide an analysis of the importance of eating behaviour on health and illness and the factors that may influence people to engage in a healthy diet.

Important points to include

To begin, you first need to define what is meant by a healthy diet and why this is important for health status. Then you can critically discuss the influences on eating behaviour, discussing the empirical research in the area and different perspectives that try to explain eating behaviour from a bio-psycho-social perspective. You should consider the usefulness of applying health psychology models and theories to the promotion of healthy eating and link this to an applied setting. Conclude by evaluating the key considerations when promoting a healthy diet and make suggestions as to how the field of health psychology can improve knowledge, research and interventions in this area.

Make your answer stand out

Try to avoid simply describing the above information, or just discussing one viewpoint. A good answer will remember to take a critical stance, evaluating the strengths and limitations of the literature. It is important to show original thinking by considering the overlaps of the understanding of eating behaviour from the different disciplines (bio-psycho-social), and how these may overlap to influence eating behaviour. You should conclude by making recommendations to challenge the current empirical evidence and advance understanding in this area.

Explore the accompanying website at www.pearsoned.co.uk/psychologyexpress

→ Prepare more effectively for exams and assignments using the answer guidelines for questions from this chapter.

→ Test your knowledge using multiple choice questions and flashcards.

→ Improve your essay skills by exploring the You be the marker exercises.

Notes

Health risk behaviours: substance misuse

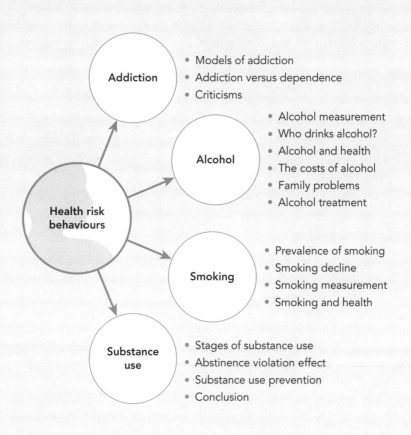

- **Addiction**
  - Models of addiction
  - Addiction versus dependence
  - Criticisms

- **Alcohol**
  - Alcohol measurement
  - Who drinks alcohol?
  - Alcohol and health
  - The costs of alcohol
  - Family problems
  - Alcohol treatment

- **Health risk behaviours**

- **Smoking**
  - Prevalence of smoking
  - Smoking decline
  - Smoking measurement
  - Smoking and health

- **Substance use**
  - Stages of substance use
  - Abstinence violation effect
  - Substance use prevention
  - Conclusion

A printable version of this topic map is available from
www.pearsoned.co.uk/psychologyexpress

Introduction

Have you ever thought about the reasons why people smoke? Do you think an alcoholic is ill, or that they drink of their own free choice?

One area that links health psychology closely to clinical psychology is substance misuse. This chapter covers the key health risk behaviours – alcohol misuse and smoking cigarettes – that are linked to the leading causes of death in the UK: coronary heart disease, stroke and cancer.

Think about your own behaviours. Let's take smoking as an example. *Have you ever tried a puff of a cigarette?* Consider to yourself, why. *Why did you or didn't you try it? And if you did ever try a cigarette, did you become a smoker?* Again, consider to yourself, why. We are all different, and motivated to behave in different ways for different reasons. Individual differences are essential to consider in health psychology because, while five people reading this book may have answered no to the questions above, another five would have answered yes.

 Revision checklist

Essential points you should know by the end of this chapter are:
❏ The different theoretical models that attempt to explain addiction
❏ The link between individual differences, health risk behaviours and the leading causes of mortality
❏ The process of initiation, maintenance, cessation and relapse.

Assessment advice

When you are writing an essay or answering an exam question on this topic, you should consider the following points:

- *Content*. What is the connection between health risk behaviours and health status? Are there factors (biological/psychological/social) that may put someone more at risk? Why do some people engage in detrimental behaviours while others engage in those that protect their health? What cognitions are involved in health risk behaviours? What are the different models of addiction? Does treatment differ based on these models?

- *Evidence* is always required, so ensure you *back up your argument with references* to relevant research. Unsupported generalisations and statements based on your own opinion will not achieve a very high mark and might even fail.

- *Be critical* of the evidence. Is there conflicting evidence? Do researchers consider a theoretical viewpoint? Could this impact on practical settings? Are there other aspects that we still don't fully understand in this field? What more could be done?

- *Read widely* on the topics, and aim for primary sources (such as journal articles) where evidence is written by the author rather than secondary sources (such as textbooks) which are describing what someone else has done. Imagine you are working in the field: what would you need to know as a practitioner to support your clients? If it isn't in the literature, there is a case for future research.

Sample question

Could you answer this question? Below is a typical problem question that could rise on this topic.

 Sample question   *Essay*

Critically evaluate the differing models of addiction with reference to empirical evidence to explain the aetiology and treatment of alcoholism.

Guidelines on answering this question are included at the end of this chapter, whilst guidance on tackling other exam questions can be found on the companion website at **www.pearsoned.co.uk/psychologyexpress**

Addiction

Before we can understand health risk behaviours, we need to understand addiction. It should be noted that not everyone who smokes or drinks too much alcohol is addicted, but the ones who are, are likely to be putting their long-term health at risk.

The term 'addiction' is derived from the Latin word *addicere*, which translates as 'to sentence'. Anyone who has ever had contact with someone suffering with an addiction will truly be able to sympathise with this translation.

Models of addiction

There are several models of addiction, and which model you draw from will determine how you conceptualise addiction, the person addicted and the treatment approach. We will use alcohol as an example. To read more on what follows, see Ogden (2012).

Moral model of addiction

In the nineteenth century, John Snow (Snow, 2002) made one of the most infamous epidemiological findings: he discovered that cholera was transmitted through water. At this time, water was seen as unsafe, and alcohol was often seen as a safer alternative:

- Alcohol consumption was acceptable and a result of free choice.
- Excessive alcohol consumption was seen as a 'chosen' behaviour.

- This was thought to deserve *punishment* when it became a problem.
- Alcoholics were seen as having a weakness and a *'lack of moral fibre'*.

Those who blame individuals for becoming an alcoholic are often adopting a moral model of addiction, assuming that their behaviour is freely chosen and that they could stop if they wanted to.

First disease concept of addiction

In the later nineteenth century, people began to fear alcohol as an evil substance that would make people who drank it succumb to its power. Here lay the foundations for the first disease concept, which tapped into the biomedical view.

- Alcoholism was seen as an *illness* that needed medical treatment.
- The substance was seen as the problem; the individual as an innocent victim.
- Alcoholics were seen to have *no control* over their condition.

Second disease concept of addiction

Because of this fear, prohibition became widespread in the early twentieth century. But this was problematic due to the black market, and it became clear that a complete ban on alcohol was difficult to uphold. It also became apparent that, while some individuals drank excessively, not everyone did. So the law was relaxed. Attitudes towards alcoholism also changed, but they still maintained a biomedical approach.

- Alcoholism was seen as an *illness* developed by only certain people.
- Addiction was thought to occur for three differing reasons:
  - pre-existing physical abnormalities;
  - pre-existing psychological abnormalities;
  - acquired dependency.
- Those who became alcoholics were now seen to need *support and treatment*.
- There was a clear focus on *abstinence*, and this is still a view held by well-known treatment providers such as Alcoholics Anonymous (AA).
- However, there is some criticism of this biomedicalisation, as creating stigmatisation and limiting control of the sufferer (Berghmans, de Jong, Tibben, & de Wert, 2009).

Social learning theory

In the 1970s psychologists (Bandura, 1977b) began to provide evidence that behaviours can be learned, through modelling and reinforcement, and, therefore, can be unlearned.

- From this viewpoint, addiction was seen as an *acquired habit*. Addictive behaviours were thought to be learned due to one of four processes:
  1 *Classical conditioning* – when an unconditioned stimulus (e.g. pub) elicits an unconditioned response (e.g. feeling relaxed), and the unconditioned stimulus is linked to a conditioned stimulus (e.g. alcohol), then eventually

this conditioned stimulus (alcohol) will lead to a conditioned response (feeling relaxed). Remember Pavlov and his dog!

- This continues to be an explanation for alcohol dependence (Drobes, Saladin, & Tiffany, 2001).

    2 *Operant conditioning* – behaviour is more likely to occur if it is positively reinforced by a positive event (e.g. feeling good or social acceptance), or negatively reinforced by the removal of a negative event (e.g. withdrawal or stress). So if the behaviour gives you something good or takes away something bad, you are more likely to do it again. Remember Skinner and his rats!

- This may explain why there are strong co-morbidities between anxiety disorders and alcohol abuse, whereby an individual may drink to take away negative affect (Kushner, Abrams, & Borchardt, 2000).

    3 *Observational learning* – modelling behaviour on significant others (e.g. copying parents' or friends' behaviour). Remember Bandura and the Bobo doll!

- This may explain why children of problem drinkers are more susceptible to alcoholism (Green, MacIntyre, West, & Ecob, 1991).

    4 *Cognitive processes* – linked to problem solving and maladaptive coping mechanisms (e.g. performing the behaviour to escape from something).

Addiction versus dependence

'Addiction' and 'dependence' are often used interchangeably. However, it is argued (Maisto, Galizio, & Connors, 2004) that they are two different things.

- *Addiction* is seen as seeking out activities that are pleasurable even though they are bad for health or social life.
- *Dependence* is when the body needs (craves) the substance to bring it back to its 'normal' state, avoiding an unpleasant state. This often includes:
    - *Tolerance* – a need for increased amounts of the substance to achieve the desired effect or a diminished effect with continued use of the same amount.
    - *Withdrawal* – often the opposite of what the substance produces.

Criticisms

As with everything in psychology, there are criticisms of these theories:

- The disease model, which comes from a biomedical viewpoint, does not acknowledge the individual as a whole, ignoring social and psychological influencers. Relapse is seen as a failure rather than a learning experience in a process of change. This is an 'all or nothing' way of thinking and can lead to unrealistic targets and reduced motivation to try again. Abstinence is seen as the safest form of treatment, creating the assumption that the individual has no control over their behaviour except to avoid it.

- The social learning theory stance also has its drawbacks. Viewing a behaviour as learned detracts from any biological influence there may be in terms of genetic predisposition or biological abnormality.

A good practitioner will understand all concepts and consider a bio-psycho-social approach which aims to guide their client to the best style of treatment for them.

Test your knowledge

5.1 What is the second disease concept?

5.2 How can the bio-psycho-social model be applied to substance misuse?

Answers to these questions can be found on the companion website at:
www.pearsoned.co.uk/psychologyexpress

Further reading Addiction

Topic	Key reading
Overview of addiction models	Ogden, J. (2012). *Health Psychology: A textbook* (5th ed.). Maidenhead: Open University Press, Chapter 4.
One of the 'Clinical Psychology' series of textbooks – on addiction	Teesson, M., Hall, W., Proudfoot, H., & Degenhardt, L. (2012). *Addictions* (2nd ed.). Hove: Psychology Press.

 **Sample question**   *Essay*

Critically discuss the philosophy 'Once a drunk, always a drunk'.

Alcohol

Alcohol is the second most commonly used substance in the world after caffeine (Julien, 1996). Although often perceived as a stimulant in the short term, alcohol acts by depressing the central nervous system, thus inducing unconsciousness and potential death at high levels.

It is now a socially acceptable behaviour to drink alcohol in moderation. But how much is 'safe'? Public health authorities recommend daily benchmarks with alcohol-free days in between:

- *Women* should drink no more than *2–3 units* per day.
- *Men* should drink no more than *3–4 units* per day.

This has changed from previous recommendations due to the concern of 'binge drinking' (defined as drinking over twice the recommended level) behaviour (Moore, Smith, & Catford, 1994). Previously it was recommended that:

- Women should drink no more than 14 units per week.
- Men should drink no more than 21 units per week.

In England, one unit is equal to 8g (10ml) of pure alcohol. This equates to:

- a typical glass (125ml) of wine;
- a pub measure of spirits; or
- a half-pint of standard strength beer.

Alcohol measurement

The most commonly used assessment for alcohol use is the Alcohol Use Disorders Identification Test (AUDIT: Saunders, Aasland, Babor & Grant, 1993), developed to screen alcohol misuse in medical settings. For a brief assessment, there is also the AUDIT-C (Bush, Kivlahan, McDonell, Fihn, & Bradley, 1998).

Who drinks alcohol?

In a 2009 national survey (NHS Health and Social Care Information Centre: NHS HSCIC, 2011), cross-sectional data revealed that:

Adults

- 87% of men and 81% of women drink alcohol at least occasionally.
- 69% of men and 55% of women reported drinking at least once a week.
- 10% of men and 6% of women reported drinking every day.
- 37% of men drank over 4 units and 29% of women drank more than 3 units, on at least one day in the week prior to interview.
- In 2007, 33% of men and 16% of women (around a quarter of all adults) were classified as hazardous drinkers.
- This includes 6% of men and 2% of women classified as harmful drinkers, and 9% of men and 4% of women showed signs of alcohol dependence, both likely to be damaging to health status.

The misuse and abuse of alcohol is a major social, economic and public health problem. There is concern over young people who drink heavily or binge drink; however, this is reducing. In the same survey (NHS HSCIC, 2011):

Children

- 18% of secondary school pupils aged 11 to 15 reported drinking alcohol in the week prior to interview, compared with 26% in 2001.
- Around half of pupils had ever had an alcoholic drink (51%), compared with 61% in 2003.

Alcohol and health

The misuse of alcohol can have a number of detrimental effects:

- The withdrawal effects of alcohol include shaking, sweating, nausea (which many would experience as a hangover), anxiety, sleep disturbance, hallucination and seizure (more common with chronic alcohol problems).

- Approximately 10% of people who consume alcohol will develop a problem with it (Fleming, Mihic, & Harris, 2001).
- Alcohol-use disorders are the most common psychiatric problems treated by mental health professionals (Gold & Miller, 1997).
- There are often co-morbidities with other mental health problems such as anxiety and depression (Grant et al., 2004) and an increased risk of suicide.
- The frequent use of alcohol disturbs the natural absorption of nutrients from the gastrointestinal tract (Fleming et al., 2001).
- The organ that takes the most alcohol-induced damage is the liver and alcohol is the most common cause of liver disease (Walsh & Alexander, 2000).
- A 'fatty' liver, alcoholic hepatitis and cirrhosis are also common risk factors for alcohol misuse. Cirrhosis can develop by drinking just 2–4 drinks a day for 10 days (Karsan, Rojter, & Saab, 2004).
- Alcohol is associated with several forms of cancer, including: upper digestive tract, respiratory system, mouth, pharynx, larynx, oesophagus, bowel, breast and liver. Due to its links with cancer, it has been classified as co-carcinogenic (Bagnardi, Blangiardo, La Vecchia, & Corrao, 2001).
- Alcohol has been found to be associated with 75% of all oesophagus cancer deaths (Rice, 1993).
- Consuming more than 35 units of alcohol a week makes you twice as likely to die of a stroke than light to moderate drinkers (Hart, Davey Smith, Hole, & Hawthorne, 1999).
- Abstainers and heavy drinkers are more at risk of coronary heart disease than light/moderate drinkers (Corrao, Bagnardi, Zambon, & La Vecchia, 2004).
- There is also an increased risk of coronary heart disease for binge drinkers (Murray et al., 2002).
- Extensive alcohol misuse can lead to neurological damage. Alcohol-induced blackouts can occur, where the individual can appear conscious to the people around them, but they have no memory after the event. It is believed this occurs due to alcohol preventing the coding of a memory from developing (Browning, Hoffer, & Dunwiddie, 1993).
- Chronic alcohol use can lead to severe brain damage, such as alcohol-induced dementia. This, mixed with thiamine (vitamin B) deficiency, can lead to Wernicke's encephalopathy, causing confusion and disorientation (Day, Bentham, Callaghan, Kuruvilla, & George, 2004) and Korsakoff's syndrome.

The costs of alcohol

Alcohol misuse can have a number of consequences for the individual, their family and the economy. Based on 2009/10 figures (NHS HSCIC, 2011):

- There were 1,057,000 alcohol-related admissions to hospital in the UK. This is an increase of 12% on the 2008/09 figure (945,500) and more than twice as many as in 2002/03 (510,800).

- There were 6,584 deaths in the UK directly related to alcohol in 2009. This is a 3% decrease on the 2008 figure (6,769) but an increase of 20% from 2001 (5,477).
- Of these, the majority (4,154) died from alcoholic liver disease.
- It is estimated that the cost of alcohol misuse to the NHS is £2.7 billion.

The Cabinet Office (2003) reports that alcohol misuse is responsible for:

- £6.4 billion in lost productivity;
- £7.3 billion in criminal activity.

Family problems

Alcoholism is difficult not just for the individual, but also for their family, and it has been linked to both spousal and child neglect. Research (Gilvarry, 2005) on data from the network to support children of alcoholics (COA) found that:

- An estimated 920,000 children live in families where one or both parents have problems with alcohol.
- Alcoholism is often a family secret, with fear of disclosure or asking for help.

Alcohol treatment

Treatment for alcohol dependence will depend on what model of addiction the approach draws from and should also consider drinking motives. Those with moderate drinking issues seem to be associated with social motives; however, when drinking becomes more dependent, it is often related to coping mechanisms (Kuntsche, Knibbe, Gmel, & Engels, 2005). The first thing to consider is the treatment goal: is it controlled drinking (to use in moderation) or abstinence? Controlled drinking may be suitable for some individuals but not others. It also goes against one of the biggest support networks for alcoholics, Alcoholics Anonymous (AA), who suggest that no alcoholic is able to moderate alcohol use over time (Teesson et al., 2012).

Detoxification

To reach abstinence, the person first needs to detoxify. *Detoxification* is the removal of a substance from the body. It can lead to serious and, in the case of alcohol, life-threatening withdrawal, so medical guidance should be sought for those with severe alcohol dependency. Detoxification is often confused with treatment and it is noted (Mattick & Hall, 1996) that this is just the first step towards recovery. Adding psychological intervention can significantly improve outcome (Alwyn, John, Hodgson, & Phillips, 2004).

Psycho-social intervention

The most efficacious psycho-social treatments found in a meta-analysis of clinical trials (Miller & Wilbourne, 2002) were: brief interventions, social skills training, the community reinforcement approach, behaviour contracting, behavioural marital therapy and case management. The least effective were interventions that aimed to educate, confront, shock or foster insight regarding the nature and causes of alcoholism. Project MATCH (Kadden, Carbonari, Litt, Tonigan, & Zweben, 1998) found 12-step facilitation therapy (TSF), motivational enhancement therapy (MET) and cognitive behavioural therapy (CBT) to be successful treatment options. Self-efficacy and readiness to change were seen as the most important cognitive factors for alcohol reduction outcomes.

 Sample question   *Problem-based learning*

Alcohol treatment (Ferri, Amato, & Davoli, 2006)

Below are the 12 steps of Alcoholics Anonymous (AA General Service Office, 1952). Consider the approach they are drawn from. What strengths and weaknesses does this type of treatment have? Does a person who is treated with the 12 steps need to believe in God?

1 We admitted we were powerless over alcohol – that our lives had become unmanageable.
2 Came to believe that a Power greater than ourselves could restore us to sanity.
3 Made a decision to turn our will and our lives over to the care of God as we understood Him.
4 Made a searching and fearless moral inventory of ourselves.
5 Admitted to God, to ourselves and to another human being the exact nature of our wrongs.
6 Were entirely ready to have God remove all these defects of character.
7 Humbly asked Him to remove our shortcomings.
8 Made a list of all persons we had harmed, and became willing to make amends to them all.
9 Made direct amends to such people wherever possible, except when to do so would injure them or others.
10 Continued to take personal inventory and when we were wrong promptly admitted it.
11 Sought through prayer and meditation to improve our conscious contact with God as we understood Him, praying only for knowledge of His will for us and the power to carry that out.
12 Having had a spiritual awakening as the result of these steps, we tried to carry this message to alcoholics and to practise these principles in all our affairs.

Real-life case – Russell Brand

The 12 steps are supported by those who have suffered with addiction helping each other. Although not an academic, peer-reviewed article, a summary of the journey to sobriety published in March 2013 by the *Guardian*, written by well-known comedian and actor Russell Brand, is certainly worth a read. Entitled 'My life without drugs' he takes you on a journey of his alcohol and heroin dependency, saying: 'Drugs and alcohol are not my problem, reality is my problem, drugs and alcohol are my solution'. Although sober now for 10 years, he admits drugs can still come to the forefront of his mind and he describes true strength in his ability to overcome this (http://www.guardian.co.uk/culture/2013/mar/09/russell-brand-life-without-drugs).

Test your knowledge

5.3 How many units of alcohol is the government's recommended limit?

5.4 Name three health complications that can occur from alcohol misuse.

Answers to these questions can be found on the companion website at:
www.pearsoned.co.uk/psychologyexpress

Further reading Alcohol misuse

Topic	Key reading
Project MATCH	Kadden, R., Carbonari, J., Litt, M., Tonigan, S., & Zweben, A. (1998). Matching alcoholism treatments to client heterogeneity: Project MATCH three-year drinking outcomes. *Alcoholism: Clinical and Experimental Research, 22*(6), 1300–1311.
Meta-analysis on treatment approaches to alcohol dependency	Miller, W. R., & Wilbourne, P. L. (2002). Mesa Grande: A methodological analysis of clinical trials of treatments for alcohol use disorders. *Addiction, 97*(3), 265–277.

 Sample question   *Essay*

Critically evaluate the individual differences involved in the initiation, maintenance OR cessation of smoking OR alcohol.

Smoking

Nicotine, derived from tobacco leaves, has an almost immediate pharmacological action (Maisto et al., 2004). Absorbed within 10–16 seconds, it activates nicotinic acetylcholine receptors which increase dopamine in the brain (Jarvis, 2004). It is as toxic as cyanide (Rose, 1991) and can be fatal at doses over 60 milligrams (mg).

However, the average cigarette contains 6–11 mg (Henningfield, 1995), with only 1–3 mg being absorbed. Nicotine causes physical dependence and is more addictive than cocaine (Doweiko, 2006).

Prevalence of smoking

Smoking rates have declined since the 1970s and smoking is now seen as a minority activity (NHS HSCIC, 2012b). Statistics show that:

- In 2010, 20% of the UK population aged 16 and over (men = 20%; women = 19%) were engaging in the behaviour (down from 39% in 1980).
- Looking at the statistics over the last few decades from the General Household Survey (Robinson & Harris, 2011), smoking behaviour in the UK has reduced in:
  - men: 51% (1974); 31% (1990); 26% (2004);
  - women: 41% (1974); 29% (1990); 23% (2004).

Smoking decline

This decline in smoking behaviour may be due to a number of reasons:

- The advertising of tobacco has been banned from the media since 2003 and from sponsorship since 2005 (Tobacco Advertising and Promotion Act, 2002).
- A smoking ban has been introduced in public places (Smoke-Free England, from July 2007).
- Purchase age has changed, with a law to prosecute anyone selling cigarettes to under 18s (increased from 16 years in October 2007).
- Smokers may also be dying!

Smoking measurement

Assessment of motivation to stop smoking may be done using direct questioning (West, 2004) and motivational interviewing (Rubak, Snadbaek, Lauritzen, & Christensen, 2005). The level of dependence allows you to estimate the likelihood of quit attempt success. A common measurement used is the Fagerström Test for Nicotine Dependence (Heatherton, Kozlowski, Frecker, & Fagerström, 1991).

Smoking and health

Smoking is the single greatest cause of avoidable illness and preventable death in England (DH, 2004a). Approximately 6 million people worldwide die each year as a result of cigarettes (World Health Organisation: WHO, 2011). Doll and Hill (1952) were the first to report the link between smoking and lung cancer. This work led to the development of the pressure group Action on Smoking and Health (ASH) and the white paper *Smoking kills* (DH, 1998b). ASH (2012) suggests that cigarette smoking is linked to:

- 17% of deaths from coronary heart disease (CHD);
- 86% of deaths from lung cancer;

- more than 25% of other cancer deaths, including cancer of the lung, mouth, lip, throat, bladder, kidney, stomach, liver and cervix;
- 80% of deaths from bronchitis and breathing diseases;
- 25% of lung cancer deaths among non-smokers due to passive smoking.

These risks have been confirmed in the 34-year follow-up Framingham study (Freund, Belanger, D'Agostino, & Kannel, 1993) and diet is seen as important in smokers, as there are high levels of antioxidants found in fruit, vegetables and tea which may *reduce* the risk of cancer. Furthermore, one in two long-term smokers will die prematurely as a result of smoking, half in middle age (Wald & Hackshaw, 1996). UK national statistics for 2011 (NHS HSCIC, 2012b) suggest that:

- Around 459,900 patients are admitted to NHS hospitals each year due to diseases caused by smoking.
- Around 79,100 people are killed by smoking every year, accounting for 18% of all UK deaths in over-35-year-olds.

Half of all teenagers who are currently smoking will die from diseases caused by tobacco if they continue to smoke. Someone who starts smoking at 15 is three times as likely to die from cancer due to smoking than someone who starts smoking in their mid-twenties. Furthermore, of 1,000 20-year-old UK smokers (Peto, 1994):

- 1 will be murdered;
- 6 will die in road traffic accidents;
- 250 will die from a smoking-related illness in middle age (35–69 years);
- 250 will die from smoking in older age (70yrs+).

Substance use

Stages of substance use

No matter what substance is being used/misused, the user goes through the following process: *recruitment/initiation*, *maintenance*, *cessation* and *relapse* (see Ogden, 2012, p. 83). We will use smoking as an example now, but these stages are relevant for many other substances (e.g. alcohol, cocaine, heroin) and behaviours (e.g. overeating).

Recruitment and initiation

This phase refers to the take-up of a behaviour. Recent statistics from the NHS Health and Social Care Information Centre (2012b) suggest that:

- Smoking often begins in childhood and adolescence.
- Girls are more likely to have tried smoking and be regular smokers than boys.
- The prevalence of smoking increases with age, from less than 0.5% of 11-year-olds to 11% of 15-year-olds.

The models discussed in Chapter 2 explain some of the psychological cognitions involved in initiation, such as attitude and perceived behavioural control from the theory of planned behaviour (McMillan, Higgins, & Connor, 2005). Parental smoking has also been found to significantly predict children's smoking intention (McMillan et al., 2005), although contradictory reports exist (Li, Pentz, & Chou, 2002; De Vries et al., 2003). Avenevoli and Merikangas (2003) suggest that the effect of parental behaviour diminishes when other factors (such as cognitions) are taken into account.

There is a popular notion that initiation begins through peer pressure, from both friends (Jarvis, 2004) and siblings (Mercken, Candel, Willems, & De Vries, 2007). However, adolescents have rejected this idea (Denscombe, 2001). A positive smoker stereotype (i.e. a prototype or perceived image that is seen as cool and exciting) may also predict uptake (Gibbons & Gerrard, 1995; Van den Eijnden, Spikerman, & Engels, 2006; Rivis, Sheeran, & Armitage, 2006).

Twin and adoption studies suggest there might be a genetic link, showing that smoking runs in families (Heath, Madden, Slutske, & Martin (1995). However, this may be confounded by socially learned influences. Stressful events such as parental separation have also been suggested as a reason for initiation (Kirby, 2002).

Maintenance

The maintenance of smoking is underpinned by many interacting factors. Nicotine contained in cigarettes is highly addictive and it is thought that this is one of the key reasons that people continue to smoke (Jarvis, 2004). Smoking has serious health costs, yet fulfils important functions for smokers. The prevalence of smoking is linked to social economic status, gender, ethnicity and social support. Statistics (NHS HSCIC, 2012b) show:

● Smoking status is lower among households classified as professional and managerial (15%) than among manual (26%).

● Divorced or separated people were most likely to smoke (30%), with widowed smoking the least (13%).

Wilkinson and Abraham (2004) have found a significant link between smoking behaviour and peer smoking status, extraversion and self-esteem. Stress and high job strain are also linked to smoking behaviour (Kouvonen, Kivimäki, Virtanen, Pentti, & Vahtera, 2005). Some smokers underestimate the health risk of smoking, showing a degree of unrealistic optimism, believing they have less risk than an average smoker of being affected by lung cancer and that exercise can reduce the ill effects of their smoking-related behaviour (Weinstein, Marcus, & Moser, 2005). Others smoke to relieve boredom, because they enjoy it, to help them to concentrate or to keep withdrawal effects at bay (McEwen, West, & McRobbie, 2008).

Cessation

The beneficial effects of stopping smoking on health status are well documented (Kenfield et al., 2010). Cessation relates to stopping a behaviour and is seen as a process of change involving *pre-contemplation, contemplation, preparation, action* and *maintenance* (transtheoretical model of change: Prochaska & DiClemente, 1983; see Chapter 3).

Smokers find it very difficult to stop. From the 2004 General Household Survey (Goddard & Green, 2004):

- 66% want to stop but 58% say it would be difficult to go without smoking for a whole day.
- 17% report lighting up within five minutes of waking up.
- Performance of deprived smokers is impaired.
- Health concerns are the most common reason for cessation (86%), followed by cost (27%), family pressure (20%) and the effect on children (15%).
- It is important to use the term 'stopping' (which suggests choice) rather than 'giving up' (which suggests taking something away).

Disease models of cessation would treat the physical addiction with therapies such as nicotine replacement, which has been found to be effective over and above a placebo (Stead, Perera, Bullen, Mant, & Lancaster, 2008). Antidepressant medication such as bupropion is also commonly used and is more effective than a nicotine patch or placebo (Jorenby et al., 1999).

Social learning techniques would use strategies (see Ogden, 2012, pp. 90–91) such as:

- *aversion therapies*, which aim to punish the behaviour (e.g. rapid smoking);
- *contingency contracting*, which aims to punish the behaviour, and create a contract to provide a reward for behaviour change (e.g. money);
- *cue exposure*, which aims to create new coping mechanisms to external cues;
- *self-management* (e.g. diary keeping – monitoring behaviour, triggers and frequency – and creating self-awareness);
- *multi-perspective cessation clinics*, which incorporate all of the above.

Relapse or lapse

From the disease model, which has an 'all or nothing' perspective of abstinence, relapse is a failure of the given pathway of change. However, from a social learning perspective it is a learning experience. Relapse prevention should be just as important as cessation interventions. Marlatt and Gordon (1985; Marlatt and Donovan, 2005) developed the *relapse prevention model* which suggested that:

- Addictive behaviours are learned and can therefore be unlearned.
- Addictions are not 'all or nothing' but exist on a continuum.
- Lapses from abstinence are likely and acceptable.
- There is a difference between a 'lapse' or minor slip (e.g. one cigarette) and a 'relapse' or return to the former behaviour (e.g. 20 cigarettes).
- For no relapse to occur, the individual needs to develop good coping strategies (including self-efficacy) and have a negative outcome expectancy.
- Relapse is more likely if there are poor coping strategies and positive outcome expectancies (i.e. thinking the behaviour will be good).

Abstinence violation effect

The transition between a lapse and relapse is determined by (Curry, 1987):

● *Dissonance conflict.* Conflict between the self-image of someone who no longer smokes and smoking behaviour (triggering that all-or-nothing thinking).

● *Self-attribution.* If a lapse is blamed on self, it increases feelings of guilt and shame and thus lowers self-efficacy. However, if a lapse is blamed on the external world (such as the situation), guilt and shame are reduced, control is maintained and relapse is less likely.

Substance use prevention

This goes back to the premise of the last chapter in terms of health promotion. Ideally, what we want as health professionals is for people not to engage in a health risk behaviour in the first place. Chapter 2 can assist with the cognitions involved that are important for this. One approach that is often used is social 'inoculation' (McGuire, 1964). This aims to protect people from the social pressures that could result in them abusing a substance. It has four common features:

● knowledge about the consequences of a substance;

● an understanding of how attitudes towards the substances are developed through peers, family and the media;

● the development of refusal training: 'Just Say No';

● enabling people to tell their peers/family that they have a commitment not to engage in substance abuse.

Conclusion

There are many approaches to addictive behaviour; however, they can be broken down into four distinct stages: *recruitment, maintenance, cessation* and *relapse*. Many different factors influence the behaviour at each stage, and the way in which these are interpreted depends upon the model of addiction that you draw from: that is, the disease model (biomedical) or social learning (bio-psycho-social). What is clear is that lifestyle and individual differences play a key role in these behaviours, and that treatment approaches need to acknowledge this.

Test your knowledge

5.5 Why do people smoke?

5.6 What are the four stages of substance misuse?

Answers to these questions can be found on the companion website at:
www.pearsoned.co.uk/psychologyexpress

CASE STUDY

Alcohol misuse and smoking behaviour

The clients

Edwina (aged 40) and Spencer (aged 45) are well respected in their work lives, have a teenage daughter and to the outside world have the perfect, happy life. However, behind closed doors things are difficult. They are both alcoholics and heavy smokers, putting their own and their daughter's health at risk.

After consultation with the couple, their GP uncovered the death of their son, which was a major trigger for their drinking behaviour. They often smoked when they drank, and they reported that drinking took their pain away. However, they wanted to stop for their daughter's sake.

Advice

If the couple were referred to you as a health psychologist for alcohol reduction and smoking cessation, what things would you consider to be influencing their health risk behaviours? And what treatment options would you consider?

Further reading Smoking behaviour

Topic	Key reading
Manual to support smoking cessation	McEwen, A., Hajek, P., McRobbie, H., & West, R. (2008). *Manual of smoking cessation: A guide for counsellors and practitioners.* Wiley-Blackwell.
Background to why people smoke and how to help them stop	Jarvis, M. J. (2004). ABC of smoking cessation: Why people smoke. *British Medical Journal, 328*(7434), 277–279.

Chapter summary – pulling it all together

→ Can you tick all of the points from the revision checklist at the beginning of this chapter?

→ Attempt the sample question from the beginning of this chapter using the answer guidelines below.

→ Go to the companion website at **www.pearsoned.co.uk/psychologyexpress** to access more revision support online, including interactive quizzes, flashcards, You be the marker exercises as well as answer guidelines for the Test your knowledge and Sample questions from this chapter.

Answer guidelines

 *Sample question*   *Essay*

Critically evaluate the differing models of addiction with reference to empirical evidence to explain the aetiology and treatment of alcoholism.

Important points to include

- Begin by outlining the prevalence of the behaviour that you are going to discuss (how big the problem is and who is affected).
- Then critically discuss the influences on the behaviour:
  - Discuss the empirical research that informs this.
  - Evaluate the different perspectives from a biomedical and bio-psycho-social approach.
- You should then consider the usefulness of applying health psychology to an applied setting. Link to prevention or treatment and the health behaviours.
- Conclude by making suggestions about how the field of health psychology can improve knowledge, research and treatment, and suggest future directions.

Make your answer stand out

Try to avoid simply describing the above information. A good answer will remember to take a critical stance, evaluating the strengths and limitations of the literature. A good student would also show original thinking by considering the overlaps in the understanding of addiction and addictive behaviours from the different disciplines (bio-psycho-social) and the research that supports them, their differences and future considerations, in order to challenge the current empirical evidence and advance development.

Explore the accompanying website at www.pearsoned.co.uk/psychologyexpress

→ Prepare more effectively for exams and assignments using the answer guidelines for questions from this chapter.

→ Test your knowledge using multiple choice questions and flashcards.

→ Improve your essay skills by exploring the You be the marker exercises.

Notes

6

Preventive health behaviours

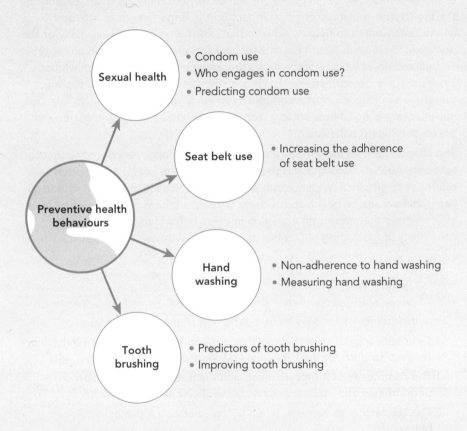

Sexual health
- Condom use
- Who engages in condom use?
- Predicting condom use

Seat belt use
- Increasing the adherence of seat belt use

Preventive health behaviours

Hand washing
- Non-adherence to hand washing
- Measuring hand washing

Tooth brushing
- Predictors of tooth brushing
- Improving tooth brushing

A printable version of this topic map is available from
www.pearsoned.co.uk/psychologyexpress

Introduction

Would you practise safe sex with a new partner? Do you always put your seat belt on before the car is put into gear to drive off? Do you always remember to brush your teeth twice a day or wash your hands after going to the toilet?

Preventive health behaviours can be characterised as behaviours that are considered beneficial and protective to health, thus allowing individuals to make positive steps towards healthy living. But is it that easy?

We cannot forget as health psychologists that individuals do not always act as they know they should. Therefore, we need to have a full understanding of the health behaviours in question, and of ways to enhance them. Exploring the bio-psycho-social factors that impact on the engagement of preventive health behaviours can help us achieve that. Furthermore, by using many of the dominant theories in health psychology, we can endeavour to gain a theoretical understanding of what contributes to the engagement of these behaviours. Essentially, we cannot assume that it is a one-size-fits-all approach. We must therefore aim to uncover the complexity of each health behaviour, to increase our understanding of how society, communities and individuals engage with preventive health behaviours.

This chapter focuses on key preventive health behaviours: namely, condom use, seat belt use, hand washing and tooth brushing. There will be a discussion with reference to empirical evidence and policies to determine the impact of these health behaviours on health status. Furthermore, a critical overview will be given of the factors that impact on engaging in these behaviours, uncovering the complexity of motivating population sub-groups in preventative health behaviour.

 Revision checklist

Essential points you should know by the end of this chapter are:

❏ The prevalence of the problems that not engaging in preventive behaviours can lead to both for the individual and for the wider community

❏ The complexity of bio-psycho-social influences that impact upon the performance and maintenance of preventive health behaviours

❏ The key factors to consider when trying to enhance protective health behaviours.

Assessment advice

When you are writing an essay or answering an exam question on this topic, you should consider the following points:

● *Content.* Be explicit in *providing context* to the topic. What do the national and international epidemiological data tell us in relation to the performance of preventive health behaviours? If not performed, what is the cost in terms of morbidity? Mortality? Quality of life? Health care? Consider, if the problem has improved, what may have contributed to this? Only by knowing the cost of the problem will we know the benefits of engaging in preventive health behaviour.

- *Evidence* is always required, so ensure you back up your argument with *references to relevant research*. Consult a wide range of primary sources to produce a good, well-developed critique to support your arguments. You will need to look in more than just health psychology journals for this topic area, so make sure you consult other key areas such as public health, nursing and epidemiology.

- *Be critical* of studies and the nature of evidence. For example, when uncovering the factors that impact on the use of condoms, has longitudinal or prospective research been conducted to establish relationships, or is research limited to correlational and cross-sectional data? Have control groups been used in research studies which look at the effectiveness of interventions that aim to improve hand-washing rates? And if so, were these groups randomised or clustered, and are the control groups active or passive? It is important in any writing that you do that you are not descriptive; you need to tell a story that shows that you understand the evidence and can create a good argument from it, rather than simply being able to put what you have read into your own words.

Sample question

Could you answer this question? Below is a typical problem question that could rise on this topic.

 Sample question   **Essay**

Critically discuss the contribution that preventive health behaviours make to current mortality and morbidity rates with reference to at least two behaviours.

Guidelines on answering this question are included at the end of this chapter, whilst guidance on tackling other exam questions can be found on the companion website at **www.pearsoned.co.uk/psychologyexpress**

Sexual health

To begin to evaluate the importance of preventive health behaviours when it comes to sexual health, the best place to start is the epidemiological evidence: that is, what is the scope of the problem? Taking HIV (human immunodeficiency virus) as an example, the Health Protection Agency (HPA, 2012) estimated that, by the end of 2010, there were 91,500 people living with HIV in the UK. Approximately one-quarter (22,200, 24%) of these were unaware of their condition (undiagnosed) with a further 640 AIDS (acquired immunodeficiency syndrome) diagnoses reported. By the end of 2012, it was estimated that more than 100,000 people were living with HIV in the UK (Health Protection Agency, 2012). Statistics suggest that just over half (51%, 35,280) of HIV-diagnosed people in 2010 were infected via heterosexual intercourse (13,100 men and 22,180 women), dispelling myths that the infection is predominantly contracted through homosexual intercourse and IV (intravenous) drug use. Of these, 65% (22,940) were black African and 21% (7,550) were white (Health Protection Agency, 2012).

Since 1996 antiretroviral drugs have been available for the treatment of HIV/AIDS. These are often taken in combination, known as HAART (highly active antiretroviral therapy), and essentially work by inhibiting the virus at different phases of its life cycle (Hazenberg et al., 2000). The use of this therapy has not only been able to increase the life expectancy of people living with HIV/AIDS but helped to prevent the mother-to-child transmission of HIV during pregnancy. However, this treatment depends on strict adherence, which is a core issue for this regime – low adherence is often attributed to the adverse side-effects of the medication (for more information on what influences adherence behaviours, see Chapter 9).

HIV is a well-known infection and many campaigns have aimed to educate the public, so why do there continue to be increasing numbers of infected individuals? It has been suggested that, as treatment options have improved, HIV/AIDS has changed from being seen as a terminal virus and disease to a now manageable condition, diminishing the perceived threat. Research conducted by Stolte, Dukers, Geskus, Coutinho and Wit (2004) investigated health beliefs of homosexual men following the HAART programme towards protected and unprotected sexual intercourse (n = 213). Results indicated that most men held less perceived threat following the HAART programme, thus perceiving less need for condom use.

There is also increased risk with regards to other sexually transmitted infections (STIs), with the epidemiological trend increasing over the last decade (2002–12). Data from the Health Protection Agency confirm that the annual rise from 2010 to 2011 was associated with an increased diagnosis of gonorrhoea (25%; 16,835 to 20,965 infected), infectious syphilis (10%; 2,650 to 2,915 infected) and genital herpes (5%; 29,794 to 31,154 infected). During the same time chlamydia fell by 2% (189,314 to 186,196) but it still remains significantly prevalent, with more infected by this than the other mentioned STIs (HPA, 2012). It is worthy to note, however, that although these increases may well be due to a lack of condom use, they may also be attributed to better screening methods and more people attending for screening to be diagnosed.

Condom use

The risk of HIV infection and other STIs can be reduced through safe sexual intercourse via the use of latex condoms. Research assessing likelihood of infection suggests that heterosexual couples are at 2% risk of contracting HIV when consistently practising safe sex, compared to 15% risk when only using condoms occasionally. Similarly, homosexual men who used condoms only some of the time were six times more likely to contract the infection than when using condoms all time (Stroebe, 2011).

Who engages in condom use?

One predominant survey that was carried out with 19,000 adults living in Britain was the National Survey of Sexual Attitudes and Lifestyles, which highlighted that females tend to engage in condom use less often than males with younger people using condoms more commonly than older people. Gender differences also found that condom use declined with males who had new multiple partners and was lowest when multiple partners were not new. Conversely, condom use for females was not affected if multiple partners were new or not (Wellings, Field, & Johnson, 1994). This is in contrast to recent figures from the Health Protection Agency that suggest that young people (under the age of 25 years) and men who have sex with men (MSM) are the most likely to not use condoms and become infected with an STI (HPA, 2012).

This survey was repeated in 2001, and found a significant increase in condom use for both males and females. However, 'high-risk' individuals with multiple partners were now the most likely to report condom use. When accounting for ethnicity and religion, results suggested that those who were of non-white ethnicity and of a non-Christian religion were more likely to use condoms, suggesting an important cultural aspect to condom use (Cassell, Mercer, & Imriel, 2006).

Understanding psycho-social health beliefs may help to uncover the influences on condom use (Sheeran, Abraham, & Orbell, 1999). A plethora of studies have linked condom use with constructs such as the health belief model (HBM; Downing-Matibag & Geisinger, 2009) and the theory of planned behaviour (TPB; Bennett & Bozionelos, 2000). However, we should also consider that the key outcome variable of these models is sometimes an intention rather than actual behaviour, and there is evidence to suggest that intending to use a condom does not always lead to the practice of safe sex (de Visser & Smith, 2004). It is therefore also worth considering the factors of behaviour change discussed in Chapter 3.

Comparing many theoretical constructs, Reid and Aiken (2011) report that perceived susceptibility, benefits and barriers from the HBM, self-efficacy from social cognitive theory (SCT) and partner norms and attitudes from the TPB served as indirect or direct predictors of condom use. These relationships changed dependent on relationship status: for example, self-efficacy significantly predicted condom use for women with casual partners, with attitude and partner norms significantly predicting condom use in women with 'steady' partners.

Effective interventions to increase condom use have included message framing and visual aids to increase affective reactions, risk perceptions and more favourable attitudes towards condom use (Garcia-Retamero & Cokely, 2011) and increasing knowledge through health promotion and education programmes (DiCenso, Guyatt, Willan, & Griffith, 2002). The government has also conducted health education campaigns; however, these have been met with marked criticism: for example, showing that slogans such as 'You know the risks: the decision is yours' is contradictory to the research, which highlights that individuals have a low risk appraisal of HIV (Ingham, Woodcock, & Stenner, 1991).

Community-based interventions have been used and have been shown to be successful in creating peer norms towards safer sex (Gutierrez, McPherson, Fakoya, Matheou, & Bertozzi, 2010). However, interventions need to address personal and structural factors: for example, lack of negotiating skills, availability of condoms, opinions of peers, attitudes of society and deprivation (Sarkar, 2008). They also need to ensure that people know how to use a condom effectively, as it is reported that up to 40% of people apply a condom imperfectly (Hatherall, Ingham, Stone, & McEachran, 2007). More research is now needed to uncover the complexity of sub-groups who engage in 'risky sexual behaviour' among both heterosexual and homosexual individuals to ensure that interventions are specifically targeted to those at risk.

KEY STUDY

Predicting condom use (Garcia-Retamero & Cokely, 2011)

Background

This study aimed to effectively promote prevention and detection of STDs (sexually transmitted diseases) in a young, high-risk population.

Method

In a two-phase longitudinal experiment, the effects of a brief risk awareness intervention (in the form of a sexual health information brochure) were examined in a large sample ($n = 744$) of sexually active young adults.

Intervention

The experiment had two phases using either a gain- or loss-framed approach (in brief, gain-framed messages focus on the benefits and loss-framed focus on the costs). In the first phase, participants read a brochure about STDs and indicated their affective reactions to the brochure, their perceptions of the risk of contracting an STD, their attitudes toward the recommended behaviour in the brochure, and their behavioural intentions. In the second phase conducted six weeks later, participants reported whether they had performed any of the behaviours during this period.

Findings

Results indicated that gain-framed messages induced greater adherence to condom use, whereas loss-framed messages were more effective in promoting illness-detecting behaviours (e.g. making an appointment with a doctor to discuss STD screening). The influence of the framed messages on prevention and detection of STDs was mediated by changes in participants' attitudes toward the health behaviours along with changes in their behavioural intentions.

Conclusion

The study concludes that well-constructed visual aids are a highly effective, transparent, fast, memorable and ethically desirable means of risk communication and that the frame of the message should be taken into consideration.

CASE STUDY

Risky sexual behaviour

The client

Callum is a 22-year-old student. He likes to go out after uni, have a few drinks and 'hook up' with a girl, be it a friend or stranger, often engaging in unprotected sex. From what we know about risky sexual behaviour, Callum's profile makes him at high risk of being infected with an STI (HPA, 2012). Callum confides in his university GP about his behaviour but declines a sexual health screen. If Callum was referred to you as a health psychologist by his GP, what would you need to consider in promoting safer sexual behaviour and engagement in screening, and how would you address this?

Advice

Callum may have negative attitudes towards using condoms. To support Callum to engage in safer sex we need to support him to reduce perceived barriers that he may have, so that he has more positive attitudes towards the behaviour. Furthermore, it could be that Callum does not feel confident in using condoms – a concept that Reid and Aiken (2011) suggest is closely related to low use.

But not only does Callum have to feel confident to use a condom, he has to feel confident in negotiating condom use with his partner. For example, research conducted by Kordoutis, Loumakou and Sarafidou (2000) found that when condoms had not been used, they were not negotiated in 80% of the cases, clearly highlighting the importance of negotiation in condom use.

Increasing levels of confidence and knowledge may deal with only some of the boundaries. What you first need to do is find out from Callum his reasons for not engaging in condom use or screening. From there, you can develop a tailored approach to help support him to practise safe sex.

Test your knowledge

6.1 Which population sub-groups have the highest incidence of HIV in England?

6.2 What health beliefs help us understand why some people don't engage in safe sex?

Answers to these questions can be found on the companion website at: **www.pearsoned.co.uk/psychologyexpress**

Further reading Sexual health

Topic	Key reading
Paper giving an overview of condom use and STIs	Cassell, J. A., Mercer, C. H., & Imriel, J. (2006). Who uses condoms with whom? Evidence from national probability sample surveys. *Sexually Transmitted Infections, 82*, 467–473.
The government's approach to HIV/AIDS	Department of Health (2001a). *Better services, better sexual health: The national strategy for sexual health and HIV*. London: HMSO.
Research incorporating health psychology theories in condom use	Reid, A. E., & Aiken, L. S. (2011). Integration of five health behaviour models: Common strengths and unique contributions to understanding condom use. *Psychology and Health, 26*, 1499–1520.

Condom use is one of the most obvious preventive health behaviours. However, there are many other behaviours that are part of our day-to-day routine, such as wearing seat belts, washing our hands and brushing our teeth, which we should also consider to protect our health.

 Sample question   *Essay*

Discuss with reference to the literature the key factors that are associated with at least one preventive health behaviour.

Seat belt use

Seat belt use, promoted in the UK since 1973, was made compulsory in 1983 following international objectives to reduce both the number and severity of casualties in road traffic accidents (Department of Transport, 2011). Furthermore, in 2006 legislative change required all children to wear an appropriate type of restraint.

In 2008, an observation survey (Knowles, Walter, & Buckle, 2008) in Greater London of 30,850 cars and taxis alongside 5,314 vans found that 89% of car drivers wore seat belts – an increase from 87% in 2007 (Walter, Broughton, & Buckle, 2007) and 82% in 2006 (Broughton & Buckle, 2006). This increase brings London just below the national average of 92%. However, rear seat passengers showed a decline to 63%, which remains lower than the national average (82%).

If seat belt usage were 100%, it is estimated that 590 casualties would be saved each year (Knowles, Walter, & Buckle, 2008). Seat belt use has been shown to reduce the risk of mortality by 72% in a head-on collision (Crandall, Olson, & Sklar, 2001), and it is not just the life of the person wearing the seat belt that could be saved. There is evidence to suggest that there is a significant risk to the person belted in the front seat if the rear passenger does not have their seat belt on in an accident. Research (Ichikawa, Nakahara, & Wakai, 2002) shows that 80% of deaths of front seat occupants could have been avoided if the back seat passenger had been wearing their seat belt. The risk of mortality to rear seat passengers is also improved by 55–75% if they wear a seat belt (Zhu, Cummings, Chu, & Cook, 2007).

So, although both the legal and health benefits of seat belt use are well known, why do people still not 'buckle up'? A range of factors have impacted on intention to use seat belts, including drug and alcohol use (Steptoe et al., 2002). A range of psycho-social factors, such as attitudes, beliefs and intentions, have also been used to explain non-use of seat belts (Chliaoutakis, Gnardellis, Drakou, Darviri, & Sboukis, 2000). Simsekoglu and Lajunen (2008), for example, found the theory of planned behaviour to be a good model at explaining seat belt use behaviour when compared to other models such as the health belief model. Schwarzer et al. (2007) found that uptake could be explained through the variables in the health action process approach, most specifically self-efficacy and planning. Begg and Langley (2000), however, found that the main reasons for not using a seat belt were forgetfulness, laziness, a perceived low risk of injury and discomfort. In contrast, Calisir and Lehto (2002) argued that seat belt use was mainly affected by a person's age, gender and beliefs in usefulness in a possible accident.

Increasing the adherence of seat belt use

Historically, interventions to increase seat belt use have focused on fear campaigns to increase risk susceptibility (National Cooperative Highway Research Program, 2007). However, critics argue that fear is often ineffective in achieving desired behaviour change, and a positive reinforcement approach is viewed as more effective (Soames-Job, 1988). Morrison, Petticrew, and Thomson (2003) evaluated both published and unpublished systematic reviews to determine the effectiveness of interventions relating to seat belt use among other transport interventions. The highest-quality reviews indicated that the most effective interventions are health promotion campaigns, alongside education driver courses. This is in support of Steptoe et al. (2002), who confirm that legislative change alongside changing attitudes among student populations is needed to improve seat belt use adherence.

Test your knowledge

6.3 What is the proportion of the population who wear seat belts?

6.4 Explain the reasons for non-seat belt use.

Answers to these questions can be found on the companion website at:
www.pearsoned.co.uk/psychologyexpress

Further reading Seat belt use

Topic	Key reading
Applying health psychology models to seat belt use	Tayafian, S. S., Aghamolaei, T., Gregory, D., & Madani, A. (2011). Prediction of seat belt use among Iranian automobile drivers: Application of the theory of planned behaviour and the health belief model. *Traffic Injury Prevention, 12,* 48–53.
Seat belt use in young adults	Begg, D. J., & Langley, J. D. (2000). Seat-belt use and related behaviours among young adults. *Journal of Safety Research, 31,* 211–220.

Another preventive health behaviour that we (should) engage in on a daily basis is washing our hands. But imagine if this behaviour was also part of your job to protect lives. The next section will evaluate research in this area.

? Sample question   *Essay*

Critically evaluate the bio-psycho-social factors that impact on the uptake of hand washing in a hospital setting, in light of the current evidence in the field of health psychology.

Hand washing

The importance of hand washing and lack of hand-cleanliness in the transmission of hospital infections is accepted world-wide (Nogueras, Marinsalta, Roussell, & Notario, 2001). A key editorial by the Handwashing Liaison Group (1999) published in the *British Medical Journal* sparked a huge surge of interest in the effectiveness of hand washing in eradicating hospital acquired infection. For example, one intervention study which spanned over 150 years found that when doctors washed their hands before the delivery of babies, the mortality of Streptococcal puerperal sepsis reduced from 22% to 3% (Rotter, 1997). Support was also provided by a literature review which evaluated the impact of hand washing on infection through 107 years and over 423 articles. A causal association was found in both experimental and non-experimental studies; thus the author concluded that the practice of hand washing as a primary infection control measure should continue (Larson, 1988).

However, many studies suggest that health-care workers fail to wash their hands, with many observational studies in intensive care highlighting low rates of hand washing, especially among doctors (Gould, 1996). For example, Bartzokas, Williams and Slade (1995) conducted an observational study of doctors and found that they only washed their hands twice despite frequent patient contact among a total of 21 ward rounds. Erasmus et al. (2010) conducted a systematic review of 96 empirical studies published pre-2000 and highlighted that there was an overall median adherence rate of 40%, with adherence rates lower in intensive care units (30–40%) than in other settings (50–60%), lower among physicians (32%) than nurses (48%), and lower before (21%) than after (47%) patient contact.

So if hand washing is viewed as the cornerstone of reducing hospital infections, why is adherence so low? Hammond, Eckles, Gomez and Cunningham (1990) observed only a 16% adherence rate to hand washing in 81 trauma residents. During surgical procedures (endotracheal intubation) adherence was less than 40%. The main reasons given for this included no knowledge of the protocol, forgetting and insufficient time.

Non-adherence has also been related to the type of setting and activity. Denman, Dwyer, Israel and Vacek (1993) found that hand washing after an interaction in the long-term care setting varied from 50% (changing soiled linen) to 100% (wound care). Risk appraisal has also been viewed as a factor, whereby the higher the perception of risk of infection, the more likely individuals are to wash their hands and pay more attention to infection control (Schillo & Reischl, 1993). Further studies have highlighted that organisational factors such as leadership involvement, reminders, convenient availability of products, and staff workload have a big influence on hand washing (Consensus Measurement in Hand Hygiene: CMHH, 2009). Health psychologists have a role in intervening with this behaviour to enhance global health.

Test your knowledge

6.5 What key factors impact on hand-washing adherence?

6.6 When is hand washing at its highest among health professionals?

Answers to these questions can be found on the companion website at:
www.pearsoned.co.uk/psychologyexpress

Further reading Hand washing

Topic	Key reading
Hand washing and hospital-acquired infections	Bartzokas, C. A., Williams, E. E., & Slade, P. D. (1995). *A psychological approach to hospital-acquired infections: Studies in health and human sciences.* London: Edward Mellen.
Hand washing liaison group	Handwashing Liaison Group (1999). Hand washing: A modest measure-with big effects. *British Medical Journal, 318,* 686.

CRITICAL FOCUS

Measuring hand washing

Critics argue there are methodological issues relating to the measurement of hand-washing behaviour. Let's say, for example, one hospital's statistics confirm 95% adherence compared to another which has a rate of 65%. You would think that the first hospital is better. However, is it that clear cut? Firstly, there is no standardised method for collecting and reporting rates of hand hygiene. Furthermore, organisations measure and report hand washing in many different ways, varying in sample group size, and hand hygiene pre-and post-interaction, thus the adherence rate is greatly influenced by what indications are chosen for measurement (CMHH, 2009).

Observation methods have been viewed as the gold standard, and although it is accepted that this has the advantage of linking the activity to the indication, there have also been many criticisms. There are potential biases such as the Hawthorne effect (Benson, 2001), in which people change behaviour because they know they are being observed. Furthermore, collecting reliable observation data requires a highly structured method of both observing care and documenting data. McAteer et al. (2008) propose a hand-hygiene observation tool (HHOT), which has been found to have good inter-rater reliability and should be considered when researching this area. However, at present there remains no perfect method.

 Sample question   *Essay*

Discuss with reference to the literature the key factors that are associated with the performance of health protective behaviours.

One final thing to consider in this chapter is something we are told to do from childhood, twice a day ... brushing our teeth. But like so many other health behaviours, we don't always do what we know we should be doing. And if we do it, are we doing it right?

Tooth brushing

Regular tooth brushing is a recommended preventive behaviour for oral plaque control (Aunger, 2007). Around three-quarters of the British public claim they engage in the recommended twice-daily tooth-brushing regime (Faculty of Dental Surgery, 1997). However, the prevalence of plaque and periodontal disease contradicts this, with statistics highlighting that over 70% of adults have visible plaque (Kelly, Steele, & Nuttall, 2000). Thus research in the realm of health psychology has attempted to explore factors that impact on this behaviour and also to develop theoretically based interventions to increase the engagement of the population in oral hygiene self-care.

Tolvanen, Lahti, Miettunen and Hausen (2012) explored socio-cognitive factors that impact on tooth brushing in adolescents. Measures were taken for knowledge, attitudes and self-reported tooth-brushing behaviour from 8th and 9th graders (14–16 years) in Finland (n = 827). Results suggested that knowledge influenced behaviour directly and through attitudes related to 'concern'. Anagnostopoulos, Buchanan, Frousiounioti, Niakas and Potamianos (2011) supported this, with results suggesting that greater perceived severity of oral diseases was related to increased tooth-brushing frequency, which in turn was associated with better oral health status. Furthermore, results highlighted that stronger self-efficacy beliefs were also an important factor that impacts on tooth-brushing behaviour.

Claessen, Bates, Sherlock, Seeparsand and Wright (2008) highlight that the health belief model, the theory of planned behaviour and the transtheoretical model have provided useful theoretical frameworks that have successfully increased tooth-brushing behaviour through targeting cognitions such as: attitudes, pre-contemplation beliefs, norms, perceived behavioural control and learning. Furthermore, implementation-intentions (Gollwitzer, 1999) have enabled the maintenance of behaviour, highlighting regular tooth brushing not as a one-off behaviour but as a habit (Claessen et al., 2008).

Tooth brushing is not just important for oral health. Large-scale longitudinal research (de Oliveira, Watt, & Hamer, 2010) from Scotland has found that those who do not brush their teeth regularly are at a heightened risk of cardiovascular disease, while other research shows that those with diabetes have significantly worse oral health than those who do not have the condition (Kanjirath, Kim, &

Inglehart, 2011). Therefore, promoting this behaviour is important for overall health.

Further reading Tooth brushing

Topic	Key reading
Oral health, knowledge and attitudes in young people	Tolvanen, M., Lahti, S., Miettunen, J., & Hausen, H. (2012). Relationship between oral health-related knowledge, attitudes and behavior among 15–16-year-old adolescents: A structural equation modelling approach. *Acta Odontologica Scandinavia, 70,* 169–176.
Theory of reasoned action and tooth brushing	Syrjälä, A. M. H., Niskanen, M. C., & Knuuttila, M. L. (2002). The theory of reasoned action in describing tooth brushing, dental caries and diabetes adherence among diabetic patients. *Journal of Clinical Periodontology, 29,* 427–432.

? *Sample question*   *Problem-based learning*

KeKe is a 12-year-old boy who still has some baby teeth left in his mouth. He has recently visited the dentist for his six-month check-up and the dentist has noted that he has plaque on his teeth, including his adult teeth. When he was asked how often he brushes his teeth, he replied, 'Some of the time.' His mother confirmed that he does not brush his teeth every morning and evening, and said that she did not know what to do to encourage him to engage in this preventive health behaviour. When the dentist asked KeKe why he doesn't brush his teeth every day, he said that he knows that brushing his teeth is important, but that he forgets, and his mother confirmed that when she reminds him, he does brush his teeth. He also said that he doesn't like the taste of the toothpaste.

As a health psychologist, what would you need to consider in encouraging adolescents like KeKe to engage in regular tooth brushing?

Conclusion

This chapter has covered some of the key preventive health behaviours that can be responsible for reducing a number of diseases and illnesses. A running theme among all these behaviours is that, although the prevalence for ill-health is high (i.e. in terms of the number of diagnoses of STIs/hospital acquired infections/periodontal disease), and people often know the risks to their (and other people's) health if they do not perform a health protective behaviour (e.g. condom use, hand washing, seat belt use, teeth brushing), there is still a high proportion of people who do not engage in these behaviours and are non-adherent. Understanding the psychological mechanisms behind this lack of engagement can assist policy makers and intervention designers to support people to make better choices for their health.

Further reading Preventive health	
Topic	*Key reading*
Sex	Thirlaway, K.& Upton, D. (2009). *The psychology of lifestyle: Promoting health behaviour*. Abingdon: Routledge, Chapter 7.
The government's approach to HIV/AIDS	Department of Health (2001). *Better services, better sexual health: The national strategy for sexual health and HIV*. London: HMSO.
Research incorporating health psychology theories in condom use	Reid, A. E., & Aiken, L. S. (2011). Integration of five health behaviour models: Common strengths and unique contributions to understanding condom use. *Psychology and Health, 26*, 1499–1520.
A multi-behavioural study including dental health and seat belt use	Schwarzer, R., Schuz, B., Ziegelmann, J. P., Lippke, S., Luszczynska, A., & Scholz, U. (2007). Adoption and maintenance of four health behaviours: Theory-guided longitudinal studies on dental flossing, seat belt use, dietary behaviour, and physical activity. *Annals of Behaviour Medicine, 33*, 156–166.

Chapter summary – pulling it all together

→ Can you tick all of the points from the revision checklist at the beginning of this chapter?

→ Attempt the sample question from the beginning of this chapter using the answer guidelines below.

→ Go to the companion website at www.pearsoned.co.uk/psychologyexpress to access more revision support online, including interactive quizzes, flashcards, You be the marker exercises as well as answer guidance for the Test your knowledge and Sample questions from this chapter.

Answer guidelines

 ? *Sample question* *Essay*

> Critically discuss the contribution that preventive health behaviours make to current mortality and morbidity rates with reference to at least two behaviours.

Approaching the question

Your answer should aim to provide a definition of what preventive health behaviours are, aiming to evaluate a range of health behaviours and putting the problem into context: for example, what are the morbidity/mortality rates of illness, diseases and accidents that can be prevented (e.g. HIV, hospital-acquired infections, accidents, gum disease)? Who uses condoms? What influences performance? What implications does non-engagement with hand washing or tooth brushing have? What does a lack of protective behaviours cost the economy? By critically evaluating research and the use of theoretical models to explain uptake of these health behaviours, you will be able to provide arguments for the importance of preventive health behaviours in health status (mortality and morbidity).

Important points to include

Introduction

- Begin by outlining two/three preventive health behaviours.
- For each preventative behaviour you will need to:
  - set the context using current research and statistics.

Body

- Discuss the empirical research which has explored the factors that impact on performance, and the theoretical frameworks that have been used to explain health behaviour. Be explicit in which cognitions are relevant for the health behaviours: for example, perceived severity may be important in one behaviour but not as important for another.

- Discuss and evaluate interventions and how these impact on both mortality and morbidity. Have psychologically based interventions been successful? What separates the successful ones from the unsuccessful ones? Try to be critical here and don't be afraid to discuss the strengths and limitations of the methodology adopted. It would also be useful to discuss systematic reviews and meta-analyses which provide a more rigorous evaluation and overview of the area.

Conclusion

- Conclude by making suggestions about what future research should focus on, how our theoretical understanding could be improved and future considerations.

Make your answer stand out

Try not simply to describe different preventive health behaviours as this will not achieve a very high mark. A good answer will remember to take a critical stance and show a good engagement with a wide range of evidence to present an argument about to what extent preventive health behaviours impact on health status. For the highest marks you will need to present original insightful thinking, using well-balanced, evidence-based arguments.

Explore the accompanying website at www.pearsoned.co.uk/psychologyexpress

→ Prepare more effectively for exams and assignments using the answer guidelines for questions from this chapter.
→ Test your knowledge using multiple choice questions and flashcards.
→ Improve your essay skills by exploring the You be the marker exercises.

Notes

Assisted prevention: screening and immunisation

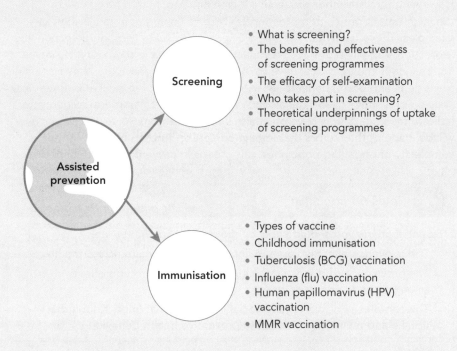

- **Assisted prevention**

- **Screening**
  - What is screening?
  - The benefits and effectiveness of screening programmes
  - The efficacy of self-examination
  - Who takes part in screening?
  - Theoretical underpinnings of uptake of screening programmes

- **Immunisation**
  - Types of vaccine
  - Childhood immunisation
  - Tuberculosis (BCG) vaccination
  - Influenza (flu) vaccination
  - Human papillomavirus (HPV) vaccination
  - MMR vaccination

A printable version of this topic map is available from
www.pearsoned.co.uk/psychologyexpress

Introduction

Think about the types of preventive health behaviour that you engage in and perhaps the ones you don't. Have you eagerly gone for an immunisation? Ladies, did you rush to book yourself in for your last cervical smear test? Gentlemen, when was the last time you gave yourself a check?

In the area of preventive health behaviour, as with many health behaviours, we do not always make rational decisions about our health. As health professionals, we need to understand the less than obvious decisions that people make when it comes to their health. The preventive health behaviours discussed in the previous chapter are those that are mainly under the individual's sole control. No other person need be involved in the decision to wash your hands, brush your teeth or wear a seat belt, while there is joint control in the use of condoms.

However, there are other preventive health behaviours that often need the involvement of health professionals. Take screening or immunisation as examples. These behaviours can help to prevent disease through detection and protection, and will thus have an impact on mortality and morbidity. However, not only does the individual have to 'buy in' to these behaviours, they also have to visit a health professional to take them up. This chapter focuses on these key assisted preventive health behaviours, with reference to empirical evidence to indicate the impact they have on health status. Furthermore, a critical overview will be made of the factors that impact on uptake, further uncovering the complexity of engaging population sub-groups in preventive health behaviour.

Revision checklist

Essential points you should know by the end of this chapter are:
- ❏ The relevance of screening and immunisation to health across the lifespan
- ❏ The prevalence of disease that could be reduced through effective screening and immunisation
- ❏ The complexity of bio-psycho-social influences that impact upon the uptake and maintenance of these preventive health behaviours.

Assessment advice

When you are writing an essay or answering an exam question on this topic, you should consider the following points:

- *Content.* Be explicit in *providing context* to the topic. Use national and international epidemiological data to help present the problem. What is the cost in terms of morbidity? Mortality? Quality of life? Health care? If the problem has improved, what may have contributed to this? Only by knowing the cost of the problem will we know the benefits of engaging in preventive health behaviour.

- *Evidence* is always required, so ensure you *back up your argument with references* to relevant research. Consult a wide range of primary sources to provide a good, well-developed critique to support your arguments. If you wish to reference any of the studies we have reviewed in this book, you should try to find and read them yourself to show you have gone to the primary source. You should not include *anecdotal details* about personal experiences (e.g. stating why you did or did not engage in a preventive health behaviour) and usually for scientific reports you should write in the *third person*.

- *Be critical* of theories and the nature of evidence. For example, when uncovering the factors that impact on uptake of screening, has longitudinal or prospective research been conducted to establish cause and effect or is research limited to correlational/cross-sectional studies? Have control groups been used in research studies that look at the effectiveness of improving immunisation rates?

Sample question

Could you answer this question? Below is a typical problem question that could rise on this topic.

 Sample question   **Essay**

Critically discuss the contribution that screening OR immunisation makes to current mortality and morbidity rates.

Guidelines on answering this question are included at the end of this chapter, whilst guidance on tackling other exam questions can be found on the companion website at **www.pearsoned.co.uk/psychologyexpress**

Screening

What is screening?

Screening is known as *secondary prevention*, defined as the process of actively seeking to identify precursors to disease in those who are presumed to be healthy as a means of preventing disease (Naidoo & Willis, 2005). There are two broad types of screening, as outlined by Ogden (2012). The first is *opportunistic screening*, which involves taking measures of an individual's health when they have used a medical service: for example, taking a patient's blood pressure when they have gone to the doctor with a rash. The other type is *population screening*, which involves a programme of screening, related to:

- mass screening of whole population groups – for example, prostate cancer screening in men above the age of 55 (Kiellman, Akre, Norming, Tomblom, & Gustafsson, 2009);

- selective screening of high-risk groups – for example, screening obese patients for diabetes mellitus (Teh et al., 2011);
- anonymous screening – for example, to detect trends;
- genetic screening; or
- routine screening in childhood.

All of these aim to identify health risk and detect a problem at the symptomatic stage (Armstrong, 2012).

Primary screening aims to discover a risk of a disease: for example, pre-cancerous cells (cervical intraepithelial neoplasia: CIN) found in cervical Pap smear tests suggest a risk for the development of cervical cancer (Nieminen, Vuorma, Viikki, Hakama, & Anttila, 2004), while genetic screening may give an estimated risk of producing a child with a genetic disorder such as Down's syndrome (Haddow et al., 1992). However, such screening is not always welcomed and there may be psycho-social factors to consider (Marteau & Croyle, 1998; Waller, McCaffery, Forrest, & Wardle, 2004). *Secondary screening* seeks to detect the illness itself, for example, a mammogram may detect breast cancer and bowel screening may detect bowel cancer (Ogden, 2004).

The benefits and effectiveness of screening programmes

The benefits of screening have recently come into question, in the sense that it is not clear if these benefits are applicable to wider society (Morrison & Bennett, 2009). It is accepted that screening is cost effective if the incidence is high and early treatment can reduce associated mortality and morbidity. However, we need to consider that screening may at times be drawing attention away from the primary problem (i.e. the cause). Take cervical cancer as an example: it has been associated with a number of factors, including smoking, contraceptive pill use, age of first sexual intercourse, number of sexual partners and a range of viruses, particularly the human papillomavirus (HPV) (Waggoner, 2003). Therefore, it could be argued that it would be more cost effective and beneficial to the population and less intrusive if greater focus was placed on primary prevention through increasing awareness and adaption of these factors. The same could be said for the screening of STIs and the primary preventive nature of the use of condoms. Screening has also been challenged as to the extent to which detecting early disease progression can outweigh the financial costs of large-scale screening programmes (McLaren, 2009).

Nevertheless, screening can save lives. To ensure cost effectiveness of screening programmes, Austoker (1994) described criteria that should form the basis for screening programmes relating to ovarian, prostate and testicular cancer. These are that:

1 The condition should be an important health problem, i.e. prevalent and/or serious.

2 There should be a recognisable early stage to the condition.

3 Treatment at an early stage should have clear benefit to the individual (reduced mortality) compared to at a later stage.

4 A suitable test should be used with good sensitivity and specificity.

5 The test should be considered acceptable to the population.

6 Adequate facilities should be available for diagnosis and treatment.

7 Issues of screening frequency and follow-up should be agreed on.

8 The costs (individual and health care) should be considered in relation to the benefits (individual and public health).

9 Any particular sub-groups to target should be identified.

The effectiveness of screening programmes is shown in their ability to reduce mortality. For example, breast cancer is the largest cause of death in women aged 65 and under, accounting for over 11,000 deaths each year (Cancer Research UK, 2012a). This is alongside cervical cancer, which occurs in 4,000 women each year and causes over 1,000 deaths, the majority in those who have never had a smear test (Cancer Research UK, 2012b). Furthermore, bowel cancer, the third most common cancer in the UK, is diagnosed in more than 41,000 new cases every year, and 16,000 died from it in 2010. However, it is estimated that there could be up to 20,000 fewer deaths over the next 20 years if just 60% took up screening (Cancer Research UK, 2012c). Therefore, screening is seen as an important process for many forms of cancer (Zoorob, Anderson, Cefalu, & Sidani, 2001).

The efficacy of self-examination

Self-examination is a type of screening behaviour that has been advocated in the early detection of several types of cancer, such as breast, testicular and skin cancer. Breast cancer is commonly detected through self-examination (Cancer Research, UK, 2007). Previous research has supported the efficacy of breast self-examination (BSE), amid controversy that it does not reduce mortality (Thomas et al., 2002). For example, Wolden et al. (2000) reported that in 65 survivors of Hodgkin's lymphoma, 63% of breast cancers were discovered by patient BSE and only 30% by mammography. There is, however, some research that challenges the effectiveness of BSE (Baxter, 2001), suggesting that it may in fact cause more harm (increased visits to the GP, anxiety) than good (detecting breast cancer).

KEY STUDY

Breast self-examination (Cox et al., 2008)

Background

Females who have had childhood cancer are at more risk of developing breast cancer, with breast self-examination (BSE) being the main route of detection in early onset breast cancer. This research determined the efficacy of a behavioural intervention which aimed to increase the frequency of BSE in female survivors of childhood cancer.

Method

Data on female survivors from a children's outpatient clinic (*n* =149), aged 12–18 years, were examined 11 years (median) after diagnosis of leukaemia or lymphoma (59%) or solid tumour (41%). The research variables explored included: BSE frequency, health risk perceptions, motivation, and fears or worries.

Findings

Baseline BSE frequency was the strongest influence on follow-up BSE. Other influential variables included age, motivation for behaviour change, motivation to commit to health promotion, concern about appearance, and the mother's education.

Conclusion

The results highlight that survivors least likely to perform BSE are fearful about cancer and are not motivated to change health behaviours. Therefore, interventions should target and ease fears about cancer and late treatment effects to address misconceptions, use modelling techniques with demonstrations to ensure competency in BSE, and tailor risk information to each survivor's demographic, biological (age, gender), psychological (cognitive: disease and treatment knowledge, risks; affective: fears) and social (socioeconomic status, support) profiles to increase BSE motivation.

Who takes part in screening?

As a health professional, it is important to understand the reasons why some people do not take part in screening behaviour. There are a wide range of patient factors associated with non-uptake of screening programmes alongside the practice of self-examination. Morrison and Bennett (2009) outline nine factors that impact on low uptake:

1 lower levels of education and income;
2 age (e.g. younger women tend not to attend);
3 lack of knowledge about the condition;
4 lack of knowledge regarding purpose of screening;
5 lack of knowledge about potential outcomes of screening;
6 embarrassment regarding procedures involved;
7 fear of what will be detected;
8 fear/discomfort regarding the procedure;
9 lack of self-efficacy in terms of practising self-examination.

Theoretical underpinnings of uptake of screening programmes

Socio-cognitive theoretical frameworks have been used to predict screening behaviour. Norman and Brain (2005) analysed the effectiveness of applying the health belief model to predict breast self-examination in 833 women. Findings suggested that women who perform BSE infrequently showed lower self-efficacy, higher emotional barriers and lower perceived benefits. Therefore, interventions should target these cognitions to enhance BSE and reduce anxiety relating to breast cancer.

However, the health belief model has been criticised for its limited ability to explain variance in BSE behaviour. Bish, Sutton and Golombok (2000) compared the health belief model and the theory of planned behaviour (TPB), against the uptake of a cervical smear test. Findings suggested that the TPB predicted 51% of women's intentions to go for a smear test, while the HBM accounted for only 4%. This suggests that while the HBM may explain some of the reason why people attend screening, the TPB explains more. In contrast, Sutton et al. (2000) found that, when invited for colorectal screening, it was lower barriers and greater benefits that were significant at predicting screening attendance, which fits with some elements of the HBM.

Self-efficacy and barriers are viewed as the most powerful predictors of breast and cervical screening (Murray & McMillan, 1993), while self-efficacy and outcome expectancies are influential in prostate cancer screening (Cormier, Kwan, Reid, & Litwin, 2002) and colorectal cancer screening uptake (Kremers, Mesters, Pladdet, van den Borne, & Stockbrügger, 2000). Therefore, interventions must consider how to increase confidence in performing the behaviours, and beliefs in the usefulness of the procedure, while reducing barriers such as anxiety.

CRITICAL FOCUS

Screening research

Here are some issues you may want to consider in the area of screening research:

- Medical-technological advances in screening are viewed by health professionals as a positive development, but is this always the case? It could be argued that just because something can be done, does not mean it should be done; therefore, polarised research often leads to contradictory findings.
- What about the ethical issues relating to screening? For example, screening could move an individual who believed themselves to be healthy, to a state of being diagnosed with a disease. It could be that some people do not wish to know that anything is wrong with them; thus, balancing the ethical positions can be difficult.
- Screening may cause psychological distress (e.g. fear and anxiety) through the involvement of invasive procedures/treatments. This may impact on uptake and health outcomes and could contribute to contradictory findings.

Test your knowledge

7.1 List the factors that impact on low uptake of screening programmes.

7.2 What theoretical models have been applied to understanding screening uptake behaviour and what do they suggest?

Answers to these questions can be found on the companion website at:
www.pearsoned.co.uk/psychologyexpress

Further reading **Screening behaviour**

Topic	Key reading
Article explaining considerations for screening	Austoker, J. (1994). Screening for ovarian, prostate and testicular cancers. *British Medical Journal*, *309*, 315–320.
Cost effectiveness of screening	McLaren, E. H. (2009). Is screening cost effective? *British Medical Journal*, *339*, b3040.

? *Sample question*   ***Problem-based learning***

Think of your own preventive health behaviours. Do you go for regular screening? Are you up to date on your vaccinations? Consider your answer. If you answered yes, what motivates you? If you answered no, what influences your decision? How can health psychology explain your responses? Reflect on your answers from a bio-psycho-social approach.

Screening is one way to protect health through early identification, but what about being able to immunise against a disease?

? *Sample question*   ***Essay***

Critically discuss the bio-psycho-social factors that impact on the uptake of immunisation.

Immunisation

Immunisation is outlined by the Department of Health as one of the most important 'weapons' for protecting individuals and the community from serious diseases, and has been a key strategy in the decline of infectious diseases (Department of Health: DH, 2007). Based on data from the World Health Organisation (WHO, 1999) which confirmed that infectious diseases (such as measles, diarrhoea, tuberculosis and malaria) account for one-third of all deaths worldwide, the Department of Health (2002) introduced a UK strategy to combat infectious diseases: *Getting Ahead of the Curve*.

Immunisation is achieved through two basic mechanisms. One is *active immunity*, usually acquired through natural disease or through a vaccination, which provides immunity by a smaller dose but similar to that provided by the natural infection. The other is *passive immunity*, achieved by the transfer of antibodies from immune individuals – for example, from mother to child for infections such as measles – although this protection is temporary and normally lasts only a short time.

Types of vaccine

There are two main types of vaccine: live and non-live. The *live (attenuated) vaccines* introduce a weakened version of the disease into the body to allow the immune system to build antibodies to fight the disease. Immunisation programmes such as the MMR use live vaccines and, as a result of this, there is a small risk of side-effects that are similar to the symptoms of the disease, such as a fever or rash (Isozaki et al., 1982). In contrast, programmes such as the annual influenza injection use *inactivated (dead) vaccines* that produce mainly side-effects around the entry of the injection, such as a sore arm or swelling (Nichol et al., 1996), but do not lead to symptoms of the flu. These are important aspects to consider, particularly as some people will not engage in immunisation programmes because they fear immunisation will make them ill (Bish, Yardley, Nicoll, & Michie, 2011).

Although the primary aim of vaccination is to protect the individual who receives the vaccine, it also works by reducing the risk of unvaccinated individuals being exposed to infection. For example, if 90% of the population are immunised from measles, it will protect the 10% who are not. This is referred to as population (or 'herd') immunity (DH, 2007) and is known as the *prevention paradox* (Rose, 1993).

Childhood immunisation

The focus of immunisation is often in the infant years when our immune system is most effective. The Department of Health (2007) published the 'Green Book', which provides the immunisation schedule for children in the UK (see Table 7.1), the overall aim being to immunise children routinely against a number of infections.

Tuberculosis (BCG) vaccination

Those of you who were in the UK as an adolescent may remember being vaccinated against tuberculosis (TB), through the BCG immunisation programme. It was the 'big' needle that often led to a prominent scar on the top of the arm. This programme was stopped in 2005 following continued decline in TB rates in the indigenous UK population (Zwerling et al., 2011), and it is now only given to those who are at a heightened risk, often through family, travel or occupation (Department of Health, 2007; NICE, 2011).

Influenza (flu) vaccination

There are many strains of flu and it can be deadly, as we saw in the 2009 A/H1N1 influenza pandemic, where the mortality rate was 26 per 100,000 (Donaldson et al., 2009). The flu virus is seen as seasonal because outbreaks often occur during the winter period. It is spread quickly, through sneezing and coughing. The influenza vaccination is offered to those at the highest risk of

Table 7.1 **Schedule for the UK's routine childhood immunisations (Department of Health, 2007)**

When to immunise	What vaccine is given	How it is given
Two months old	Diphtheria, tetanus, pertussis (whooping cough), polio and Hib (DTaP/IPV/Hib)	One injection
	Pneumococcal (PCV)	One injection
Three months old	Diphtheria, tetanus, pertussis (whooping cough), polio and Hib (DTaP/IPV/Hib)	One injection
	Meningococcal C (MenC)	One injection
Four months old	Diphtheria, tetanus, pertussis (whooping cough), polio and Hib (DTaP/IPV/Hib)	One injection
	MenC	One injection
	PCV	One injection
Between 12 and 13 months of age	Hib/MenC	One injection
	PCV	One injection
	Measles, mumps and rubella (MMR)	One injection
Three years four months to five years old	Diphtheria, tetanus, pertussis and polio (DTaP/IPV or dTaP/IPV)	One injection
	Measles, mumps and rubella (MMR)	One injection
Girls aged 12 to 13 years old	Human papillomavirus (HPV)	Three injections
From 13 to 18 years old	Tetanus, diphtheria and polio (Td/IPV)	One injection

infection, falling into the categories: over 65, immuno-suppressed, pregnant women, and those with an underlying health condition (such as heart or respiratory difficulties, including asthma). There is evidence to show that death rates from flu are higher among these groups than the general population (Mytton et al., 2012), so it is important to promote preventive behaviour to those at risk.

Armstrong, Berlin, Schwartz, Propert and Ubel (2001) explored the barriers to immunisation against influenza, for which over one-third of elderly Americans are not immunised each year. A cross-sectional survey of a random sample ($n = 486$) of elderly individuals (aged $\geq$ 65 years) found that perceived concern appeared to impact on uptake. The influenza vaccine was inversely associated with the belief that immunisation is inconvenient and that it is painful alongside the history of previous side-effects. Among pregnant mothers, a major barrier to immunisation uptake is the worry of acquiring the virus (Edmonds, Coleman, Armstrong, & Shea, 2011), while Byrne, Walsh, Kola and Sarma (2012) found that lack of uptake in a sample of university students was due to a low belief in outcome efficacy, attitude and threat.

However, immunisation was viewed more positively when associated with physician recommendation. Smailbegovic, Laing and Bedford (2003) support this, concluding that both health beliefs and health professional attitudes impact on uptake. Therefore, as health professionals we should consider both the barriers and beliefs of the individual and the normative influence of those around them on their decision to engage in immunisation.

Human papillomavirus (HPV) vaccination

HPV is a sexually transmitted virus that has no symptoms. There is now a large body of research that links HPV with cervical cancer (Bosch, Lorincz, Munoz, Meijer, & Shah, 2002; Waller et al., 2004), with data showing that 93% of cervical cancer cases were infected with HPV (Walboomers et al., 1999). In an attempt to prevent the spread of this virus, a new vaccine was developed and rolled out in the UK in 2008. It is now offered to schoolgirls aged 12–13 years (year 8) through three doses at zero, one and six months over one school year. This prophylactic vaccination (to ward off disease) is provided to immunise against HPV 16 and 18 and has been found to be safe with good efficacy (Lu, Kumar, Castellsagué, & Giuliano, 2011). However, this strategy alone, even if there is a level of cross-protection against other oncogenic viruses, cannot completely prevent cervical cancer (Adams, Jasani, & Fiander, 2007). There may also be a potential to increase protection by immunising young men, who are not currently included in the immunisation programme in the UK, but who are carriers of the virus.

Brabin et al. (2008) assessed the feasibility and acceptability of this vaccination in girls, through a prospective cohort study focusing on vaccination uptake in 36 secondary schools in Greater Manchester (n = 2,817). Results found that uptake was 70.6% for the first dose and 68.5% for the second dose. Uptake was significantly lower in schools with a higher proportion of ethnic minority girls and those entitled to free school meals, showing a culture and socioeconomic divide. Of those who did not take up the vaccination, in 20.3% of cases the parents did not respond to the invitation, while 8.1% replied with a refusal letter. The main reason for parents' refusal was insufficient information about the vaccine and its long-term safety.

Marlow, Waller and Wardle (2007) supported these findings, suggesting that concerns about too many vaccinations or vaccine side-effects and worry about increasing promiscuity emerged as deterrents. Although the issue of promiscuity is shown as a concern in only a minority of parents, the media's representation of the HPV vaccination may have increased this as a barrier to uptake (Forster, Wardle, Stephenson, & Waller, 2010). Therefore, as health professionals, we must be in tune with what could be influencing the decision making of the people we work with. In a 'catch-up' programme for 16–18-year-olds, the key reasons for not intending to take up the HPV vaccination were beliefs in risk, lack of information and a fear of needles (Forster, Marlow, Wardle, Stephenson, & Waller, 2010).

Measles, mumps and rubella (MMR) vaccination

The MMR vaccine was introduced to the UK in 1988. The World Health Organisation set the target that by the year 2000 there would be universal vaccination and population immunity in Britain from 97% uptake of the MMR vaccination (Bellaby, 2003). However, this changed following the speculation that MMR was linked to autism in children, and after reaching an all-time low of 79%

in 2003 (Health Protection Agency, 2003) this vaccination has steadily increased to a recent uptake of 85% (Health Protection Agency, 2007).

The media debate linked to the research of the MMR/autism link caused concern to parents, with many refusing to take up the MMR vaccine for their children. These concerns were based on a study (Wakefield et al., 1998), which has since been withdrawn from publication (Eggertson, 2010) due to being methodologically flawed, limited by both sample size and speculation. And while more rigorous research concluded that no link was apparent (Peltola, Patja, & Leinikkii, 1998; Taylor & Seeman, 1999), the effect of the speculation highlights the importance of perceived dangers and beliefs.

Socioeconomic variables have also been found to impact on the uptake of vaccination. The following key study examines the uptake of the MMR vaccine and the use of single antigen vaccinations (Pearce, Law, Elliman, Cole, & Bedford, 2008). The findings highlight that, whilst uptake of immunisations is high in the UK, there are still sub-groups of the population that are not immunising their children. Therefore, it remains important to explore the barriers to uptake across these population sub-groups to feed into specifically targeted campaigns.

Hamilton-West (2006) outlined that emotional and cognitive factors impact on MMR immunisation uptake, highlighting that beliefs of the risks and benefits of the vaccine varied considerably and individuals were unlikely to uptake when perceived risks of immunising were equivalent to perceived risks of not immunising. These results suggest that interventions should address attitudes and outcome expectancies towards the vaccine and perceptions of barriers to uptake.

KEY STUDY

MMR vaccination uptake (Pearce et al., 2008)

Background

This was a UK cohort study that aimed to determine factors relating to the uptake of the MMR vaccine and single antigen vaccines.

Method

Immunisation data from children born between 2000 and 2002 (n = 14,578) were used to assess immunisation status at three years, defined as 'immunised with MMR', 'immunised with at least one single antigen vaccine' and 'unimmunised'.

Findings

Results indicated that 88.6% (n = 13,013) were immunised with MMR and 5.2% (634) had received at least one single antigen vaccine. Children were more likely to be unimmunised if they lived in a household with other children or a lone parent, or if their mother was under 20 or over 34 at the child's birth. Those more likely to be immunised were children of more highly educated parents, self-employed or not employed. Use of single vaccines increased with household income and maternal age. Children were less likely to have received single vaccines if they lived with other children, or had mothers who were Indian, Pakistani, Bangladeshi or black, or aged under 25. Nearly three-quarters (74.4%, *n* = 1,110) of parents who did not immunise with MMR made a 'conscious decision' not to immunise.

Conclusion

Although MMR uptake in this cohort is high, a substantial proportion of children remain susceptible to avoidable infection, largely because parents consciously decided not to immunise their children. Social differentials in uptake could be used to inform targeted interventions to promote uptake.

Test your knowledge

7.3 What are the costs and benefits that need to be considered for immunisation programmes?

7.4 What psychological factors impact on non-uptake to immunisation programmes?

Answers to these questions can be found on the companion website at: **www.pearsoned.co.uk/psychologyexpress**

Conclusion

The key points from this chapter are that preventive health behaviours that aim to detect precursors or immunise against disease can significantly reduce mortality and morbidity. However, although many people have knowledge around these behaviours, there are still a number of people who do not engage in them. There are many bio-psycho-social factors that may impact on uptake, including age, attitude and income, affective factors such as anxiety and fear, and more cognitive factors, such as not acknowledging the need. As health professionals, we need to understand what facilitates or restricts preventive health behaviours that we may need to assist with, so that we can develop better ways to enhance uptake.

Further reading Screens and immunisation	
Topic	*Key reading*
Overview of interventions to improve immunisation and screening	Stone, E. G., Morton, S. C., Hulscher, M. E., Maglione, M. A., Roth, E. A., Grimshaw, J. M., ... & Shekelle, P. G. (2002). Interventions that increase use of adult immunization and cancer screening services: A meta-analysis. *Annals of Internal Medicine, 136*(9), 641–651.
Strategy for combatting infectious disease	Department of Health (2002). *Getting ahead of the curve: A strategy for combating infectious diseases.* London: HMSO.

Chapter summary – pulling it all together

→ Can you tick all of the points from the revision checklist at the beginning of this chapter?

→ Attempt the sample question from the beginning of this chapter using the answer guidelines below.

→ Go to the companion website at www.pearsoned.co.uk/psychologyexpress to access more revision support online, including interactive quizzes, flashcards, You be the marker exercises as well as answer guidance for the Test your knowledge and Sample questions from this chapter.

CASE STUDY

Cervical screening

The client

Kelly is 25 and has recently been invited to make an appointment to have a cervical smear test; however, she does not make an appointment. What factors do you think have influenced her? And how would you address this to support her to engage in screening?

Background – the problem

Cervical screening aims to detect and treat early abnormalities which, if left untreated, could lead to cancer in a woman's cervix (the neck of the womb). The first stage in cervical screening is taking a sample using liquid-based cytology (LBC) from the cervix for analysis, which involves opening the woman's vagina and using a spatula to sweep around the cervix. Most women consider the procedure to be only mildly uncomfortable (NHS, 2013).

Advice

Let's relate this to the health belief model. Perhaps Kelly has low levels of susceptibility and severity? For example, Harlan, Bernstein and Kessler (1991) suggest that most women do not attend cervical screening because they do not think it necessary as they have had no symptoms. Think of the Jade Goody effect (Bowring & Walker, 2010), where the media showed a dramatic increase in uptake of screening (Lancucki, Sasieni, Patnick, Day, & Vessey, 2012) and requests for screening under the invited age (25 years) following Jade's (a reality TV star) diagnosis of cervical cancer and her subsequent death. Therefore, perhaps we need to increase Kelly's levels of susceptibility and severity – this could be via a media campaign.

Self-efficacy and barriers are viewed as the most powerful predictors of cervical screening (Murray & McMillan, 1993). Therefore, we should consider how to increase confidence in performing the behaviours and reduce anxiety. Perhaps, if Kelly is embarrassed, we could provide her with the knowledge she needs to feel more at ease.

Maybe we need to encourage her to take someone with her to increase her level of social support. She may, however, just have forgotten to make an appointment or feel she doesn't have time to attend.

What is certain is that, if Kelly has psychological factors that may be influencing her decision (whether or not it be conscious) not to attend a smear test, as health psychologists, we need to understand these factors to intervene and support her to engage in this potentially lifesaving preventive health behaviour.

Answer guidelines

 Sample question   *Essay*

Critically discuss the contribution that screening OR immunisation makes to current mortality and morbidity rates.

Approaching the question

Your answer should aim to provide an analysis of the importance of either screening or immunisation on health and illness.

Important points to include

Your answer should aim to provide a definition of what the preventive health behaviour is: for example, if it is screening, what type of screening is it and what illness does it apply to? It should then put the problem into context: for example, what are the morbidity/mortality rates of illness and diseases that can be identified early (e.g. cancer) or immunised against (e.g. measles)? What is the effectiveness of screening and immunisation behaviours? What influences uptake? What does a lack of preventive behaviours cost the economy? By critically evaluating research and the use of theoretical models to explain uptake of these health behaviours, you will be able to provide arguments to explain the importance of preventive health behaviours for health status (mortality and morbidity).

Make your answer stand out

Try not simply to describe the preventive health behaviour, such as screening or immunisation, as this will not achieve a very high mark. A good answer will remember to take a critical stance and show a good engagement with a wide range of evidence to present an argument concerning the extent to which preventive health behaviours impact on health status. For the highest marks, you will need to present original insightful thinking, using well-balanced, evidence-based arguments.

Explore the accompanying website at www.pearsoned.co.uk/psychologyexpress
- → Prepare more effectively for exams and assignments using the answer guidelines for questions from this chapter.
- → Test your knowledge using multiple choice questions and flashcards.
- → Improve your essay skills by exploring the You be the marker exercises.

Notes

Stress and psychoneuroimmunology

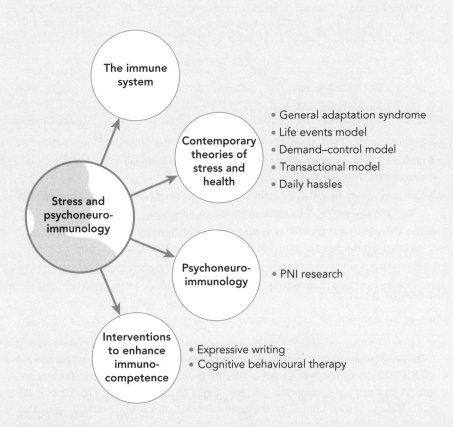

A printable version of this topic map is available from
www.pearsoned.co.uk/psychologyexpress

Introduction

Do you ever notice feeling unwell around times of stress – especially when you are over-tired? Do you get a sore throat or mouth ulcers around exam period?

This all has to do with our immune system not working quite as it should. The immune system is essentially the surveillance system of the body. Its primary function is to distinguish what is *self* and what is *foreign* and then to attack and rid the body of invaders (Elgert, 2009).

This chapter examines the complex connection between the immune system, psycho-social factors (such as stress) and the nervous, cardiovascular and endocrine systems, evaluating contemporary theories of stress and potential mechanisms by which psycho-social stressors can lead to illness. The development of an area of research called psychoneuroimmunology (PNI) will be introduced and the features of the immune system will be outlined. Biological pathways by which stressors can impact on health will be identified, drawing on research in the areas of herpes simplex, wound healing, HIV/AIDS and breast cancer.

 Revision checklist

Essential points you should know by the end of this chapter are:

❑ Features of the immune system and biological pathways by which stressors can impact on health

❑ Contemporary theories of stress and illness, and potential mechanisms by which psycho-social stressors can lead to illnesses

❑ The development of PNI as a discipline and research in the field that has focused on herpes simplex, wound healing, HIV/AIDS and breast cancer.

Assessment advice

When you are writing an essay or answering an exam question on this topic, you should consider the following points:

● *Content.* There are many theories in this area that you may be asked to evaluate, such as the *transactional theory of stress*, the *general adaption model* and the *life events model*. You might be asked to consider the relative contribution of the models to the development of our understanding of the stress–illness link. Alternatively, you may be asked to assess the importance of PNI. This latter question does not explicitly mention theories of stress and illness. However, a high-achieving student will recognise that theory is an important consideration when discussing approaches to this topic, and will talk about this explicitly in order to demonstrate their understanding of the relationship between theoretical and applied psychology.

- *Evidence* is always required, so ensure you *back up your argument with references* to relevant research. Unsupported generalisations and 'everybody knows' statements will not achieve a very high mark and might even fail.

- *Be critical* of theories and the nature of evidence. It is important to remember that stress–illness takes place within a social context and is influenced by emotional and social factors as well as many individual differences, and you may want to refer to other theories that might account for this. Be explicit in relating health psychology to the topic.

Sample question

Could you answer this question? Below is a typical essay question that could rise on this topic.

 Sample question | **Essay**

Outline and evaluate research conducted in the field of psychoneuroimmunology (PNI) that explains the relationship between chronic stressors and chronic disease.

Guidelines on answering this question are included at the end of this chapter, whilst guidance on tackling other exam questions can be found on the companion website at **www.pearsoned.co.uk/psychologyexpress**

The immune system

The main organs involved in the immune response are known as *lymphoid organs*, including thymus, lymph nodes, spleen and bone marrow (Lydyard & Porakishvili, 2012).

- Optimum immune function is mainly achieved in childhood (Graham, Christian, & Kiecolt-Glaser, 2006).

- A reduced efficiency of the immune system is strongly correlated with increased age (Gomez, Boehmer, & Kovacs, 2005).

- There is a marked downward ability for adults aged 60 and over to respond to infections (Murasko, Weiner, & Kaye, 1987; Prelog, 2006).

What causes complications of the immune system? Ample research has highlighted a close link between an unhealthy lifestyle and poor immune function. For example, insufficient vitamin A or E decreases production of lymphocytes and antibodies. Furthermore, insufficient levels of vitamin C (integral in the effectiveness of phagocytes) (Marcos, Nova, & Montero, 2003), high fat and cholesterol intake alongside poor sleep impair immune functioning (Hall et al., 1998; Pressman et al., 2005). Diseases of the immune system are also implicated in infection, allergies, cancer and auto-immune disorders such as: AIDS, elephantiasis, tonsillitis, mononucleosis, lymphoma, arthritis, multiple sclerosis, and systemic lupus erythematosis (Stein & Miller, 1993).

Traditionally, the immune system was viewed as autonomous and self-regulatory, functioning independently from the rest of the body (Barrows & Jacobs, 2002). However, since the 1970s a body of research has developed evaluating the impact of emotions and perceptions on the autonomic nervous system (Selye, 1976).

Contemporary theories of stress and health

A wide range of theoretical models have been applied to account for the link between stress and illness, and these have uncovered potential mechanisms by which psycho-social stressors lead to illnesses.

General adaptation syndrome

Historically, one of the first theoretical approaches proposed with a response-based model of stress was the *general adaptation syndrome* (GAS) developed by Selye (1936) (Figure 8.1). This model focused on the emergency reaction of the *sympathetic nervous system* (SNS), *peripheral nervous system* (PNS) and *adrenocortical system*, also known as the 'fight or flight' response. Selye (1907–1983) postulated that stress occurs in all living things and is the pressure resulting from a 'disturbing environment'. It was proposed that a set of three responses were displayed in response to stress:

● *Alarm* – the body mobilises to confront a threat (SNS).

● *Resistance* – the organism attempts to cope with the threat by fleeing it or fighting it (if the threat is short term, the PNS restores homeostasis).

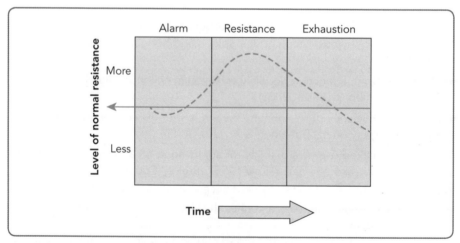

Figure 8.1 General adaptation syndrome (GAS) model

Source: A syndrome produced by diverse nocuous agents, *Nature*, 138, pp. 32–3 (Seyle H. 1936), reprinted by permission from Macmillan Publishers Ltd, copyright (© 1936).

- *Exhaustion* – the organism may deplete its physiological resources and increase allostatic load, leading to diseases of adaptation over time.

Criticism of GAS

Although the GAS model holds great historical value, critics argue that the model:

- is deterministic;
- omits psychological processes, such as emotional reactions (e.g. anger, anxiety);
- omits the impact on physiological responses (Kreibig, 2010);
- ignores the role of individual differences (Guglielmi & Tatrow, 1998);
- does not acknowledge positive factors such as that explained by Selye's concept of 'Eustress' (good stress);
- has a lack of causal accountability – for example, it fails to consider constructs such as perception (what we think) and appraisal (what we attribute things to), which are thought to be key to determining the causal pathway of stress (David, Schnur, & Belloiu, 2002).

Life events model (Holmes & Rahe, 1967)

Holmes and Rahe (1967) presented a stimulus model of stress, based on Hooke's law of elasticity (Moyer, 1977), which suggests that every substance has an elastic limit. This model reinforced the aspect of life changes as stressful events that require psychological adjustment (see Table 8.1) and is linked to work by Wyler, Masuda and Holmes (1971), who found that a person scoring between 200 and 300 Life Change Units (LCUs) in one year has a 50% increased chance of developing an illness.

Table 8.1 **Representative life event items from the social readjustment rating scale and their LCUs (Holmes & Rahe, 1967)**

Event	LCU rating (1–100)
Death of a spouse	100
Divorce	75
Death of a close family member	63
Personal injury or illness	53
Marriage	50
Being fired from work	47
Retirement	45
Sex difficulties	39
Death of a close friend	37
Change to a different job	36
Foreclosure of mortgage or loan	30
Son or daughter leaving home	29
Outstanding personal achievement	28
Begin or end school	26
Trouble with boss	23
Change in residence	20
Change in social activities	18
Vacation	13
Christmas	12

Life events research

Brown and Harris (1978) found, when interviewing 458 London women, that those showing signs of depression had experienced a serious life event (e.g. bereavement) or serious difficulty (e.g. domestic violence). Furthermore, if social support was lacking, risk of depression increased significantly. The most serious life events that triggered depression were related to loss. More recent research has confirmed the link between life events and depression, showing that this relationship is more prevalent for males (Fountoulakis, Fotiou, Lacovides, & Kaprinis, 2005). However, it may be that depressed individuals are more likely to over-report negative life events. Stressful life events have also been linked to:

- cardiovascular disease (Rosengren et al., 2004);
- infectious disease (Cohen, Tyrrell, & Smith, 1993);
- exacerbation of symptoms in people with multiple sclerosis (Ackerman, Heyman, & Rabin, 2002).

The link between life events and mortality has mixed empirical evidence. For example, Rosengren, Orth-Gomer, Wedel and Wilhelmsen (1993) found a link with all-cause mortality; however, a study of 2,000 men found that those with more events were less likely to die during a six-year follow-up (Hollis, Connett, Stevens, & Greenlick, 1990). Furthermore, longitudinal research (Phillips, Osborne, & Giles, 2008) investigating mortality found that in 28% of cases (*n* = 968), there was a direct association with life event numbers and impact scores, even when adjusted for sex, occupational status, smoking, body mass index and blood pressure (life events cards used were: health, marriage, relationships, death, work, housing, finances).

Children and young people are also significantly affected by life events, with research confirming that hospitalised children had a significantly greater number of life events than controls (Hatch & Dohrenwend, 2007; Kashani, Hodges, Simonds, & Hilderbrand, 1981). Furthermore, a three-year study found that children with three or more stressful life events were significantly more likely to develop emotional and behavioural disorders (ONS, 2008). Life events have also been associated with asthma attacks in children in the two days following a life event (Sandberg, Järvenpää, Penttinen, Paton, & McCann, 2004).

Criticism of life events model

The life events model continues to be widely used, and is considered an 'objective' approach (Phillips et al., 2008). However, to establish cause or effect there is a need for more longitudinal research. Criticism of this model focuses on the impact that individual differences play: for example, there have been age and self-efficacy differences in relation to experience of major life events (Pinquart & Sörensen, 2001) that may cause bias. Furthermore, it does not account for either cross-cultural factors or the role of individual appraisal (Diener, Oishi, & Lucas, 2003). Some critics also argue that we need some change in our lives, suggesting that this model encourages us to be static. There have been clear associations between life events and ill health but there are many methodological challenges

(Lee et al., 2005); thus, there is a need for future research to take these factors into consideration.

Demand–control model (Karasek, 1979)

The demand–control (job strain) model (Karasek, 1979) has been one of the most influential and widely used models of work stress, illustrated by its large application to epidemiological studies (e.g. Whitehall studies) conducted over the last 30 years. This model (see Figure 8.2) views stress as an interaction between the individual and the external environment. It suggests that psychological strain is caused when job demands are high and job control is low, supported by early research suggesting that stress reactions are most extreme in workers with low levels of control (Johannson, Aronsson, & Lindstrom, 1978). This model has also been extended to include social support (Johnson & Hall, 1988) in the *iso-strain model*.

Demand–control research

Marmot, Bosma, Hemmingway, Brunner and Stansfield (1997) presented findings from the first Whitehall study that confirmed the contribution of psycho-social work factors to the risk of coronary heart disease (CHD). This was further supported by a systematic review by Schnall, Landsbergis and Baker (1994) of over 36 published studies (from 1981 to 1993) which linked job strain and cardiovascular disease (CVD).

Tsutsumi, Kayaba and Ishikawa (2011) conducted a prospective study of Japanese workers and showed that men with high-strain jobs were nearly three times more likely to suffer from a stroke than men with low-strain jobs. However, job strain was linked to stroke risk for male workers in lower occupational classes only. Conversely,

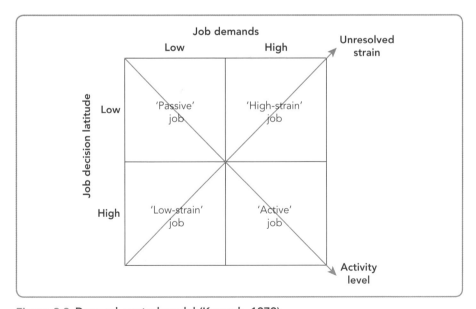

Figure 8.2 Demand–control model (Karasek, 1979)

there was a significant, over fivefold excess stroke risk for females in higher occupational class groups, highlighting clear gender and occupational class variations.

Overall, this model has developed our understanding of demands and control on health. However, the model can be viewed as rather simple: for example, research has highlighted moderations with several factors (e.g. personality, social support, gender and culture), confounded by occupational class.

> **?** *Sample question*   *Essay*
>
> Compare and contrast the application of the general adaptation syndrome model and the life events model to the understanding of the stress–illness relationship.

Transactional model

Stress is defined by Lazarus and Folkman (1984) as a result of an interaction between:

- an individual's characteristics and appraisals;
- the external or internal event (stressor) environment;
- the internal or external resources a person has available.

When developing their transactional model (see Figure 8.3), Lazarus and Folkman stated that 'An event is only stressful if it is appraised as such by an individual, that is if it is appraised as taxing or exceeding resources and endangering wellbeing' (Lazarus & Folkman, 1984). This model was based on evidence from early studies suggesting that appraisal processes mediate stress responses (Speisman, Lazarus, Mordkoff, & Davison, 1964; Lazarus, 1995).

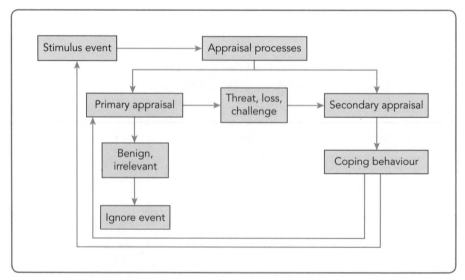

Figure 8.3 **Lazarus and Folkman's (1984) early transactional model of stress**

Thus, stress is a state that occurs when people are:

- faced with events they perceive as potentially dangerous to their physical or psychological well-being (primary appraisal);
- uncertain of their ability to deal with these stressors (secondary appraisal).

Let's go back to the question we asked at the beginning: do you ever get ill if you are stressed – for example, during exam periods? Some of you reading this may be thinking, '*Well, exams don't make me feel stressed.*' This is key for this model, as it shows that appraisal is vital. What we mean is, an individual must perceive the event as demanding and be uncertain of their ability to cope effectively, in order for them to feel stressed about it.

Lazarus and Folkman (1984) outline three methods of coping:

- *Appraisal-focused* (adaptive cognitive):
  - A person modifies the way they think (e.g. imagine you find flying in an aeroplane stressful – you may not fly, deny the stress, or alter the way you think about flying).
- *Problem-focused* (focused on reducing or eliminating a stressor):
  - This involves using problem-focused strategies to deal with the cause of stress. You may do this by finding out information on the problem, perhaps developing new skills or learning to manage the problem, aiming to change or eliminate the source of the stress (e.g. you receive a high phone bill and have no money, so it makes you feel stressed – to deal with this problem, you call the phone company and organise a payment scheme, thus reducing your stress level).
- *Emotion-focused* (aimed at changing own emotional reaction to a stressor):
  - This involves releasing pent-up emotions, distracting oneself, managing hostile feelings, meditating or using systematic relaxation procedures.
  - It deals with the emotional reactions caused by the stressor, rather than the stressor itself (e.g. you have the same high phone bill, no money, you feel stressed – rather than dealing with the problem phone bill, you deal with the negative emotion of stress and anxiety, maybe by going out for a drink to make you feel more relaxed. The emotional reaction that the stressor caused has been dealt with, but the problem still exists, thus leading to stress again later on).

Emotion-focused coping can lead to other detrimental cognitions. Five examples of emotion-focused coping strategies are:

- disclaiming;
- escape-avoidance;
- accepting responsibility or blame;
- exercising self-control;
- positive reappraisal.

Individuals can use all three types of coping strategy and these strategies can change over time and with experience of dealing with a stressor. There is no best way to deal with stress; however, there has been research to suggest that problem-focused coping strategies will enable a better adjustment to life and may increase perceived control over a person's problem, whereas emotion-focused coping may sometimes lead to a reduction in perceived control (maladaptive coping) (Folkman & Lazarus, 1988; Lazarus, 1998; Tamres, Janicki, & Helgeson, 2002).

Kristofferzon, Lindqvist and Nilsson (2011) found that those with low levels of self-efficacy who used emotion-focused coping had a poorer quality of life in a sample of end-of-stage renal disease and chronic heart failure patients. Furthermore, women were found to use emotion-focused coping more often than men.

To understand the role of appraisals, consider exams as a potential stressor. There are many ways of dealing with exams, depending on your appraisal of them and coping style. Take the following examples and links to stress:

- *'There is no way I can possibly deal with this exam – I simply know I will fail'* (threat + no resources = stress).
- *'This exam will be really hard: I am just not as clever as the other students'* (threat + limited internal resources = stress).
- *'Maybe I can manage this exam if I revise really hard'* (challenge + possible internal resources = less stress).
- *'I could perhaps do this exam if I get some help from my friends'* (challenge + external resources = less stress).

And those of you who love exams may think:

- *'This isn't a problem – I know the material really well'* (benign = no stress).
- *'I managed to pass the last time – I'll be okay this time'* (benign = no stress).

KEY STUDY

Transactional model of stress (Honey, Morgan, & Bennett, 2003)

Background

This study aimed to explore the application of the transactional model of stress to a sample of first-time mothers to examine low mood following childbirth.

Method

A longitudinal design collected data during the last trimester of pregnancy ($n = 306$) and six weeks postpartum ($n = 223$). Measures were taken for depression vulnerability, social support, appraisal and coping.

Findings

The results suggest that the transactional model was generally upheld, whereby depression scores were predicted by women's predisposition to depression, negative appraisals of an anticipated childcare stressor, perceptions of low antenatal support and a high use of avoidance coping. Furthermore, results highlighted that a high number of daily hassles (see below) were reported since the beginning of pregnancy.

▶

Conclusion

This model extends the knowledge and theoretical understanding of postnatal depression and has important implications for how this can be treated and where future research should focus to support 'high-risk' women during pregnancy.

Daily hassles

Daily hassles are based on the transactional theory of stress. Think back to a really hectic week you may have experienced. It might have included a number of daily hassles, such as: no milk for your tea in the morning, misplacing your car keys, no hot water for a shower, traffic jams or train delays, a minor disagreement with a friend or colleague, and so on. When these (demands) all add up, they can cause problems. For example, longitudinal research found that daily hassles predicted psychological/physical symptoms (Kanner, Coyne, Schaefer, & Lazarus, 1981). This research was extended to see if enjoyable interactions (e.g. good conversation, someone smiling at you), known as 'uplifts', could counterbalance daily hassles (Kanner et al., 1981). Subsequent research has supported this notion, suggesting that daily hassles are more damaging to health than serious life events, although there was no clear relationship with uplifts (DeLongis, Coyne, Dakof, Folkman, & Lazarus, 1982).

Daily hassles have been associated with:

- high fat/sugar snacking and low vegetable consumption (O'Connor, Jones, Conner, McMillan, & Ferguson, 2008);
- sleep problems (Lapierre et al., 2011);
- substance abuse (Bailey & Covell, 2011);
- obesity (Dockray, 2011);
- blood glucose levels (Riazi, Pickup, & Bradley, 2004).

While there is clear evidence of the negative effect of daily hassles, research has suggested that effects are buffered by individual differences such as optimism, conscientiousness and self-efficacy (O'Connor et al., 2009).

Overall, there are many models of stress, with evidence that life events can impact on psychological and physical health status and mortality. While the original model in this area is outdated, new models and methodologies are more promising. The transactional model has the greatest promise, but there are still difficulties in operationalising concepts.

Test your knowledge

8.1 What are the differences between life events and daily hassles?

8.2 What role does appraisal play in the stress–illness relationship?

Answers to these questions can be found on the companion website at: **www.pearsoned.co.uk/psychologyexpress**

<table>
<tr><td colspan="2">Further reading Models of stress</td></tr>
</table>

Topic	Key reading
General overview of the links between stress and immunity	Glaser, R., & Kiecolt-Glaser, J. (1994). *Handbook of human stress and immunity*. London: Academic Press.
Overview of the transactional model of stress	Lazarus, R. S. (1999) *Stress and emotion: A new synthesis*. New York: Springer.

Psychoneuroimmunology

Psychoneuroimmunology (PNI) is the study of the connection between the brain and the immune system. The assumption is that psychological experiences (such as stress) can influence immune function, which has a strong impact on contracting disease and its progression. PNI was initially coined by Ader and Cohen in the 1970s (Ader & Cohen, 1975) following an influential study (see Critical Focus).

CRITICAL FOCUS

PNI

PNI research began when Ader and Cohen (1975) conditioned an illness-induced taste aversion in rats by pairing saccharin with cyclophosphamide (an immunosuppressive agent). After six days, measures were taken and it was found that animals learned to avoid these drinks, whereby the *drug* became the conditioned stimulus and *taste aversion* became the conditioned response. Then it was found that a *dose–response reaction* occurred, whereby the volume of saccharine consumed before rats were injected predicted the strength of the conditioned response (taste aversion), how long it took for extinction to occur, and the likelihood of the rats dying.

So what did this mean? The authors suggested that while conditioning rats to avoid saccharine, a suppression of the immune system was conditioned via stress, leaving them more susceptible to infection.

This finding had enormous potential, suggesting that by conditioning the immune system through mental processes, a connection in communication has been made. There was initially great resistance among the medical community to pursuing the area. However, this work has led to the now well-researched field of PNI.

PNI research

To begin, early research found that stress increases susceptibility to herpes simplex in mice (Rasmussen, Marsh, & Brill, 1957). Substantial evidence has followed showing a relationship between stress and decreased immunity in humans, with findings confirming that killer T-cells are lower during periods of high stress and that adrenalin and cortisol released during the stress process increase suppressor T-cells, and decrease helper T-cells and the functioning of phagocytes and lymphocytes (Herbert & Cohen, 1993), which are all important for the immune response. Immune response has been suggested to change with stressor duration: a meta-analysis of nearly 300 studies found enhancement of short-term stressors, and impairment for chronic stressors (Segerstrom & Miller, 2004).

Wound healing

One heavily researched area in the field of PNI is wound healing. A well-known study by Kiecolt-Glaser, Marucha, Mercado, Malarkey and Glaser (1995) showed that there was a significant effect of stress through caregiving on wound healing. Using a punch biopsy (which creates a hole in the skin like a hole-punch to paper), they showed that the wound healing process was much slower in caregivers (caring for a person with Alzheimer's) than controls. Marucha, Kiecolt-Glaser and Favagehi (1998) extended this with research to look at exam stress on students and again found a causal link between perceived stress and wound healing. A systematic review and meta-analysis (Walburn, Vedhara, Hankins, Rixon, & Weinman, 2009) has further confirmed this relationship in 17 of 21 studies reviewed.

Vaccination

Reduced immune response to the influenza vaccination has been shown in caregivers showing fewer lymphocytes (total T and helper T) (Kiecolt-Glaser et al., 1987) when showing higher levels of perceived stress. This effect has also been shown in immune response to vaccinations in elderly spousal caregivers as well as younger, healthy people (Burns, Carroll, Ring, & Drayson, 2003; Vedhara, 2003). Research has further shown similar findings linking stress and the common cold (Cohen et al., 1993; Cohen, Tyrrell, & Smith, 1991).

HIV

It has been suggested that stress increases HIV progression by increasing viral replication, suppressing immune response and inducing negative health-related behaviours (Robinson, Mathews, & Witek-Janusek, 2000). Research has explored the role of cognitive appraisal in HIV/AIDS, suggesting that negative self-appraisal leads to greater CD4 T-cell decline (Taylor, Kemeny, Reed, Bower, & Gruenewald, 2000). Negative attitudes have also been found to impact on disease progression: for example, Reed, Kemeny, Taylor, Wang and Visscher (1994) found that asymptomatic men with negative thoughts about HIV progression developed acquired immune deficiency syndrome (AIDS) quicker. This has been supported by Chida and Vedhara (2009); however, it was concluded that personality types, coping styles and psychological distress were more influential in disease progression than stress stimuli *per se*.

Cancer

Research focusing on breast cancer has similarly found that stress may enhance carcinogenesis through alterations in DNA repair and apoptosis (Kiecolt-Glaser, Robles, Heffner, Loving, & Glaser, 2002). However, the role played by life events in breast cancer is mixed and there is thought to be a complex interaction between stress and the immune system in women with breast cancer (Mundy-Bosse,

Thornton, Yang, Andersen, & Carson, 2011). Forsén (2010) presents evidence that women with breast cancer had significantly more life events prior to their diagnosis compared to controls. Furthermore, Chen et al. (1995) support an association between stress and the progression of breast cancer. However, there is a body of evidence that shows no such link (Ginzburg, Wrensch, Rice, Farren, & Spiegel, 2008; Maunsell, Brisson, Mondor, Verreault, & Deschênes, 2001; Petticrew, Fraser, & Regan, 1999). Furthermore, data from a 12-year follow-up study (Heikkilä et al., 2013) investigating work stress via self-reported job strain has shown no significant heightened risk to four types of cancer (colorectal, lung, breast and prostate cancers). Therefore, it seems that more research is needed in this area to make a more definitive argument.

In conclusion, there is a link between stress and many health conditions (Sapolsky, 2004); however, this influence is likely to be small when compared with genetic and other bio-psycho-social factors. As the field of PNI develops, more rigorous research is needed with studies that aim to confirm a cause-and-effect relationship.

 Sample question   *Problem-based learning*

Marie is a 35-year-old woman who is always 'on the go'. She is a self-confessed workaholic, and when she is not working, she is spending time with her young family or her friends. What she rarely has is down-time where she just relaxes. She is even known to take work on holiday to read on the plane or at the beach! She has also suffered several significant life events in recent times, including the death of her parents and grandparents, moving house and changing job. She has been suffering with discomfort in her stomach for some time, with bouts of bloating and nausea, and has recently been diagnosed with irritable bowel syndrome (IBS). How would psychoneuroimmunology and the bio-psycho-social approach of health psychology explain and support Marie's condition?

Test your knowledge

8.3 Explain the role of PNI with regard to stress and chronic illness.

8.4 What would you need to consider if you were developing a study in PNI?

Answers to these questions can be found on the companion website at: **www.pearsoned.co.uk/psychologyexpress**

Further reading Psychoneuroimmunology

Topic	Key reading
Overview of PNI	Ader, R. (2000). On the development of psychoneuroimmunology. *European Journal of Pharmacology, 405*, 167–176.
PNI of chronic disease	Vedhara, K., & Irwin, M. E. (2005). *Human psychoneuroimmunology.* Oxford: Oxford University Press.

Interventions to enhance immuno-competence

Expressive writing

There have been a range of interventions that have aimed to improve health outcomes. Expressive writing, developed and expanded by Pennebaker (1997), which involves a person writing about emotions and/or negative life experiences, has been shown to boost immune status in patients with terminal and life-threatening disease. For example, Petrie, Fontanilla, Thomas, Booth and Pennebaker (2004) found that patients with HIV/AIDS who completed expressive writing (about their deepest thoughts and feelings) had higher CD4 lymphocyte counts (immune response cells) than controls; however, this effect disappeared three months later.

Expressive writing has also been linked with a stronger antibody response to a hepatitis B vaccine. Petrie, Booth, Pennebaker, Davison and Thomas (1995) tested negative hepatitis B medical students ($n = 40$), and randomly assigned them to write about personal traumatic events. Compared with the control group, participants in the emotional expression group showed significantly higher antibody levels against hepatitis B at both four- and six-month follow-up periods, highlighting support for a link between emotional disclosure and immune function.

Furthermore, a meta-analysis of 85 intervention studies conducted by Miller and Cohen (2001) found that classical conditioning, hypnosis and emotional writing are most successful at enhancing the immune system, with stress management (usually group therapy) showing weaker effects but greater benefits if specifically designed for the population in question.

Cognitive behavioural therapy

Cognitive behavioural therapy (CBT) interventions have been used to increase immune function, with studies suggesting that a 10-week CBT intervention for HIV-positive men has resulted in lower urinary epinephrine and increased T lymphocytes and antibodies to the herpes simplex virus (HSV) compared with controls (Antoni, Cruess, & Cruess, 2000), with similar findings shown for women with breast cancer (Cruess et al., 2000). There is also research to indicate that using CBT and relaxation training can have a significant benefit to those who care for others (Vedhara et al., 2003).

CASE STUDY

Herpes simplex virus

The client

James, who is 22 years old, has been revising for his final-year degree exams, which he finds particularly stressful, as highlighted by an outbreak of a cold sore on his lip. James feels that his performance in exams is always poor and he does not normally obtain good grades. Consequently, he always leaves his exam preparation and revision to the last minute. He also focuses on other things to distract himself, rather than his exams.

Background – the problem

There are two types of herpes simplex virus (HSV), type 1 and type 2, both of which are highly contagious and can be transmitted from one part of the body to another. HSV is a common infection that can affect any mucus membrane in the body (most commonly mouth/lips and genitals) and causes small, painful blisters, although around 8 out of 10 people who have HSV are unaware they have been infected, as they may have never had symptoms (NHS Choices, 2012). Although the symptoms are usually mild and clear up within 7–10 days, the virus stays inactive in the nervous system and outbreaks have been shown to be triggered and exacerbated by stress (Glaser & Kiecolt-Glaser, 1997). Conversely, stress can also be increased by an outbreak (Goldmeier, Garvey, & Barton, 2008).

Advice

The first thing to note is James's coping style. What type of coping would you say this is? According to Lazarus and Folkman (1984) it appears that James is using emotion-focused coping, whereby he is changing his own emotional reaction to a stressor. In this instance he is dealing with the emotional reaction of the stress caused by the exam by distracting himself, using escape-avoidance behaviour.

As a health psychologist, how could you support James to use a better strategy? Perhaps you may support him to use appraisal-focused strategies: for example, instead of looking at the exam as a stressful event, he could look at it as a process where he can consolidate all of his learning. Perhaps you could help him to use more problem-focused strategies. Why does James procrastinate? Is it because of his previous low performance? Perhaps you could find out ways to address this by supporting him in learning new skills, improving his time management, ability to manage the problem and consequently to revise, and hopefully performing better in his exam. This may in turn reduce his stress load and the risk of a future herpes outbreak.

You might support James to activate more positive emotion-focused strategies: for example, Henderson and Huon (2002) used relaxation techniques to help students increase positive emotion-focused strategies in relation to exam stress. Results found that students receiving immune-related imagery reported fewer viral illnesses, such as colds, influenza and herpes, and enjoyed increased general well-being.

Conclusion

There is overwhelming evidence that psycho-social factors influence disease via changes in the immune system. However, we need to know more about potential pathways by which stress may be related to suppressed immunity and subsequent ill health. Prospective studies with clinical populations facing 'naturally occurring' stressors are most likely to improve our understanding of the stress–immune link.

This chapter has highlighted that interventions can enhance immune status in sick, immuno-compromised and healthy samples. However, there is a danger in using PNI data to legitimise claims for some types of holistic or alternative medicine. It may also be too simplistic to believe that all diseases have their basis in psychological/emotional reactions. Nonetheless, PNI has great potential to aid our understanding of the stress–immune response, and warrants further, more longitudinal research.

Further reading Enhancing immuno-competence

Topic	Key reading
An overview of treating stress and trauma with expressive writing	Pennebaker, J. W. (1993). Putting stress into words: health, linguistic, and therapeutic implication. *Behavioral Research Therapy, 31*, pp. 539–548.
Using CBT to improve immune enhancing	Vedhara, K., Bennett, P. D., Clark, S., Lightman, S.L., Shaw, S., Perks, P., Hunt, M.A., Philip, J.M., Tallon, D., Murphy, P.J., Jones, R.W., Wilcock, G.K., Shanks, N.M. Enhancement of antibody responses to influenza vaccination in the elderly following a cognitive-behavioural stress management intervention. *Psychotherapy and Psychosomatics, 72(5)*, pp. 245–52.

Chapter summary – pulling it all together

→ Can you tick all of the points from the revision checklist at the beginning of this chapter?

→ Attempt the sample question from the beginning of this chapter using the answer guidelines below.

→ Go to the companion website at www.pearsoned.co.uk/psychologyexpress to access more revision support online, including interactive quizzes, flashcards, You be the marker exercises as well as answer guidance for the Test your knowledge and Sample questions from this chapter.

Answer guidelines

 Sample question   *Essay*

Outline and evaluate research conducted in the field of psychoneuroimmunology (PNI) that explains the relationship between chronic stressors and chronic disease.

Approaching the question

Your answer should aim to provide an analysis of how research in the field of PNI has explained the relationship between chronic stress and chronic disease.

Important points to include

You may want to consider: What are chronic stressors? What is chronic disease? The aim is to link the practical approaches to interventions that have been used to support these factors.

> ### Make your answer stand out
>
> *It is really easy to fall into the trap of simply describing different types of model used to explain approaches to stress and illness. A good answer will remember to take a critical stance, evaluating the strengths and limitations of each method. Linking your evaluation to theory will show your ability to provide a theoretical rationale and evidence base for educational practice. A good student would also show original thinking by considering the impact of individual differences and other outside factors that may impact on the knowledge of stress and PNI, using a wide range of sources to support their arguments.*

> Explore the accompanying website at www.pearsoned.co.uk/psychologyexpress
> → Prepare more effectively for exams and assignments using the answer guidelines for questions from this chapter.
> → Test your knowledge using multiple choice questions and flashcards.
> → Improve your essay skills by exploring the You be the marker exercises.

Notes

9

Doctor–patient communication and adherence

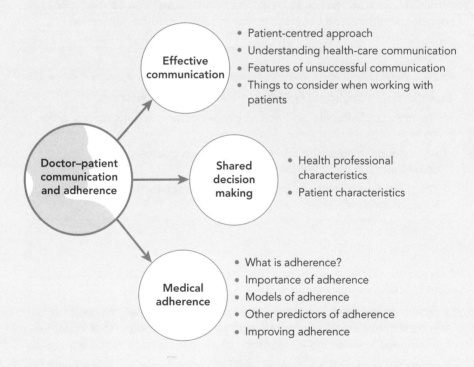

- **Effective communication**
  - Patient-centred approach
  - Understanding health-care communication
  - Features of unsuccessful communication
  - Things to consider when working with patients

- **Doctor–patient communication and adherence**

- **Shared decision making**
  - Health professional characteristics
  - Patient characteristics

- **Medical adherence**
  - What is adherence?
  - Importance of adherence
  - Models of adherence
  - Other predictors of adherence
  - Improving adherence

A printable version of this topic map is available from
www.pearsoned.co.uk/psychologyexpress

Introduction

Think back to the last time you went to see your doctor. How would you have rated the consultation? What factors would you say impacted on your satisfaction with your doctor? And did you follow their advice? If they gave you medicine, did you take it as prescribed or stop when you felt better?

Research in this area aims to understand the role of communication and health beliefs in patient behaviour: for example, adherence to treatment regimes. This chapter will ascertain why effective communication is an important aspect of medical care, and will examine the features of successful and unsuccessful communication between health-care providers and patients. Ineffective communication patterns of clinicians (such as the use of jargon, baby talk and depersonalisation) will be discussed, and the impact of poor communication on the doctor–patient relationship will be examined. The important role of communication in adherence to treatment regimens will also be examined, alongside cognitions and beliefs that may influence medical adherence.

 Revision checklist

Essential points you should know by the end of this chapter are:

❏ The impact of effective and non-effective doctor–patient communication styles

❏ An understanding of the relationship between doctor–patient communication and medical adherence

❏ The theoretical constructs that can help to understand, predict and improve medical adherence.

Assessment advice

When you are writing an essay or answering an exam question on this topic, you should consider the following points:

- *Content.* Try to develop an *awareness* of the links between the research literature in health-care communication and the contribution that individual components make to the investigation of patient satisfaction and adherence.

- Remember, *evidence* is always required. You should not include *anecdotal details* about personal experiences (e.g. 'When I went to see the doctor ...') and you should write in the *third person*. This allows you to stay objective (i.e. creating an argument from evidence that is not influenced by your own experiences) rather than subjective (creating an argument based on how you feel or think, or what you do).

- Become *critically* aware of the strengths and weaknesses of the evidence: for example, what methodologies have been used to explore communication, satisfaction and adherence? Consult a wide range of primary sources to produce a well-developed critique to create and support your arguments.

Sample question

Could you answer this question? Below is a typical problem question that could rise on this topic.

 Sample question **Essay**

Assess the importance of effective doctor–patient communication in the management of illness with reference to empirical evidence.

Guidelines on answering this question are included at the end of this chapter, whilst guidance on tackling other exam questions can be found on the companion website at **www.pearsoned.co.uk/psychologyexpress**

Effective communication

Consultations are an integral process, allowing the doctor to gain information for diagnosis and treatment, and the patient to understand their symptoms and treatment options.

The importance of good communication was highlighted in the 1991 *Toronto Consensus Statement* (Simpson et al., 1991). This detailed the relationship between patient anxiety and dissatisfaction with doctors, due to a lack of information, explanation and feedback given by doctors often as a result of their misperception of the amount and type of information that patients require. It also discussed the increased link between improved quality of communication and positive health outcomes, acknowledging the importance of understanding patients' concerns to help reduce distress.

Patient-centred approach

In 1991, the Department of Health acknowledged the importance of health-care communication in the 'Patients Charter' (Stocking, 1991). It was clearly outlined that patients should have a right to be given a clear explanation of any treatment proposed, including side-effects and risks in alternatives to the recommended treatment.

The concept of patient-centred consultations was first developed by Byrne and Long (1976), who outlined five phases present in the typical medical consultation:

1 The doctor establishes a relationship with the patient.

2 The doctor attempts to discover the reason for the patient's attendance.

3 The doctor conducts a verbal or physical examination, or both.

4 The doctor, or the doctor and the patient, or the patient considers the condition.

5 The doctor, and occasionally the patient, considers further treatment or further investigation.

The NHS now advocates a patient-centred approach, seen as the gold standard in doctor–patient communication, calling for *active partnerships* between health professionals and patients (NHS Executive, 1996). It is characterised (Coulter, 1999) by:

● a receptiveness by the doctor to the patient's opinions and expectations, and an effort to see the illness through the patient's eyes;

● patient involvement in the decision making and planning of treatment;

● an attention to the affective content of the consultation in terms of the emotions of both the patient and the doctor.

Epstein et al. (2005) further highlighted that good patient-centred communication should:

● be concordant with the patient's values, needs and preferences;

● allow patients to provide input and participate actively in decisions regarding their health and healthcare.

This style is suggested to contain four communication domains:

● the patient's perspective;

● the psychosocial context;

● shared understanding;

● sharing power and responsibility.

Roter and Hall (2006) confirm that good communication in medical care can result in:

● positive outcomes;

● better diagnosis;

● higher levels of satisfaction;

● higher levels of adherence;

● improved health.

At the same time, bad communication in medical care has been shown to result in:

● a lack of engagement with patients;

● refusal to follow recommended health behaviours;

● failure to adhere;

● failure to cope;

● psychological damage;

● physical harm.

Criticisms

There are issues when measuring patient-centred communication, as there is a lack of theoretical and conceptual clarity, unexamined assumptions, lack of adequate control for patient characteristics and social contexts, modest correlations between survey and observational measures, and overlap of patient-centred communication with other constructs.

Provider behaviour (Hall, Roter, & Katz, 1988)

Background

This meta-analysis aimed to identify the factors related to provider behaviour in medical encounters.

Method

A total of 41 independent studies were analysed, with provider behaviours grouped into the following categories: information giving, questions, competence, partnership building and socio-emotional behaviour, along with the total amount of communication.

Findings

Of all the patient variables considered, satisfaction had the most consistent relationship to provider behaviour. Satisfaction was most dramatically predicted by the amount of information that was given by providers, and was further related to greater technical and interpersonal competence, partnership building, more immediate and positive nonverbal behaviour, more social conversation, more positive talk, less negative talk and more communication overall. Only 'question asking' showed no relationship to satisfaction.

Taking into account socio-demographic differences, it appeared that patients of higher social class received more information as well as more communication overall. Furthermore, female patients received more information and more total communication than males. Older patients received more information, more total communication and more courtesy than younger patients.

Conclusion

It appears that there are a wide range of factors that correlate with provider behaviour, the most significant being satisfaction, recall and compliance. Furthermore, there were clear socio-demographic differences in relation to provider behaviours, specifically in terms of the patient's gender, age and social class.

Understanding health-care communication

Northouse and Northouse (1985) proposed a theoretical model to explain health communication (see Figure 9.1). This model emphasises the way in which a series of factors (relationships, transactions and contexts) can impact on the interaction in health-care settings. Four types of *relationships* are proposed to exist in health-care settings, comprising:

- professional–professional;
- professional–client;

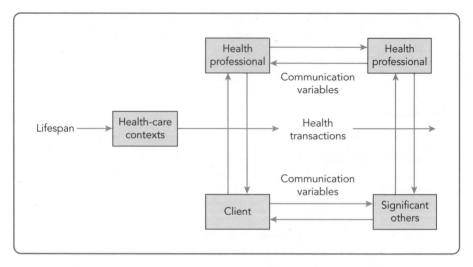

Figure 9.1 Northouse and Northouse's (1985) model of health communication

- professional–client's significant others;
- client–significant others.

Both health professionals and patients (and their families) bring unique characteristics, beliefs, values and perceptions to the health-care setting, which affect how they interact.

The second element is *transactions*, which suggests that health-related interactions occur between participants. These transactions include both verbal and non-verbal communications, as well as the content and relationship dimensions of messages. Health transactions are established within the various relationships represented by the model, and this dimension influences how the content of the messages should be interpreted.

The third core element is *health-care contexts*, outlined as the settings in which health communication occurs. Different contexts (e.g. waiting rooms) have been shown to have a significant influence on communication between participants.

Features of unsuccessful communication

Long-standing research has shown that patients often judge the quality of care by the delivery, showing limited concern about the technical quality (Ben-Sira, 1976; Johnson, Roter, Powe, & Cooper, 2004). Poor doctor–patient communication has been linked to depersonalisation, related to a biomedical communication style, often leading to less satisfaction, trust and adherence (Williams, Lawrence, Campbell, & Spiehler, 2009).

Macdonald (2004) highlights that barriers in the consultation relate to cognitive and physical factors alongside the doctor communicating with relatives rather than the patient. Northouse and Northouse (1998) suggest that doctor–patient relationships are negatively affected by:

- uncertainty over the roles;
- uncertainty over who is responsible;
- asymmetrical power;
- medical jargon.

Medical jargon has been associated with a negative influence on the doctor–patient relationship, alongside less cognitive satisfaction, comprehension and recall (Jackson, 1992). Park (2010) explored patient understanding of jargon terms used and found that from a total of 60 interviews, 26 physicians used one or more medical jargon terms; however, only 53.4% of the physicians explained them. Furthermore, findings highlighted that the level of patients' understanding of ten medical terms increased significantly according to increasing level of income, but this was not the case for age, gender or level of education.

Research has also highlighted that communication style can be poorer with older patients. Doctors have been found to be more condescending, abrupt, indifferent and dismissive with older people (Adelman, Greene, & Ory, 2000), whereas they are more egalitarian, patient, engaged and respectful with younger patients (Andelman, Greene, Charon, & Friedmann, 1992). This was also supported by Minichiello, Browne and Kendig (2000), who suggested that doctors tend to speak louder, be more patronising, and use more baby talk with older patients although this is not always the case as seen in this key study (Hall et al., 1988).

Greene, Adelman, Friedmann and Charon (1994) suggest that older patients prefer encounters where:

- there is physician supportiveness and shared laughter;
- they are questioned about and given an opportunity to provide information on their own agenda;
- physicians provide some structure for the first meeting through their use of questioning.

Things to consider when working with patients

Davis and Fallowfield (1991) suggest that the basic mistakes that professionals make when communicating with patients are:

- not introducing themselves;
- not asking for clarifications;
- not encouraging the patient;
- not asking about feelings;
- not providing information that can be understood.

Research highlights that the patient can also contribute to poor communication: for example, if he or she fails to listen to the advice, or ignores instructions with a strong misconception regarding their condition (Bensing et al., 2011). It is suggested that negative perceptions are caused by poor communication and in turn result in less effective treatment. They have been associated with lower uptake of health care such as cancer screening (Fox et al., 2009) alongside health service uptake in general (Ross & Duff, 1982).

CRITICAL FOCUS

Communication research

Here are some issues with research in the area of communication:

- The current emphasis is on patient-centredness, shared decision making and informed decisions. However, the health professional is medically trained to provide safe and expert advice on how to manage conditions, so can these clash?
- Research methods used to explore communication in the consultation normally rely upon qualitative methods such as recording and coding interactions, observations and interviews. All of these methods accept a level of subjectivity and interpretation by the researcher, which can restrict the conclusions drawn.

Test your knowledge

9.1 List potential barriers to a successful medical consultation.

9.2 Why is successful doctor–patient communication important?

Answers to these questions can be found on the companion website at: **www.pearsoned.co.uk/psychologyexpress**

Further reading Doctor–patient relationship

Topic	Key reading
Introduction to health communication	Northouse, L. L., & Northouse, P. G. (1998). An introduction to health communication. In L. L. Northouse & P. G. Northouse (Eds.), *Health communication: Strategies for health professionals* (pp. 1–11). Norwalk, CT: Appleton & Lange.
Improving communication	Roter, D., & Hall, J. A. (Eds.) (2006). *Doctors talking with patients/patients talking with doctors: Improving communication in medical visits* (2nd ed.). Westport, CT: Praeger.

Shared decision making

The medical consultation relies on the interaction between the patient and the health professional, where key decisions relating to diagnosis and treatment are made. Traditional models have placed the doctor as the key centre-point for any decisions that are made, since doctors are regarded as educated experts. However, with the patient-centred approach and patients wanting more of a role in decision making, along with the availability of medical knowledge and an increased awareness of patient autonomy, there has been a decline in the perception of physicians as all-knowing (Lee, Back, Block, & Stewart, 2002).

Ford, Schofield and Hope (2003) conducted a series of semi-structured interviews with general practitioners, hospital doctors, practice nurses and academics alongside lay people. It appeared that there had been a shift of preference from the 'doctor knows best' style to a more shared-decision approach, with six core dimensions for the health professional:

- having a good knowledge of research or medical information and being able to communicate this to the patient;
- achieving a good relationship with the patient;
- establishing the nature of the patient's medical problem;
- gaining an understanding of the patient's understanding of their problem and its ramifications;
- engaging the patient in any decision-making process: for example, treatment choices not simply being chosen by the health professional but being discussed with the patient;
- managing time so that the consultation does not appear to be rushed.

Lee et al. (2002) investigated decision-making preferences of women (n = 999) with early-stage breast cancer and a cohort (n = 141) of stem cell transplant patients. Results indicated that there were five commonly recognised models of medical decision making (see Table 9.1). The two *least desired* models were A and E. Model A was characterised by the physician being solely responsible for the medical decision, while model E is described as patient focused, whereby patients make treatment decisions by themselves and the physician is seen as providing a service rather than being involved in selecting the treatment.

The two less extreme categories (models B and D) involve both parties in the treatment decision, although one party assumes responsibility. In the doctor-as-agent model (model B), the doctor holds responsibility for making the treatment decision, using personal knowledge of the patient's values, and placing

Table 9.1 **Decision-making preferences of 999 women with early-stage breast cancer (I) and 141 stem cell transplant patients (II) (Lee et al., 2002)**

Theoretical model	Decision-making process	I(%)	II(%)
A. Paternalistic	Physician makes decisions	18	3
B. Physician-as-agent	Physician makes decisions after considering patient input	17	25
C. Shared decision making	Physician and patient make decisions together	44	40
D. Informed decision making	Patient makes decisions after considering physician input	14	30
E. Consumerism	Patient makes decisions	9	2

themselves in the role of the patient. In the informed decision-making model (model D), doctors provide patients with medical information, and the patients process this information and decide on a particular treatment, taking more responsibility for the decision.

In contrast, shared decision making (model C) was highlighted as the *most preferred* model. It aims to educate patients about potential outcomes of treatment options and to engage them fully in deciding which choice is best. It involves patients early in the process to be sure that decisions reflect both the patient's values and the doctor's medical knowledge, outlined as a collaborative process (Lee et al., 2002).

Elwyn, Edwards, Kinnersley and Grol (2000) outlined that shared decision making essentially occurs when both the patient and health professional have an equal responsibility in treatment decisions. To ensure this occurs, six steps are followed within the consultation:

1 Explore patient's ideas about the nature of the problem and potential treatments.
2 Identify how much information the patient would prefer, and tailor information to meet these needs.
3 Check the patient's understanding of ideas, fears and expectations of potential treatment options.
4 Assess the patient's decision-making preference and adopt their preferred mode.
5 Make, discuss or defer decisions.
6 Arrange follow-up.

However, there are a wide range of factors that influence the consultation process: for example, both parties involved in the consultation need to be 'speaking the same language'. Tuckett, Boulton, Olson and Williams (1985) argue that the consultation should be viewed as a 'meeting between experts' and emphasise the importance of the patient's and doctor's differing view of the problem. However, there is evidence that both parties do not adopt similar perspectives. Ogden et al. (2001) explored interactions between the doctor and the patient and found that although GPs and patients showed similar beliefs about involving the patient in decision making, GPs believed that it was less important to focus only on the patient's main problem, and was more important to acknowledge their own feelings and avoid medical language. Furthermore, GPs rated doctor receptiveness and the affective content of the relationship overall as more important for a good consultation than did the patients. The patients consistently rated information giving as more important. This suggests that, although patient-centredness may currently be the preferred style of consultation, doctors and patients favour different aspects of this interaction.

There has also been research which suggests that the quality of interaction impacts on the patient's ability to be confident in dealing with their condition. Zachariae et al. (2003) examined the relationship between the quality of a doctor's interaction with patients who had cancer and patients' satisfaction with the consultation and confidence in their ability to cope with their condition. Doctors' communication style was rated by:

- if the doctor attempted to gain an understanding of the patient's viewpoint;
- how well patients considered the doctor to understand their feelings;
- their satisfaction with the doctor's ability to handle medical aspects of their care;
- the quality of their personal contact with the doctor.

The results indicated that higher scores across all measures were associated with higher satisfaction, higher levels of confidence in coping with illness and lower levels of emotional distress. Furthermore, doctors with poor communication skills were least aware of their patient's responses and level of satisfaction.

Health professional characteristics

The type of health professional is also viewed as important in communication settings, where the style of interaction can be different: for example, stereotypes of nurses have traditionally been viewed as more empathetic and more nurturing than doctors. Nichols (1993) suggested that one reason for this could be that doctors find it more difficult to become emotionally involved with patients, preferring to remain detached, whereas nurses are often a main carer for individuals, the first port of call for many patients, and have more time to build up good relationships.

The gender of the health professional has also been viewed as an important factor for successful communication, with a meta-analysis ($n = 7$) revealing that overall, patients disclosed more, spoke more biomedically, offered psycho-social information, and made more positive statements to female physicians (Hall & Roter, 2002). Patients were also rated as more assertive towards female physicians and tended to interrupt them more. Furthermore, partnership statements were made significantly more often to female than male physicians. However, gender did not influence how emotional issues and personal feelings were discussed. It could be argued that these differences could be due to the doctor's behaviour (i.e. female physicians may ask more questions) and this is an area worthy of further investigation.

Patient characteristics

Patient factors can also influence the consultation. For example, individuals with higher levels of education who reside in more affluent areas tend to gain more information and have longer consultations than those with higher levels of deprivation (Stirling, Wilson, & McConnachie, 2001). Furthermore, a qualitative study by Ali, Atkin and Neal (2006) examining patients with South Asian and white British backgrounds showed that the approach followed by all patients and doctors, irrespective of ethnicity, was clearly a doctor-centred one. In this instance, patients did not feel that it was their place to comment upon the doctor's medical judgement and they felt that the doctors were well trained and had greater knowledge and experience than them. However, this may be to do with the class of the patients, since most of the patients were from working-class backgrounds and did not consider themselves to be consumers of medical treatment, but were content to play the traditional role of a patient.

Test your knowledge

9.3 What were the five phases Byrne and Long (1976) described to be present in the typical medical consultation?

9.4 What are the core features of shared decision making?

Answers to these questions can be found on the companion website at:
www.pearsoned.co.uk/psychologyexpress

Further reading Shared decision making

Topic	Key reading
A paper on shared decision making	Elwyn, G., Edwards, A., Kinnersley, P., & Grol, R. (2000). Shared decision making and the concept of equipoise: The competencies of involving patients in healthcare choices. *British Journal of General Practice, 50*, 892–899.
An overview of what to consider in shared decision making	Towle, A., & Godolphin, W. (1999). Framework for teaching and learning informed shared decision making. *British Medical Journal, 319*(7212), 766–771.

One aspect that communication has a significant influence on is medical adherence. The final part of this chapter will discuss this area in more detail.

 Sample question **Essay**

Critically evaluate the theoretical underpinnings which help to explain medication adherence.

Medical adherence

Medication can assist in the prevention, management and treatment of illness, yet many people do not take their medicines as prescribed (Horne, 2001). Health psychology has contributed much to our understanding of lay perceptions of health, illness and treatment and the cognitions that may facilitate or impede health behaviour, such as adherence.

What is adherence?

The concept of adherence has changed markedly over the years. It has moved from the paternalistic concept of *compliance*, defined by Haynes, Sackett and Taylor (1979) as 'The extent to which the patient's behaviour (in terms of taking medications, following diets or other lifestyle changes) coincides with medical or health advice' to a more empowered concept of adherence, which is referred to as 'The extent to which a patient's behaviour matches agreed recommendations from their health professional' (Horne, 2006; NICE, 2009). This change of term reflects the shift towards patient-centredness and shared decision making, in the context of medication taking and the extent to which a patient takes medication as prescribed. It further encapsulates *unintentional non-adherence*, which occurs when a patient simply forgets or has misunderstood the instruction, and *intentional non-adherence*, where a patient chooses not to follow a medication regime (Horne, 2001).

Importance of adherence

Think of the last time you were prescribed treatment. Did you take the full course as prescribed? Or did you start skipping doses or stop taking the medicine when you were feeling better? Maybe you thought you didn't need it? Maybe you forgot your doses after your symptoms went away? Maybe you thought it would give you unpleasant side-effects?

So, why is adherence important? Firstly, there are cost implications. It has been suggested that for the UK alone, drugs that have been prescribed and ordered but which are not taken cost around £4 billion per year. There are also, of course, the health implications. Simpson, Eurich and Majumdar (2006) outline that the odds of dying are halved if people take their medication as advised. This is further supported by DiMatteo, Giordani, Lepper and Croghan (2002), who reviewed 63 studies and found that those who adhered to the recommended medical treatment were around three times more likely to have a good treatment outcome. However, there is still evidence that between 30 and 50% of people are non-adherent (Horne et al., 2005). So what is going on?

Models of adherence

There are two main models to help us understand, predict and support change in adherence: Ley's (1989) *cognitive hypothesis model*, and Horne's (2001) *perceptions and practicalities approach* (PAPA).

Cognitive hypothesis model

Ley (1988; 1989) proposed the cognitive hypothesis model of compliance (see Figure 9.2), which suggested three strategies within the consultation that can increase knowledge about a condition and adherence to any recommended treatment. These strategies are:

- Maximise *satisfaction* with the process of treatment, having sufficient time in the consultation to discuss relevant issues fully, seeing the same health

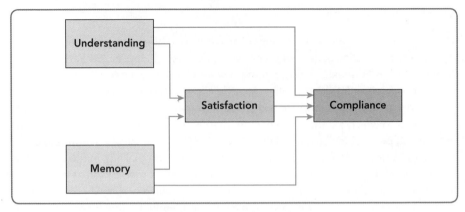

Figure 9.2 Ley's cognitive hypothesis model of compliance
Source: Based on Ley (1988, 1989).

professional on repeat visits, and allowing good accessibility to health professionals.

● Maximise *understanding* of the condition, and if treatment problems arise, the health professional 'leads' the consultation.

● Maximise *memory* for information given (i.e. the most important points should be given early or later on in the consultation to maximise primacy and recency effects).

Perceptions and practicalities approach (PAPA)

The second model, proposed by Horne (2001) and illustrated in Figure 9.3, adopts a different perspective, using the now more accepted term of 'adherence' and emphasising the influence of perceptions and practicalities. It focuses on

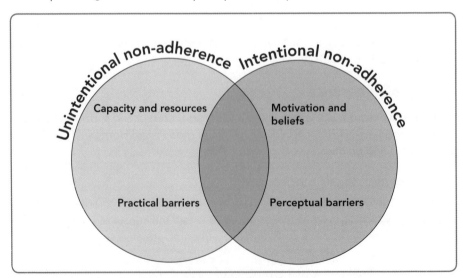

Figure 9.3 The perceptions and practicalities approach
Source: Based on Horne (2000, 2001) and Horne and Weinman (2004).

both unintentional and intentional non-adherence, and factors that are suggested to be important include:

- capacity and resource limitations (e.g. 'I have no access to my medication');
- practical barriers (e.g. 'I can't get to the pharmacy');
- motivational beliefs (e.g. 'I want to get well');
- perceptual barriers (e.g. 'My medicine is not necessary').

Other predictors of adherence

The models described above offer two different approaches which can be used to explain and understand adherence. However, there are other factors that have been researched to predict adherence, and that elaborate on the concepts in these models.

Beliefs

Beliefs can be related to the foundations of the social cognition models discussed in Chapter 2. For example, theoretical underpinnings can be a foundation for questions, such as:

- 'What barriers, if any, do you perceive in your life that might interfere with you taking this medication?' (perceived barriers, cf. health belief model PAPA).
- 'Do other people around you want you to use nicotine replacement therapy (NRT) to help you to stop smoking?' (subjective norms, cf. theory of planned behaviour, TPB).
- 'To what extent do you believe you are capable of taking your medication as prescribed?' (self-efficacy, cf. health action process approach/social cognitive theory; perceived behavioural control, cf. TPB).
- 'Do you believe that taking your medication will help you become well?' (action–outcome expectancy, cf. social cognitive theory).

Leventhal et al. (Leventhal, Meyer, & Nerenz, 1980; Leventhal, Diefenbach, & Leventhal, 1992) developed a commonsense model of illness cognitions, focusing on beliefs in an attempt to provide patients with a framework to understand their illness. This model had five core dimensions:

- Identity – related to the label/diagnosis (e.g. chickenpox) and the symptoms (e.g. a rash/spots) of the illness.
- Perceived cause of the illness – related to bio-psycho-social factors in the cause of illness (e.g. a virus, being around others with the virus).
- Time line – how long the illness will last (i.e. short term [acute] or long term [chronic]).
- Consequences – the effects of the illness (e.g. must avoid others to reduce infection).
- Cure/control – belief about whether they can be treated and/or cured, and whether this is by themselves or with powerful others (e.g. doctors).

Based on this work, Weinman, Petrie, Moss-Morris and Horne (1996) developed the Illness Perception Questionnaire (IPQ), which reflects the dimensions above.

This was later revised (IPQR) by Moss-Morris et al. (2002) and this questionnaire shows good psychometric properties. Research in this area has shown that beliefs about illness relate to adherence. Halm, Mora and Leventhal (2006) undertook a longitudinal cohort study on patients (*n* = 198) hospitalised with asthma over a 12-month period. Overall, 53% of patients believed they only had asthma when they were having symptoms, which was described as the *'no symptoms, no asthma'* belief. This belief was negatively associated with beliefs about always having asthma, having lung inflammation or the importance of using inhalers, and was positively associated with expecting to be cured. These types of beliefs, therefore, have a significant impact on adherence levels.

Beliefs about medication

Beliefs regarding medication have also been suggested to impact on adherence. Horne and Weinman (2002) suggested that beliefs regarding necessity and concerns (referred to as the necessity/concerns framework: NCF) can predict adherence. In essence, if an individual has high concerns about their medication (in terms of side-effects and future health risk) and a low belief in their need to take it, they are more likely to non-adhere.

The most commonly used measure in this area is the Beliefs about Medicines Questionnaire (BMQ; Horne, 1997; Horne, Weinman, & Hankins, 1999). Evidence has been generated in this area in the context of long-term health conditions such as:

- asthma (Horne & Weinman, 2002);
- cancer and CHD (Horne & Weinman, 1999);
- HIV (Horne, Cooper, & Gellaitry, 2007);
- rheumatoid arthritis (Neame & Hammond, 2005);
- bipolar disorder (Clatworthy, Bowskill, Rank, Parham, & Horne, 2007).

Patient satisfaction

Evidence suggests a strong and consistent relationship between patient dissatisfaction and non-adherence with medical regimens (Kaplan, Greenfield, & Ware, 1989). With data reporting that around 40% of patients were dissatisfied with their treatment, and a further 28% dissatisfied with their GP practice (Ley, 1988), this can be problematic when it comes to adherence. In support of this, Roberts (2002) interviewed 28 HIV positive patients, and found that good-quality doctor–patient relationships tended to promote adherence while lesser-quality relationships impeded it. As a way to combat this, Sala, Krupat and Rother (2002) found through recorded consultations that light humour increased satisfaction. This highlights that a range of factors impact on satisfaction, and this is influential when explaining medical adherence.

Patient recall

Poor recall has been related to non-adherence. Miller et al. (2003) conducted a longitudinal study to identify the effect of recall of HIV patients (*n* = 128) on treatment regime. Findings suggested that poor recall of regime was significantly associated with lower adherence and lower levels of literacy. Ley (1989) suggested anxiety, medical knowledge, intellectual ability and the primacy effect can influence recall, although this was not influenced by age.

> **? Sample question** — *Problem-based learning*
>
> Roger is a 64-year-old man who has recently suffered from a heart attack. His cardiology consultant has advised him to stop smoking, maintain a balanced diet and take more physical activity, alongside taking regular medication. He wants to follow this advice, as he does not want to suffer another heart attack. However, he has never needed to take medication before and is concerned about the side-effects; he also enjoys the occasional cigarette and going to the pub with his friend Ian. How would you support Roger to adhere to the consultant's advice?

Improving adherence

A number of studies have suggested ways in which adherence can be improved. Interventions have focused on improving information giving (Haynes, 1982), improving the way oral information is given – such as using primacy effects, stressing the importance of the information, simplifying, using repetition, being specific and using follow-ups (Ley, 1989) – as well as providing written information (Ley & Morris, 1984). More recently, Dulmen et al. (2007) evaluated systematic reviews of adherence interventions from 1990 to 2005 and highlighted that 23 of the 38 reviews reported a significant increase in adherence. Four approaches appeared to have the strongest impact: technical, behavioural, educational and multi-faceted/complex interventions. Technical solutions, such as a simplification of the regimen, were often found to be the most effective.

Interventions based on socio-cognitive theoretical frameworks (as outlined in Chapters 2 and 3) have been successful in improving adherence in areas such as HIV (Tuldrà et al., 2000), and have included using counselling, education, family systems therapy, motivational interviewing, implementation intentions and interventions based on stage theories. Haynes, Akloo, Sahota, McDonald and Yao (2008) completed a systematic review evaluating randomised controlled trials (RCTs) to determine the impact of interventions on medical adherence. It found that studies differed widely, making quantitative analysis scientifically difficult to compare. This reflects the difficulties of comparing and replicating intervention research, as discussed in Chapter 3. As a result, Haynes et al. (2008) used qualitative analysis and concluded that the current methods of improving adherence for chronic health problems are mostly complex and not very effective, so the full benefits of treatment are not realised. Therefore, more research is needed to support patients in following medical advice for long-term conditions.

Conclusion

It is clear from this chapter that understanding how we (as health professionals) communicate with our patients is core to a good relationship with them. Moreover, we may, in doing this, influence how readily they take up our advice, be it medication use or behaviour change, which will in turn influence their health status. It is also evident that how our patients think about the advice and treatment we give them can have an impact on whether they are willing to follow it. And if they have concerns about what they are taking, or do not see the need, then why would they engage? Adherence is key to reducing medical costs and hospital admissions, and improving health status. What is now needed is an understanding of the active components and behaviour change techniques used within intervention studies that aim to improve adherence, to ascertain what works and how it can be replicated. Further research should, therefore, link this area to the BCT research discussed in Chapter 3.

Test your knowledge

9.5 Describe the PAPA and NCF models.

9.6 Identify factors that can impact on medical adherence.

Answers to these questions can be found on the companion website at: **www.pearsoned.co.uk/psychologyexpress**

Further reading Medical adherence

Topic	Key reading
Textbook on adherence	Bosworth, H. B., Oddone, E. Z., & Weinberger, M. (Eds.) (2006). *Patient treatment adherence: Concepts, interventions, and measurement*. Hillsdale, NJ: Lawrence Erlbaum.
Edited book on adherence	Bosworth, H. (Ed.) (2010). *Improving patient treatment adherence: A clinician's guide*. New York: Springer.

CASE STUDY

Adherence

The client

Jon is 87 years old, lives alone and has complex medical needs. He has type 2 diabetes which cannot be controlled by diet alone, and has been recently diagnosed with Parkinson's, which is when levels of a chemical messenger called dopamine in your brain are low and causes symptoms such as tremors, rigidity and slowness of movement (Hoehn & Yahr, 1998). At present Jon's medical conditions are managed by medication, which he takes daily.

▶

It has become apparent that Jon has not been taking his diabetes medication. His doctor is particularly concerned, as non-adherence will eventually leave Jon insulin dependent. But why isn't Jon taking his medication?

Background – the problem

The NHS spends around 40% of the budget (around £10 billion) on people over the age of 65 (Department of Health, 2001b), with higher rates of multiple chronic health conditions, commonly: hypertension, diabetes, coronary artery disease, cancer and coronary heart disease (Fillenbaum, Pieper, Cohen, Cornoni-Huntley, & Guralnik, 2000). Non-adherence will not only be detrimental to Jon's general health; it may lead to a hospital admission and leave wasted medicines, both of which have cost implications.

Advice

Let's go back to Horne's model (2001), using the perceptions and practicalities approach, while also considering the necessity and concerns framework (Horne & Weinman, 2002).

What capacity and resource limitations might Jon have? What about practical barriers?

Perhaps Jon has forgotten to get his medication from the pharmacy – remember Jon is an older gentleman and may have some short-term memory loss. Jon also lives alone, therefore it is important to identify his support network (e.g. who helps him get his medication?). Remember, there are a lot of processes involved in ensuring you have your prescribed medication: for example, Jon has to get a repeat prescription from his doctor, and he then needs to take this to the pharmacy if the doctor's surgery does not offer a repeat/collection service. Also, he has two different medications, so he will have to remember to collect both.

Perhaps Jon can't get to the pharmacy – he may not drive and may not be aware of public transport that runs, or perhaps there is no public transport available. Perhaps Jon is unable to afford to get a taxi to the pharmacy. Perhaps he has trouble taking his medication, or even getting the lid off the bottle.

How about motivational beliefs?

Perhaps he is not motivated to get better. There is a higher level of incidence of depression in older people (Durrani, Hussain, & Ugwu, 2007). Has he been screened for this? Depression is closely related to low adherence (Cukor, Rosenthal, Jindal, Brown, & Kimmel, 2009), which has been applied to diabetes management (Ciechanowski, Katon, & Russo, 2000). Could this be an overlooked issue here?

And, finally, what about perceptual barriers?

Perhaps Jon doesn't realise the seriousness of the medication for his health and does not think that it is necessary (low need). He may have an external locus of control and believe that his health is out of his control – a common theme found in low adherence (Voils, Steffens, Flint, & Bosworth, 2005). He may feel that his medicine may do him more harm than good (concerns). How can you help Jon understand the seriousness of taking his medication? Perhaps you could provide an intervention here: for example, technical, behavioural, educational and multi-faceted/complex interventions have been viewed as the most successful (Dulmen et al., 2007).

Chapter summary – pulling it all together

→ Can you tick all of the points from the revision checklist at the beginning of this chapter?

→ Attempt the sample question from the beginning of this chapter using the answer guidelines below.

→ Go to the companion website at www.pearsoned.co.uk/psychologyexpress to access more revision support online, including interactive quizzes, flashcards, You be the marker exercises as well as answer guidance for the Test your knowledge and Sample questions from this chapter.

Answer guidelines

 Sample question   **Essay**

Assess the importance of effective doctor–patient communication in the management of illness with reference to empirical evidence.

Approaching the question

● Your answer should aim to provide an analysis of how doctor–patient communication can impact medication adherence.

Important points to include

● Begin by outlining what the key models that you are examining include.
● For each model/theory you will need to:
  ● Consider the strengths and weaknesses of the model.
  ● Discuss the empirical research that informs the theories (does it support the models?).
  ● Evaluate the methodological rigour of studies that have examined medical adherence.
  ● You should then consider the usefulness of using these models in predicting and intervening with adherence behaviour. Conclude by making suggestions for how the models could be improved and directions for future research.

Make your answer stand out

It is really easy to fall into the trap of simply describing different types of factors. A good answer will remember to take a critical stance, using a wide range of primary evidence to present an argument about what impacts on adherence. For a higher grade, original thinking is needed: try to consider the differences in the effectiveness of theoretical models and research that help explain adherence, while focusing on future considerations to challenge the current empirical evidence.

Explore the accompanying website at www.pearsoned.co.uk/psychologyexpress

→ Prepare more effectively for exams and assignments using the answer guidelines for questions from this chapter.

→ Test your knowledge using multiple choice questions and flashcards.

→ Improve your essay skills by exploring the You be the marker exercises.

Notes

Notes

And finally, before the exam...

How to approach revision from here

You should now be at a reasonable stage in your revision process – you should have developed your skills and knowledge base over your course and used this text judiciously during that period. Now, however, you have used the book to reflect on, remind yourself of and reinforce the material you have researched over the year/seminar. You will, of course, need to do additional reading and research to that included here (and appropriate directions are provided) but you will be well on your way with the material presented in this book.

It is important that in answering any question in psychology you take a research- and evidence-based approach to your response. For example, do not make generalised or sweeping statements that cannot be substantiated or supported by evidence from the literature. Remember as well that the evidence should not be anecdotal – it is of no use citing your mum, dad, best friend or the latest news from a celebrity website. After all, you are not writing an opinion piece – you are crafting an argument that is based on current scientific knowledge and understanding. You need to be careful about the evidence you present: do review the material and from where it was sourced.

Furthermore, whatever type of assessment you have to undertake, it is important to take an evaluative approach to the evidence. Whether you are writing an essay, sitting an exam or designing a webpage, the key advice is to avoid simply presenting a descriptive answer. Rather, it is necessary to think about the strength of the evidence in each area. One of the key skills for psychology students is critical thinking and for this reason the tasks featured in this series focus upon developing this way of thinking. Thus you are not expected to simply learn a set of facts and figures, but to think about the implications of what we know and how this might be applied in everyday life. The best assessment answers are the ones that take this critical approach.

It is also important to note that psychology is a theoretical subject: when answering any question about psychology, do not only refer to the prevailing theories of the field, but outline the development of them as well. It is also important to evaluate these theories and models either through comparison with other models and theories or through the use of studies that have assessed them and highlighted their strengths and weaknesses. It is essential to read widely – within each section of this book there are directions to interesting and pertinent papers relating to the specific topic area. Find these papers, read these papers and make notes from these papers. But don't stop there. Let them lead you to other sources that may be important to the field. One thing that an examiner hates to see is the same old sources being cited all of the time: be innovative and, as well as reading the seminal works, find the more obscure and interesting sources as well – just make sure they're relevant to your answer!

How not to revise

- **Don't avoid revision.** This is the best tip ever. There is something on the TV, the pub is having a two-for-one offer, the fridge needs cleaning, your budgie looks lonely . . . You have all of these activities to do and they need doing now! Really . . . ? Do some revision!
- **Don't spend too long at each revision session.** Working all day and night is not the answer to revision. You do need to take breaks, so schedule your revision so you are not working from dawn until dusk. A break gives time for the information you have been revising to consolidate.
- **Don't worry.** Worrying will cause you to lose sleep, lose concentration and lose revision time by leaving it late and then later. When the exam comes, you will have no revision completed and will be tired and confused.
- **Don't cram.** This is the worst revision technique in the universe! You will not remember the majority of the information that you try to stuff into your skull, so why bother?
- **Don't read over old notes with no plan.** Your brain will take nothing in. If you wrote your lecture notes in September and the exam is in May, is there any point in trying to decipher your scrawly handwriting now?
- **Don't write model answers and learn by rote.** When it comes to the exam you will simply regurgitate the model answer irrespective of the question – not a brilliant way to impress the examiner!

Tips for exam success

What you should do when it comes to revision

Exams are one form of assessment that students often worry about the most. The key to exam success, as with many other types of assessment, lies in good preparation and self-organisation. One of the most important things is knowing what to expect – this does not necessarily mean knowing what the questions will be on the exam paper, but rather what the structure of the paper is, how many questions you are expected to answer, how long the exam will last and so on.

To pass an exam you need a good grasp of the course material and, obvious as it may seem, to turn up for the exam itself. It is important to remember that you aren't expected to know or remember everything in the course, but you should be able to show your understanding of what you have studied. Remember as well that examiners are interested in what you know, not what you don't know. They try to write exam questions that give you a good chance of passing – not ones to catch you out or trick you in any way. You may want to consider some of these top exam tips.

- Start your revision in plenty of time.
- Make a revision timetable and stick to it.
- Practise jotting down answers and making essay plans.
- Practise writing against the clock using past exam papers.
- Check that you have really answered the question and have not strayed off the point.
- Review a recent past paper and check the marking structure.
- Carefully select the topics you are going to revise.
- Use your lecture/study notes and refine them further, if possible, into lists or diagrams and transfer them on to index cards/Post-it notes. Mind maps are a good way of making links between topics and ideas.
- Practise your handwriting – make sure it's neat and legible.

One to two days before the exam
- Recheck times, dates and venue.
- Actively review your notes and key facts.
- Exercise, eat sensibly and get a few good nights' sleep.

On the day
- Get a good night's sleep.
- Have a good meal, two to three hours before the start time.
- Arrive in good time.
- Spend a few minutes calming and focusing.

In the exam room
- Keep calm.
- Take a few minutes to read each question carefully. Don't jump to conclusions – think calmly about what each question means and the area it is focused on.
- Start with the question you feel most confident about. This helps your morale.
- By the same token, don't expend all your efforts on that one question – if you are expected to answer three questions then don't just answer two.
- Keep to time and spread your effort evenly on all opportunities to score marks.
- Once you have chosen a question, jot down any salient facts or key points. Then take five minutes to plan your answer – a spider diagram or a few notes may be enough to focus your ideas. Try to think in terms of 'why and how' not just 'facts'.

- You might find it useful to create a visual plan or map before writing your answer to help you remember to cover everything you need to address.
- Keep reminding yourself of the question and try not to wander off the point.
- Remember that quality of argument is more important than quantity of facts.
- Take 30–60-second breaks whenever you find your focus slipping (typically every 20 minutes).
- Make sure you reference properly – according to your university requirements.
- Watch your spelling and grammar – you could lose marks if you make too many errors.

→ *Final revision checklist*

❏ Have you revised the topics highlighted in the revision checklists?
❏ Have you attended revision classes and taken note of and/or followed up on your lecturers' advice about the exams or assessment process at your university?
❏ Can you answer the questions posed in this text satisfactorily? Don't forget to check sample answers on the website too.
❏ Have you read the additional material to make your answer stand out?
❏ Remember to criticise appropriately – based on evidence.

Test your knowledge by using the material presented in this text or on the companion website: **www.pearsoned.co.uk/psychologyexpress**

Glossary

addiction Seeking out activities that are pleasurable even though they are bad for health or social life.

aetiology (etiology) The cause of disease.

affective To do with affect or mood and emotions.

angina Severe pain in the chest associated with a temporary insufficient supply of blood to the heart.

antibodies Immunoglobulins produced in response to an antigen.

antigen Unique protein found on the surface of a pathogen that enables the immune system to recognise that pathogen as a foreign substance and therefore produce antibodies to fight it. Vaccinations introduce specially prepared viruses into a body, and these have antigens.

antioxidant Oxidation of low-density lipoprotein (LDL or 'bad') cholesterol has been shown to be important in the development of fatty deposits in the arteries; antioxidants are chemical properties (polyphenols) of some substances (e.g. red wine) thought to inhibit the process of oxidation.

appetite regulation From a biological point of view, there is evidence of the 'ob gene'. This gene produces leptin, which is responsible for telling us when we are full.

appraisals Interpretations of situations, events or behaviour that a person makes.

attributions A person's perceptions of what causes beliefs, feelings, behaviour and actions (based on attribution theory).

autoimmune condition A group of diseases, including type 1 diabetes, Crohn's disease and rheumatoid arthritis, characterised by abnormal functioning of the immune system in which it produces antibodies against its own tissues – it treats 'self' as 'non-self'.

avoidant coping A style of coping that involves emotional regulation by avoiding confrontation with a stressful situation. It is analogous to emotion-focused coping.

bariatric surgery There are several different surgical options available; however, the most common are the gastric band (which works by making the stomach smaller) and the Roux-en-Y gastric bypass (which both reduces the size of the stomach and the ability to absorb food).

behaviour change techniques (BCT) Described as something that aims to change behaviour and is proposed to be an 'active ingredient' of interventions.

behavioural pathogen A behavioural practice thought to be damaging to health (e.g. smoking).

behaviourism The belief that psychology is the study of observables and therefore that behaviour, not mental processes, is central.

bile A digestive juice, made in the liver and stored in the gallbladder. It is involved in the digestion of fats in the small intestine.

biological rhythm The daily rhythm that functions our wake–sleep cycle.

biomedical model A view that diseases and symptoms have an underlying physiological explanation.

biopsy The removal of a small piece of tissue for microscopic examination and/or culture, usually to help to make a diagnosis.

bio-psycho-social A view that diseases and symptoms can be explained by a combination of physical, social, cultural and psychological factors (cf. Engel 1977).

body mass index A measurement of the relative percentages of fat and muscle mass in the human body, in which weight in kilograms is divided by height in metres (squared) and the result used as an index of weight (underweight, healthy weight, overweight, obese).

bronchitis An inflammation of the bronchi, the main air passages in the lungs, which persists for a long period or repeatedly recurs.

carcinogenesis The process by which normal cells become cancer cells (i.e. carcinoma).

cardiovascular Pertaining to the heart and blood vessels.

causal attribution Where a person attributes the cause of an event, feeling or action to themselves, to others, to chance or to some other causal agent.

CD4+ cells Otherwise known as helper T cells, these are involved in the proliferation of cytotoxic T cells as part of the immune response. HIV infection impairs their ability to provide this function.

central nervous system That part of the nervous system consisting of the brain and spinal cord.

cervical smear Smear of cells taken from the cervix to examine for the presence of cell changes indicating risk of cervical cancer.

classical conditioning Attributed to Pavlov, the thought that behaviours are learned through conditioning responses to stimulus.

COM-B Model of behavior which suggests that for any behaviour to occur, the individual must have three fundamental things: (1) capability – the physical and psychological capability to enact the behaviour; (2) opportunity – the physical and social opportunity for the behaviour; and (3) motivation – be motivated to engage in/refrain from the behaviour over and above competing sources (cf. Michie, van Stralen, & West, 2011).

condition Experimental studies often involve allocating participants to different conditions: for example, information versus no information, relaxation versus no relaxation, active drug versus placebo.

CONSORT (CONsolidated Standards of Reporting Trials) guidelines.

coping effectiveness training A specialist form of stress management in which participants are taught to alter the nature of their coping efforts to suit the particular type of demands they are facing, using emotion-focused coping where the situation cannot be changed and problem-focused coping where it can.

coping self-efficacy The belief that one can carry out a particular coping response in a given set of circumstances.

coronary heart disease A narrowing of the blood vessels that supply blood and oxygen to the heart. It results from a build-up of fatty material and plaque (atherosclerosis), and can result in angina or myocardial infarction.

cortisol A stress hormone that increases the availability of energy stores and fats to fuel periods of high physiological activity. It also inhibits inflammation of damaged tissue.

Crohn's disease Autoimmune disease that can affect any part of the gastrointestinal tract but most commonly occurs in the ileum (the area where the small and large intestine meet).

cross-sectional design A study is described as being cross-sectional if the different variables are measured at the same time as each other on one occasion only.

decisional balance Where the costs of behaviour are weighed up against the benefits of that behaviour.

denial response Taking a view that denies any negative implications of an event or stimulus. If subconscious, it is considered a defence mechanism.

dependence When the body needs (craves) a substance to bring it back to its 'normal' state, avoiding an unpleasant state.

dependent variable The characteristic that appears to change as a result of the independent variable: for example, changing eating behaviour (the independent variable) causes a change in weight (the dependent variable).

diabetes (type 1 and 2) A lifelong disease marked by high levels of sugar in the blood and a failure to transfer this to organs that need it. It can be caused by too little insulin (type 1), resistance to insulin (type 2), or both.

downstream approach Biomedical models of health have been referred to as a 'downstream' approach, where medical intervention pulls drowning individuals from the river's current.

dramatic relief Relating to the experience of negative emotions evoked by the health risks of the unhealthy behaviour.

drug abuse Involves use of a drug that results in significant social or work-related problems.

drug dependence Usually a progression from drug abuse. Involves dependence on the drug to achieve a desired psychological state, withdrawal symptoms in the absence of the drug, and social and work-related problems.

dual process model Fear-arousing messages point to two sets of cognitive processing: danger and fear control (cf. Leventhal, 1984).

dualism The idea that the mind and body are separate entities (cf. Descartes).

efficacy Bandura's technical term analogous to confidence.

egocentric Self-centred, such as in the pre-operational stage (age 2–7) of children, when they see things only from their own perspective (cf. Piaget).

elaboration likelihood model Suggests that persuasive communication will work only if people are interested in the message, it is relevant to them and they can cognitively process it.

emotional expression The disclosure of emotional experiences as a means of reducing stress; often achieved by describing the experience in writing.

endocrine glands Glands that produce and secrete hormones into the blood or lymph systems. They include the pituitary and adrenal glands, and the islets of Langerhans in the pancreas. These hormones may affect one organ or tissue, or the entire body.

endorphins Naturally occurring opiate-like chemicals released in the brain and spinal cord. They reduce the experience of pain and can induce feelings of relaxation or pleasure. They are associated with the so-called 'runner's high'.

environmental re-evaluation Realising the negative impact of an old behaviour or the positive impact of a behaviour change on the individual's social and physical environment.

epidemiology The study of patterns of disease in various populations and the association with other factors, such as lifestyle factors. Key concepts include mortality, morbidity, prevalence, incidence, absolute risk and relative risk. Type of question: Who gets this disease? How common is it?

exercise programme A key element of most cardiac rehabilitation, including a progressive increase in physical activity usually starting in a gym, sometimes developing into exercise in the home and beyond.

experimental design This involves a controlled study in which variables are manipulated in order specifically to examine the relationship between the independent variable (the cause) and the dependent variable (the effect).

exposure therapy A form of therapy involving exposure to traumatic memories, based on the theoretical assumption that continued exposure will result in a gradual reduction in the level of fear associated with such memories.

general adaptation syndrome A sequence of physiological responses to prolonged stress, from the alarm stage through the resistance stage to exhaustion.

health action process approach (HAPA) A theoretical model which suggests that the adoption, initiation and maintenance of behaviour is conceptualised through two stages: a motivation phase and a volition (action) phase (cf. Schwarzer, 1992).

health behaviour Behaviour performed by an individual, regardless of their health status, as a means of protecting, promoting or maintaining health (e.g. exercise).

health belief model (HBM) First proposed by Rosenstock (1966) and further developed by Becker, Haefner and Maiman (1977), the HBM suggests that behaviour is a result of a set of core beliefs which are the individual's perceptions of their susceptibility, severity, costs vs. benefits, cues to action and health motivation.

health differential A term used to denote differences in health status and life expectancy across different groups.

health locus of control The perception that one's health is: under personal control; controlled by powerful others such as health professionals; or under the control of external factors such as fate or luck.

health value Reports the extent to which an individual places a high value on their health.

heart failure A state in which the heart muscle is damaged or weakened and is unable to generate a cardiac output sufficient to meet the demands of the body.

holistic Root word 'wholeness', holistic approaches are concerned with the whole being and its wellbeing, rather than addressing the purely physical or observable.

human papillomavirus (HPV) A family of over 100 viruses, of which 30 types can cause genital warts and be transmitted by sexual contact. Some HPV infections may markedly elevate the risk for cancer of the cervix.

humoural theory A theory which suggests that when someone becomes ill it is due to an imbalance of flour fluids (blood, black bile, yellow bile and phlegm) (cf. Hippocrates).

hypertension A condition in which blood pressure is significantly above normal levels.

hypothalamus Area of the brain that regulates appetite, sexual arousal and thirst. It also appears to have some control over emotions.

illness behaviour Behaviour that characterises a person who is sick and who seeks a remedy (e.g. taking medication). It usually precedes formal diagnosis, when behaviour is described as sick role behaviour.

illness cognition The cognitive processes involved in a person's perception or interpretation of symptoms or illness and how they represent it to themselves (or to others).

illness representations Beliefs about a particular illness and state of ill health – commonly ascribed to the five domains described by Leventhal: identity, timeline, cause, consequences and control/cure.

implementation–intentions A goal-setting theory based on the form of 'if–then' planning, relating to the anticipated situation and the response (cf. Gollwitzer & Sheeran, 2006).

incidence The number of new cases of disease occurring during a defined time.

independent variable The characteristic that appears to cause a change in the dependent variable: for example, smoking (the independent variable) causes lung cancer (the dependent variable).

individual differences Aspects of an individual that distinguish them from other individuals or groups (e.g. age, personality).

individualistic A cultural philosophy that places responsibility at the feet of the individual; thus behaviour is often driven by individual needs and wants rather than by community needs or wants.

inflammatory bowel disease A group of inflammatory conditions of the large intestine and, in some cases, the small intestine. The main forms of IBD are Crohn's disease and ulcerative colitis.

intention A conscious decision reflecting a person's motivation to exert effort into the performance or avoidance of behaviour.

interval The amount of time between two specified events, points or states.

intervention mapping Provides a protocol for considerations that may improve the development and evaluations of interventions.

irritable bowel syndrome A disorder of the lower intestinal tract. Symptoms include pain combined with altered bowel habits, resulting in diarrhoea, constipation or both. It has no obvious physiological abnormalities, so diagnosis is by the presence and pattern of symptoms.

life events A term used to describe occurrences in a person's life which may be viewed positively or negatively but which inherently require some adjustment on the part of the person (e.g. marriage, loss of job). Such events are implicated in the experience of stress.

locus of control A personality trait thought to distinguish between those who attribute responsibility for events to themselves (i.e. internal LoC) or to external factors (external LoC).

longitudinal (design) Responses assessed in a study that have been taken on more than one occasion over time, either prospectively (future-oriented) or retrospectively (based on recall of past events). Prospective longitudinal studies are more powerful, and such methods are important to studies where assessment of change is important.

lymphocyte A type of white blood cell. Lymphocytes have a number of roles in the immune system, including the production of antibodies and other substances that fight infection and disease. Includes T and B cells.

mammography A low-dose X-ray procedure that creates an image of the breast. The X-ray image can be used to identify early stages of tumours.

mediate/mediator Some variables may mediate the effects of others upon an outcome: for example, individual beliefs may mediate the effects of gender upon behaviour, thus gender effects would be said to be indirect, rather than direct, and beliefs would be mediator variables.

message framing The way in which we communicate health relevant messages can influence uptake of health behaviours. Messages can be framed in terms of either their losses or their gains.

meta-analysis A review and re-analysis of pre-existing quantitative datasets that combines the analysis so as to provide large samples and high statistical power from which to draw reliable conclusions about specific effects.

monism The concept that the mind and the body are part of the same system or unit and can interact and work together.

morbidity Costs associated with illness, such as disability and injury.

mortality Death. It is generally presented as mortality statistics, i.e. the number of deaths in a given population and/or in a given year ascribed to a given condition (e.g. number of cancer deaths among women in 2000).

motivation Memories, thoughts, experiences, needs and preferences that act together to influence (drive) the type, strength and persistence of our actions.

motivational interviewing Developed by Miller and Rollnick, a set of procedures designed to increase motivation to change behaviour by resolving ambivalence (feeling two ways about something).

multiple regression A statistical test that can tell us how much of the variance in the outcome variable (i.e. dependent variable) can be explained by the predictor variable (i.e. the independent variable).

multiple sclerosis A disorder of the brain and spinal cord caused by progressive damage to the myelin sheath covering of nerve cells. This results in decreased nerve functioning, which can lead to a variety of symptoms, including weakness, paralysis, tremor, pain, tingling, numbness and decreased coordination.

myocardial infarction Death of the heart muscle due to a stoppage of the blood supply. It is more often known as a heart attack.

natural killer (NK) cells Cells move in the blood and attack cancer cells and virus-infected body cells.

negative affectivity A dispositional tendency to experience persistent and pervasive negative or low mood and self-concept (related to neuroticism).

neophobia A persistent and chronic fear of anything new (such as food).

neurotransmitter A chemical messenger (e.g. adrenaline, acetylcholine) used to communicate between neurons and other neurons and other types of cell.

nicotine replacement therapy (NRT) Replacement of nicotine to minimise withdrawal symptoms following the cessation of smoking. It is delivered in a variety of ways, including a transdermal patch placed against the skin, which produces a measured dose of nicotine over time.

noradrenaline This catecholamine is a neurotransmitter found in the brain and in the sympathetic nervous system. It is also known as norepinephrine.

objective Real, visible or systematically measurable (e.g. adrenaline levels). The term generally pertains to something outside the body that can be seen by others (as opposed to subjective).

observational learning Modelling behaviour of significant others (e.g. parents or friends); behaviour commonly associated with the Bandura Bobo doll studies.

operant conditioning Attributed to Skinner, this theory is based on the assumption that behaviour is directly influenced by its consequences (e.g. rewards, punishments, avoidance of negative outcomes).

optimistic bias An egocentric, selective and irrational perception thought to be contributed by lack of personal experience of the problem, belief that the problem is preventable, belief that the problem has not yet appeared and will not appear, and belief that the problem is infrequent.

outcome expectancies The outcome that is expected to result from behaviour (e.g. exercise will make me fitter).

parasympathetic nervous system Arm of the autonomic nervous system that is responsible for rest and recuperation.

participants These are the individuals who are involved in the study. They may also be referred to as subjects, clients, respondents or cases.

pathogen A collective name for a variety of challenges to our health and immune system, including bacteria and viruses.

perceived behavioural control One's belief in personal control over a certain specific action or behaviour.

phagocyte An immune system cell that can surround and kill micro-organisms and remove dead cells. Phagocytes include macrophages.

placebo An intervention designed to simulate a real intervention (i.e. a pill that does not contain any active ingredients to treat a specific condition).

PRECEDE/PROCEED This model has nine stages to support intervention design. The first five cover diagnosis: (1) social assessment; (2) epidemiological assessment; (3) behavioural and environmental assessment; (4) educational and organisational assessment; (5) operational and policy-making assessment. The last four cover implementation and evaluation: (6) implementation; (7) process evaluation; (8) impact evaluation; and (9) results/outcome evaluation (cf. Green & Kreuter, 1999).

predisposing factors Factors that increase the likelihood of a person engaging in a particular behaviour, such as genetic influences on alcohol consumption.

premature mortality Death before the age it is normally expected; usually set at deaths under the age of 75.

prevalence The number of established cases of a disease in a population at any one time. It is often described as a percentage of the overall population or cases per 100,000 people.

primary prevention Intervention aimed at changing risk factors prior to disease development.

problem-focused coping A style of coping that involves active planning and dealing with any source of stress.

prognosis The predicted outcome of a disease.

prospective design This involves following up subjects over a period of time (sometimes called longitudinal or cohort design).

protection motivation theory (PMT) Focuses on two cognitive factors: threat appraisal and coping appraisal, often used to explain how fear-arousing communications are processed and acted upon.

prototype willingness model (PWM) A concept that focuses on perceived image. It has been applied successfully to the study of the decision making and initiation of health risk behaviour in young people, focusing on the image they have of the type of person who engages in a health behaviour (cf. Gibbons & Gerrard, 1995).

psychoneuroimmunology (PNI) The study of the interaction between psychological processes and the nervous and immune systems of the human body.

psycho-social An approach that seeks to merge a psychological (more micro- and individually oriented) approach with a social (macro-, more community and interaction-oriented) approach, for example to health.

qualitative study This involves methodologies such as interviews in order to collect data from subjects. Qualitative data are a way of describing the variety of beliefs, interpretations and behaviours from a heterogeneous group without making generalisations to the population as a whole. It is believed that qualitative studies are more able to access the participants' beliefs without contaminating the data with the researcher's own expectations. Qualitative data are non-numerical and are often described in terms of themes and categories.

quantitative study This involves collecting data in the form of numbers using methodologies such as questionnaires and experiments. Quantitative data are a way of describing the beliefs, interpretations and behaviours of a large population and generalisations are made about the population as a whole. Quantitative data are described in terms of frequencies, means and statistically significant differences and correlations.

randomly allocated Participants are randomly allocated to different conditions in order to minimise the effects of any individual differences: for example, to ensure that subjects who receive the drug versus the placebo versus nothing are equivalent in age and gender. If all the participants who received the placebo happened to be female, this would obviously influence the results.

reinforcement management Rewarding positive behaviour change and reducing any reward for the unwanted behaviour.

reinforcers Factors that reward or provide a positive response following a particular behaviour or set of behaviours (positive reinforcers); or enable the removal or avoidance of an undesired state or response (negative reinforcers).

relapse prevention A set of skills taught to people needing to achieve long-term behavioural change that prepare them to resist temptation and to minimise the impact of any relapse should it occur. It is often used with people using addictive substances.

repeated-measures design This involves asking subjects to complete the same set of measures more than once: for example, before and after reading a health information leaflet.

rheumatoid arthritis A chronic autoimmune disease with inflammation of the joints and marked deformities. Something (possibly a virus) triggers an attack of the synovium in the joint by the immune system, which stimulates an inflammatory reaction that can lead to destruction of the joint.

self-attribution If a lapse is blamed on self, it increases feelings of guilt and shame and thus lowers self-efficacy. However, if a lapse is blamed on the external world (such as the situation), guilt and shame are reduced, control is maintained and relapse is less likely.

self-concept Those conscious thoughts and beliefs about yourself that allow you to feel are distinct from others and that you exist as a separate person.

self-efficacy The belief that one can perform a particular action in a given set of circumstances.

self-liberation Making a firm commitment to change.

self-re-evaluation A realisation that behaviour change is important to self-identity.

self-regulation The process by which individuals monitor and adjust their behaviour, thoughts and emotions in order to maintain a balance or a sense of normal function.

self-talk Talking to oneself (internally). This can be negative and add to stress. Therapeutically, individuals are taught to use self-talk in a way that helps them to keep calm.

social cognition A model of social knowledge and behaviour that highlights the explanatory role of cognitive factors (e.g. beliefs and attitudes).

social cognitive theory (SCT) Assumes that human motivation and action are based on three types of expectancy: situation–outcome, action–outcome and perceived self-efficacy (cf. Bandura).

social comparison The process by which a person or group of people compare themselves (their behaviour or characteristics) with others.

social desirability bias The tendency to answer questions about oneself or one's behaviour in a way that is thought likely to meet with social (or interviewer) approval.

social identity A person's sense of who they are in a group, rather than at a personal, individual level (e.g. you are a student, you are a female/male).

social learning theory A theory that has at its core the belief that a combination of outcome expectancy and outcome value will shape subsequent behaviour. Reinforcement is an important predictor of future behaviour.

socio economic status A measure of the social class of an individual. Different measures use different indicators, including income, job type or years of education. Higher status implies a higher salary or higher job status.

stages of change model See TTM.

stem cell A 'generic' cell that can make exact copies of itself indefinitely. In addition, such cells have the ability to produce specialised cells for various tissues in the body, including blood, heart muscle, brain and liver tissue. Stem cells are found in the bone marrow.

stem cell transplant Procedure in which stem cells are replaced within the bone marrow following radiotherapy or chemotherapy, or diseases such as leukaemia, where they may be damaged.

stimulus control Removing cues to the unhealthy behaviour, and adding reminders to support behaviour change.

stress management training A generic term for interventions designed to teach participants how to cope with stress.

stress reactivity The physiological arousal, such as increased heart rate or blood pressure, experienced during a potentially stressful encounter.

stroke Damage to the brain as a result of a bleed into the brain tissue or a blockage in an artery, which prevents oxygen and other nutrients reaching parts of the brain. It is more scientifically known as a cerebro-vascular accident (CVA).

subjective Personal, i.e. what a person thinks and reports (e.g. excitement) as opposed to what is objective. Subjective is generally related to internal interpretations of events rather than observable features.

subjective norm A person's beliefs regarding whether important others (i.e. parents) would think that they should or should not carry out a particular action. It is an index of social pressure, weighted generally by the individual's motivation to comply with the wishes of others (see theory of planned behaviour).

sympathetic nervous system The part of the autonomic nervous system involved in mobilising energy to activate and maintain arousal (e.g. increased heart rate).

taxonomy The practice and science (study) of classification of things or concepts, including the principles that underlie such classification.

T cell A cell that recognises antigens on the surface of a virus-infected cell, binds to that cell and destroys it.

theory A general belief or beliefs about some aspect of the world we live in or those in it, which may or may not be supported by evidence (e.g. women are worse drivers than men).

theory of planned behaviour (TPB) An extension of the theory of reasoned action, incorporating the inclusion of perceived behavioural control.

theory of reasoned action (TRA) Importance of social cognitions through attitudes and subjective norms.

tolerance Defined by either of the following: (1) a need for markedly increased amounts of the substance to achieve intoxication or the desired effect; (2) markedly diminished effect with continued use of the same amount of the substance.

transdermal patch A method of delivering a drug in a slow release form. The drug is impregnated into a patch, which is stuck to the skin and gradually absorbed into the body.

transtheoretical model of change (TTM) A stage theory which suggests that a person could be in one of five stages (pre-contemplation, contemplation, preparation, action and maintenance) with the option of relapse between these stages (cf. Prochaska & DiClemente, 1983).

type 1 diabetes See diabetes.

type 2 diabetes See diabetes.

unrealistic optimism Also known as 'optimistic bias', whereby a person considers themselves as being less likely than comparable others to develop an illness or experience a negative event.

upstream approach Health promotion is viewed as an 'upstream' approach when intervening early to reduce the risk of people 'falling into dangerous rivers'.

variable A characteristic that can be measured (e.g. age, beliefs, fitness).

vicarious learning Learning from the observation of others.

volition Action or doing (the post-intentional stage highlighted in the HAPA model of health behaviour change).

withdrawal A negative physical effect, often from substance use, manifested by either of the following: (1) the characteristic withdrawal syndrome for the substance; (2) the same (or a closely related) substance is taken to relieve or avoid withdrawal symptoms.

within-subjects design This involves making comparisons within the same group of participants.

written emotional expression A writing technique in which participants write about upsetting incidents either in their past or related to specific issues.

References

AA General Service Office (1952). *Twelve steps and twelve traditions.* New York: BPCC Hazell Books.

Abraham, C., & Michie, S. (2008). A taxonomy of behavior change techniques used in interventions. *Health Psychology, 27*(3), 379–387.

Abraham, C., & Sheeran, P. (2005). Health belief model. In M. Conner & P. Norman (Eds.), *Predicting health behaviour: Research and practice with social cognition models* (2nd ed.). Buckingham: Open University Press.

Abraham, C., Conner, M., Jones, F., & O'Connor, D. (2008). *Health psychology: Topics in applied psychology.* London: Hodder Education.

Abraham, C., Sheeran, P., Norman, P., Conner, M., Vries, N., & Otten, W. (1999). When good intentions are not enough: Modeling postdecisional cognitive correlates of condom use. *Journal of Applied Social Psychology, 29*(12), 2591–2612.

Abraham, S. C. S., Sheeran, O., Abrams, D., & Spears, R. (1996). Health beliefs and teenage condom use: A prospective study. *Psychology and Health, 11,* 641–655.

Academy of Medical Royal Colleges (2013). *Measuring up: The medical profession's prescription for the nation's obesity crisis.* London: AMRC.

Ackerman, K. D., Heyman, R., & Rabin, B. S. (2002). Stressful life events precede exacerbations of multiple sclerosis. *Psychosomatic Medicine, 64,* 916–920.

Action on Smoking and Health (ASH) (2012). *Smoking and disease: Facts at a glance.* London: ASH.

Adams, M., Jasani, B., & Fiander, A. (2007). Human papilloma virus (HPV) prophylactic vaccination: Challenges for public health and implications for screening. *Vaccine, 25*(16), 3007–3013.

Ader, R. (2000). On the development of psychoneuroimmunology. *European Journal of Pharmacology, 405,* 167–176.

Ader, R., & Cohen, N. (1975). Behaviourally conditioned immunosuppression. *Psychosomatic Medicine, 37*(4), 333–340.

Ajzen, I. (1985). From intentions to action: A theory of planned behaviour. In J. Kuhl & J. Beckham (Eds.), *Action control: From cognitions to behaviors* (pp. 11–39). New York: Springer.

Albery, I. P., & Munafò, M. (2008). *Key concepts in health psychology.* London: Sage Publications.

Ali, N., Atkin, K., & Neal, R. (2006). The role of culture in the general practice consultation process. *Ethnicity and Health, 11*(4), 389–408.

Allender, S., Cowburn, G., & Foster, C. (2006). Understanding participation in sport and physical activity among children and adults: A review of qualitative studies. *Health Education Research, 21*(6), 826–835.

Allender, S., Peto, V., Scarborough, P., Boxer, A., & Rayner, M. (2006). *Coronary heart disease statistics.* London: British Heart Foundation.

Alwyn, T., John, B., Hodgson, R. J., & Phillips, C. J. (2004). The addition of a psychological intervention to a home detoxification programme. *Alcohol and Alcoholism, 39*(6), 536–541.

American Psychiatric Association (1994). *Diagnostic and statistical manual of mental disorders* (4th ed.). Washington, DC: APA.

Anagnostopoulos, F., Buchanan, H., Frousiounioti, S., Niakas, D., & Potamianos, G. (2011). Self-efficacy and oral hygiene beliefs about toothbrushing in dental patients: A model-guided study. *Behavioral Medicine, 37*(4), 132–139.

References

Andelman, R. D., Greene, M. G., & Ory, M. G. (2000). Communication between older patients and their physicians. *Clinics in Geriatric Medicine*, *16*(1), 1–24.

Andelman, R. D., Greene, M. G., Charon, R., & Friedmann, E. (1992). The content of physician and elderly patient interaction in the medical primary care encounter. *Communication Research*, *19*, 370–380.

Antoni, M. H., Cruess, S., & Cruess, D. G. (2000). Cognitive-behavioral stress management reduces distress and 24-hour urinary free cortisol output among symptomatic HIV-infected gay men. *Annals of Behaviour Medicine*, *22*, 29–37.

Arden, M. A., & Armitage, C. J. (2008). Predicting and explaining transtheoretical model stage transitions in relation to condom-carrying behaviour. *British Journal of Health Psychology*, *13*(4), 719–735.

Armitage, C. J. (2009). Is there utility in the transtheoretical model? *British Journal of Health Psychology*, *14*(2), 195–210.

Armitage, C. J., & Arden, M. A. (2010). A volitional help sheet to increase physical activity in people with low socioeconomic status: A randomised exploratory trial. *Psychology and Health*, *25*(10), 1129–1145.

Armitage, C. J., & Conner, M. (2001). Efficacy of the theory of planned behaviour: A meta-analytic review. *British Journal of Social Psychology*, *40*, 471–499.

Armstrong, D. (2012). Screening: Mapping medicine's temporal spaces. *Sociology of Health and Illness*, *34*(2), 177–193.

Armstrong, K., Berlin, M., Schwartz, J., Propert, K., & Ubel, P. A. (2001). Barriers to influenza immunization in a low-income urban population. *American Journal of Preventive Medicine*, *20*(1), 21–25.

Arnow, B., Kenardy, J., & Agras, W. S. (1995). The Emotional Eating Scale: The development of a measure to assess coping with negative affect by eating. *International Journal of Eating Disorders*, *18*, 79–90.

Atkins, L., & Michie, S. (2013). Changing eating behaviour: What can we learn from behavioural science? *Nutrition Bulletin*, *38*(1), 30–35.

Aunger, R. (2007). Tooth brushing as routine behaviour. *International Dental Journal*, *57*(S5), 364–376.

Austoker, J. (1994). Screening for ovarian, prostate and testicular cancers. *British Medical Journal*, *309*, 315–320.

Avenell, A., Sattar, N., & Lean, M. (2006). Management: Part 1 – Behaviour change, diet and activity. *British Medical Journal*, *333*, 740–743.

Avenevoli, S., & Merikangas, K. R. (2003). Familial influences on adolescent smoking. *Addiction*, *98*, 1–20.

Bagnardi, V., Blangiardo, M., La Vecchia, C., & Corrao, G. (2001). Alcohol consumption and the risk of cancer. *Alcohol, Research and Health*, *25*, 263–270.

Bagozzi, R. P., & Edwards, E. A. (2000). Goal-striving and the implementation of goal intentions in the regulation of body weight. *Psychology and Health*, *15*, 255–270.

Bailey, S. J., & Covell, K. (2011). Pathways among abuse, daily hassles, depression and substance use in adolescents. *New School Psychology Bulletin*, *8*(2), 4–14.

Bandura, A. (1977a). Self-efficacy: Toward a unifying theory of behavioural change. *Psychological Review*, *28*(2), 191–215.

Bandura, A. (1977b). *Social learning theory*. Englewood Cliffs, NJ: Prentice Hall.

Bandura, A. (1982). Self-efficacy mechanism in human agency. *American Psychologist*, *37*, 122–147.

Bandura, A. (1986). *Social foundations of thought and action: A social cognitive theory*. Englewood Cliffs, NJ: Prentice Hall.

Bandura, A. (1992). Self-efficacy mechanism in psychobiologic functioning. In R. Schwarzer (Ed.), *Self-efficacy: Thought control of action*. Washington, DC: Hemisphere.

Barrows, K. A., & Jacobs, B. P. (2002). Mind–body medicine: An introduction and review of the literature. *Medical Clinics of North America*, *86*(1), 11–31.

Bartholomew, L. K., Parcel, G. S., Kok, G., Gottlieb, N. H., & Fernandez, M. E. (2011). *Planning health promotion programs: An intervention mapping approach* (3rd ed.). San Francisco: Jossey-Bass.

Bartzokas, C. A., Williams, E. E., & Slade, P. D. (1995). *A psychological approach to hospital-acquired infections: Studies in health and human sciences.* London: Edward Mellen.

Bastien, J. W. (1989). Differences between Kallawaya-Andean and Greek-European humoral theory. *Social Science and Medicine, 28*(1), 45–51.

Baughcum, A. E., Powers, S. W., Johnson, S. B., Chamberlin, L. A., Deeks, C. M., Jain, A., & Whitaker, R. C. (2001). Maternal feeding practices and beliefs and their relationships to overweight in early childhood. *Journal of Developmental and Behavioral Pediatrics, 22*(6), 391–408.

Baxter, N. (2001). Preventive health care, 2001 update: Should women be routinely taught breast self-examination to screen for breast cancer? *Canadian Medical Association Journal, 164*(13), 1837–1846.

Becker, M. H. (1974). The health belief model and personal health behaviour. *Health Education Monographs, 2*, 324–508.

Becker, M. H., & Maiman, L. A. (1975). Sociobehavioral determinants of compliance with health and medical care recommendations. *Medical Care, 13*(1), 10–24.

Becker, M. H., & Rosenstock, I. M. (1984). Compliance with medical advice. In A. Steptoe & A. Matthews (Eds.), *Health care and human behavior* (pp. 135–152). London: Academic Press.

Becker, M. H., Haefner, D. P., & Maiman, L. A. (1977). The health belief model in the prediction of dietary compliance: A field experiment. *Journal of Health and Social Behavior, 18*, 348–366.

Begg, D. J., & Langley, J. D. (2000). Seat-belt use and related behaviours among young adults. *Journal of Safety Research, 31*(4), 211–220.

Bellaby, P. (2003). Communication and miscommunication of risk: Understanding UK parents' attitudes to combined MMR vaccination. *British Medical Journal, 327*, 725–728.

Belloc, N. B., & Breslow, L. (1972). Relationship of physical health status and health practices. *Preventive Medicine, 1*, 409–421.

Ben-Sira, Z. (1976). The function of the professionals, affective behavior in client satisfaction: A revised approach to social interaction theory. *Journal of Health and Social Behavior, 17*, 3–11.

Bennett, P., & Bozionelos, G. (2000). The theory of planned behaviour as predictor of condom use: A narrative review. *Psychology, Health and Medicine, 5*(3), 307–326.

Bennett, P., & Murphy, S. (1997). *Psychology and health promotion.* Buckingham: Open University Press.

Bennett, P., Moore, L., Smith, A., Murphy, S., & Smith, S. (1994). Health locus of control and value of health as predictors of dietary behaviour. *Psychology and Health, 10*, 41–54.

Bennett, P., Norman, P., Murphy, S., Moore, L., & Tudor-Smith, C. (1998). Beliefs about alcohol, health locus of control, value for health and reported consumption in a representative population sample. *Health Education Research, 13*, 25–32.

Bensing, J. M., Deveugele, M., Moretti, F., Fletcher, I., Vliet, L. V., Bogaert, M. V., & Rimondini, M. (2011). How to make the medical consultation more successful from a patient's perspective? Tips for doctors and patients from lay people in the United Kingdom, Italy, Belgium and the Netherlands. *Patient Education and Counselling, 84*(3), 287–293.

Benson, P. G. (2001). The Hawthorne effect. In W. E. Craighead & C. B. Nemeroff (Eds.), *The Corsini encyclopedia of psychology and behavioural science* (pp. 667–668). New York: John Wiley & Sons.

Berghmans, R., de Jong, J., Tibben, A., & de Wert, G. (2009). On the biomedicalization of alcoholism. *Theoretical Medicine and Bioethics, 30*(4), 311–321.

Biddle, S. J., & Ekkekakis, P. (2005). Physically active lifestyles and wellbeing. In F. A. Huppert, N. Baylis, & B. Kaverne (Eds.), *The science of wellbeing.* Oxford: Oxford University Press.

Biddle, S. J., Gorely, T., & Stensel, D. J. (2004). Health-enhancing physical activity and sedentary behaviour in children and adolescents. *Journal of Sports Sciences, 22*(8), 679–701.

Biddle, S. J., Whitehead, S., O'Donovan, T. M., & Nevill, M. E. (2005). Correlates of participation in physical activity for adolescent girls: A systematic review of recent literature. *Journal of Physical Activity and Health, 2*(4), 421–432.

Biddle, S., Cavill, N., & Sallis, J. (1998). Policy framework for young people and health-enhancing physical activity. In S. Biddle, N. Cavill, & J. Sallis (Eds.), *Young and active* (pp. 3–16). London: Health Education Authority.

Birch, L. L., Zimmerman, S. I., & Hind, H. (1980). The influence of social-affective context on the formation of children's food preferences. *Child Development, 51*, 856–861.

Bish, A., Sutton, S., & Golombok, S. (2000). Predicting uptake of a routine cervical smear test: A comparison of the health belief model and the theory of planned behaviour. *Psychology and Health, 15*(1), 35–50.

Bish, A., Yardley, L., Nicoll, A., & Michie, S. (2011). Factors associated with uptake of vaccination against pandemic influenza: A systematic review. *Vaccine, 29*(38), 6472–6484.

Borrelli, B., Sepinwall, D., Ernst, D., Bellg, A. J., Czajkowski, S., Bregel, R., ... Orwig, D. (2005). A new tool to assess treatment fidelity and evaluation of treatment fidelity across 10 years of health behaviour research. *Journal of Consulting and Clinical Psychology, 73*(5), 852–860.

Bosch, F., Lorincz, A., Munoz, N., Meijer, C., & Shah, K. (2002). The causal relation between human papillomavirus and cervical cancer. *Journal of Clinical Pathology, 55*(4), 244–265.

Bosworth, H. (Ed.) (2010). *Improving patient treatment adherence: A clinician's guide.* New York: Springer.

Bosworth, H. B., Oddone, E. Z., & Weinberger, M. (eds.). (2006). *Patient treatment adherence: Concepts, interventions, and measurement.* Hillsdale, NJ: Lawrence Erlbaum.

Bowring, J., & Walker, P. (2010). The 'Jade Goody effect': What now for cervical cancer prevention? *Journal of Family Planning and Reproductive Health Care, 36*(2), 51–54.

Brabin, L., Roberts, S. A., Stretch, R., Baxter, D., Chambers, G., Kitchener, H., & McCann, R. (2008). Uptake of first two doses of human papillomavirus vaccine by adolescent schoolgirls in Manchester: Prospective cohort study. *British Medical Journal, 336*(7652), 1056–1058.

Brand, R. (2013). Life without drugs. *Guardian.* Accessed on 12 March 2013. http://www.guardian.co.uk/culture/2013/mar/09/russell-brand-life-without-drugs

Breslow, L., & Enstrom, J. E. (1980). Persistence of health habits and their relationship to mortality. *Preventive Medicine, 9*, 469–483.

Bridle, C., Riemsma, R. P., Pattenden, J., Sowden, A. J., Mather, L., Watt, I. S., & Walker, A. (2005). Systematic review of the effectiveness of health behavior interventions based on the transtheoretical model. *Psychology and Health, 20*(3), 283–301.

British Heart Foundation (2004). *Coronary heart disease statistics.* London: British Heart Foundation.

British Heart Foundation (2010). *Coronary heart disease statistics.* London: British Heart Foundation.

Brobeck, J. R., Tepperman, J., & Long, C. N. (1943). Experimental hypothalamic hyperphagia in the albino rat. *Yale Journal of Biological Medicine, 15*, 831–853.

Broughton, J., & Buckle, G. (2006). *Mobile phone and seat belt usage rates in London.* Wokingham: TRL Ltd.

Brown, G. W., & Harris, T. (1978). *Social origins of depression: A study of psychiatric disorders in women.* London: Tavistock.

Brown, R., & Ogden, J. (2004). Children's eating attitudes and behaviour: A study of the modelling and control theories of parental influence. *Health Education Research, 19*(3), 261–271.

Brownell, K. D. (1991). Personal responsibility and control over our bodies: When expectation exceeds reality. *Health Psychology, 10*, 303–331.

Browning, M., Hoffer, B. J., & Dunwiddie, T. V. (1993). Alcohol, memory and molecules. *Alcohol Health and Research World, 16*(4), 280–284.

Burish, T. G., Carey, M. P., Wallston, K. A., Stein, M. J., Jamison, R. N., & Lyles, J. N. (1984). Health locus of control and chronic disease: An external orientation may be advantageous. *Journal of Social and Clinical Psychology, 2*(4), 326–332.

Burkhart, P. V., & Rayens, M. K. (2005). Self-concept and health locus of control: Factors related to children's adherence to recommended asthma regimen. *Pediatric Nursing, 31*(5), 404–409.

Burkhauser, R. V., & Cawley, J. (2008). Beyond BMI: The value of more accurate measures of fatness and obesity in social science research. *Journal of Health Economics, 27*(2), 519–529.

Burns, V. E., Carroll, D., Ring, C., & Drayson, M. (2003). Antibody response to vaccination and psychosocial stress in humans: Relationships and mechanisms. *Vaccine, 21*(19–20), 2523–2534.

Bush, K., Kivlahan, D. R., McDonell, M. B., Fihn, S. D., & Bradley, K. A. (1998). The AUDIT alcohol consumption questions (AUDIT-C): An effective brief screening test for problem drinking. *Archives of Internal Medicine, 158*(16), 1789–1795.

Busick, D. B., Brooks, J., Pernecky, S., Dawson, R., & Petzoldt, J. (2008). Parent food purchases as a measure of exposure and preschool-aged children's willingness to identify and taste fruit and vegetables. *Appetite, 51*(3), 468–473.

Bussières, A. E., Patey, A. M., Francis, J. J., Sales, E., & Grimshaw, J. (2012). Identifying factors likely to influence compliance with diagnostic imaging guideline recommendations for spine disorders among chiropractors in North America: A focus group study using the theoretical domains framework. *Implementation Science, 7*, 82.

Byrne, C., Walsh, J., Kola, S., & Sarma, K. M. (2012). Predicting intention to uptake H1N1 influenza vaccine in a university sample. *British Journal of Health Psychology, 17*(3), 582–595.

Byrne, P., & Long, B. (1976). *Doctors talking to patients: A study of the verbal behaviour of general practitioners consulting in their surgeries.* London: HMSO.

Byrne, S., Cooper, Z., & Fairburn, C. G. (2003). Weight maintenance and relapse in obesity: A qualitative study. *International Journal of Obesity and Related Metabolic Disorders, 27*, 955–962.

Cabinet Office (2003). *Interim Analytical Report.* Strategy Unit Alcohol Harm Reduction Project. London: Cabinet Office.

Calisir, F., & Lehto, M. (2002). Young drivers' decision making and safety belt use. *Accident Analysis and Prevention, 34*, 793–805.

Campbell, M. K., Elbourne, D. R., & Altman, D. G. (2004). CONSORT statement: Extension to cluster randomised trials. *British Medical Journal, 328*, 702–708.

Cancer Research UK (2007). *Breast Cancer.* London: CancerStats.

Cancer Research UK (2012a). *CancerStats key facts: Breast cancer.* London: Cancer Research UK.

Cancer Research UK (2012b). *CancerStats key facts: Cervical cancer.* London: Cancer Research UK.

Cancer Research UK (2012c). *CancerStats key facts: Bowel cancer.* London: Cancer Research UK.

Cane, J., O'Connor, D., & Michie, S. (2012). Validation of the theoretical domains framework for use in behaviour change and implementation research. *Implementation Science, 7*(1), 37.

Cannon, B., & Washburn, A. L. (1912). An explanation of hunger. *American Journal of Physiology, 12*, 441–454.

Carpenter, C. J. (2010). A meta-analysis of the effectiveness of health belief model variables in predicting behavior. *Health Communication, 25*(8), 661–669.

Carver, C. S., & Scheier, M. F. (2001). *On the self-regulation of behavior.* New York: Cambridge University Press.

Cassell, J. A., Mercer, C. H., & Imriel, J. (2006). Who uses condoms with whom? Evidence from national probability sample surveys. *Sexually Transmitted Infections, 82*, 467–473.

Cavill, N., Biddle, S., & Sallis, J. (2001). Health enhancing physical activity for young people: Statement of the United Kingdom Expert Consensus Conference. *Pediatric Exercise Science, 13*(1), 12–25.

Chapin, J. (2001). It won't happen to me: The role of optimistic bias in African American teens' risky sexual practices. *Howard Journal of Communication, 12*(1), 49–59.

Chaput, J., Brunet, M., & Tremblay, A. (2006). Relationship between short sleeping hours and childhood overweight/obesity: Results from the 'Quebec en Forme' Project. *International Journal of Obesity, 30*(7), 1080–1085.

References

Chater, A., Stein, S., & Chowdhury, U. (2012). Take note of the fuss: Selective eating and autistic spectrum disorders. *Community Practitioner, 85*(12), 37–39.

Chen, C., David, A., Nunnerley, H., Michell, M., Dawson, J., Berry, H., … Fahy, T. (1995). Adverse life events and breast cancer: Case-control study. *British Medical Journal, 311*(7019), 1527–1530.

Chida, Y., & Vedhara, K. (2009). Adverse psychosocial factors predict poorer prognosis in HIV disease: A meta-analytic review of prospective investigations. *Brain, Behavior and Immunity, 23*(4), 434–445.

Chliaoutakis, E. J., Gnardellis, C., Drakou, I., Darviri, C., & Sboukis, V. (2000). Modelling the factors related to the seatbelt use by the young drivers of Athens. *Accident Analysis and Prevention, 32*, 815–825.

Ciechanowski, P. S., Katon, W. J., & Russo, J. E. (2000). Depression and diabetes: Impact of depressive symptoms on adherence, function, and costs. *Archives of Internal Medicine, 160*(21), 3278–3285.

Claessen, J.-P., Bates, S., Sherlock, K., Seeparsand, F., & Wright, R. (2008). Designing interventions to improve tooth brushing. *International Dental Journal, 58*(5), 1–14.

Clatworthy, J., Bowskill, R., Rank, T., Parham, R., & Horne, R. (2007). Adherence to medication in bipolar disorder: A qualitative study exploring the role of patients' beliefs about the condition and its treatment. *Bipolar Disorders, 9*(6), 656–664.

Cohen, S., Tyrrell, D. A. J., & Smith, A. P. (1991). Psychological stress and susceptibility to the common cold. *New England Journal of Medicine, 325*(9), 606–612.

Cohen, S., Tyrrell, D. A., & Smith, A. P. (1993). Negative life events, perceived stress, negative affect, and susceptibility to the common cold. *Journal of Personality and Social Psychology, 64*(1), 131–140.

Conner, M., & Norman, P. (1995). *Predicting health behaviour*. Buckingham: Open University Press.

Conner, M., & Norman, P. (1998). Special issue: Social cognition models in health psychology. *Psychology and Health, 13*, 179–185.

Conner, M., & Norman, P. (2005). *Predicting health behaviour* (2nd ed.). Buckingham: Open University Press.

Conner, M., & Sparks, P. (2005). The theory of planned behaviour and health behaviours. In M. Conner & P. Norman (Eds.), *Predicting health behaviour*. Buckingham: Open University Press.

Consensus Measurement in Hand Hygiene (CMHH) (2009). *Measuring hand hygiene adherence: Overcoming the challenges*. Oakbrook Terrace, IL: Division of Quality Measurement and Research.

Cook, E., Gaitán, A., & Chater, A. (2010). From unhelpful to helpful: The role of implementation intentions in a weight-loss intervention. *Health Psychology Update, 19*(1), 11–17.

Cormier, L., Kwan, L., Reid, K., & Litwin, M. S. (2002). Knowledge and beliefs among brothers and sons of men with prostate cancer. *Urology, 59*(6), 895–900.

Corrao, G., Bagnardi, V., Zambon, A., & La Vecchia, C. (2004). A meta-analysis of alcohol consumption and the risk of 15 diseases. *Preventive Medicine, 38*, 613–619.

Coulter, A. (1999). Paternalism or partnership?: Patients have grown up – and there's no going back. *British Medical Journal, 319*(7212), 719–720.

Cox, C. L., Montgomery, M., Rai, S. N., McLaughlin, R., Steen, B. D., & Hudson, M. M. (2008). Supporting breast self-examination in female childhood cancer survivors: A secondary analysis of a behavioural intervention. *Oncology Nursing Forum, 35*(3), 423–430.

Craig, P., Dieppe, P., Macintyre, S., Michie, S., Nazareth, I., & Petticrew, M. (2008). Developing and evaluating complex interventions: The new Medical Research Council guidance. *British Medical Journal, 337*, 979–983.

Crandall, C. S., Olson, L. M., & Sklar, D. P. (2001). Mortality reduction with air bag and seat belt use in head-on passenger car collisions. *American Journal of Epidemiology, 153*(3), 219–224.

Croll, J. K., Neumark-Sztainer, D., & Story, M. (2001). Healthy eating: What does it mean to adolescents? *Journal of Nutrition Education, 33*(4), 193–198.

Crosby, R., Salazar, R., DiClemente, R., & Wingwood, G. (2005). Overview of health promotion. In J. Kerr, R. Weitkunat & M. Moretti (Eds.), *ABC of behaviour change: A guide to successful disease prevention and health promotion* (pp. 3–16). London: Elsevier.

Cruess, D. G., Antoni, M. H., McGregor, B. A., Kilbourn, K. M., Boyers, A. E., & Alferi, S. M. (2000). Cognitive behavioural stress management reduces serum cortisol by enhancing benefit finding among women being treated for early stage breast cancer. *Psychosomatic Medicine, 62*(3), 304–308.

Cukor, D., Rosenthal, D. S., Jindal, R. M., Brown, C. D., & Kimmel, P. L. (2009). Depression is an important contributor to low medication adherence in hemodialyzed patients and transplant recipients. *Kidney International, 75*(11), 1223–1229.

Curry, S. (1987). Abstinence violation effect: Validation of an attributional construct with smoking cessation. *Journal of Consulting and Clinical Psychology, 55*(2), 145–49.

Curry, S. J., & Emmons, K. M. (1994). Theoretical models for predicting and improving compliance with breast cancer screening. Mini-series: Advances in behavioural medicine research on breast cancer. *Annals of Behaviour Medicine, 16*, 302–316.

Danielzik, S., Czerwinski-Mast, M., & Langnäse, K. (2004). Parental overweight, socioeconomic status and high birth weight are the major determinants of overweight and obesity in 5–7y-old children: Baseline data of the Kiel Obesity Prevention Study (KOPS). *International Journal of Obesity, 28*(11), 1494–1502.

David, D., Schnur, J., & Belloiu, A. (2002). Another search for the 'hot' cognitions: Appraisal, irrational beliefs, attributions, and their relation to emotion. *Journal of Rational-Emotive and Cognitive-Behavior Therapy, 20*(2), 93–131.

Davis, H., & Fallowfield, L. (1991). *Counselling and comminication in health care.* Chichester: John Wiley & Sons.

Day, E., Bentham, P., Callaghan, R., Kuruvilla, T., & George, S. (2004). Thiamine for Wernicke-Korsakoff Syndrome in people at risk from alcohol abuse. *Cochrane Database of Systematic Reviews, 2*.

de Oliveira, C., Watt, R., & Hamer, M. (2010). Toothbrushing, inflammation, and risk of cardiovascular disease: Results from Scottish Health Survey. *British Medical Journal, 340*, c2451.

de Visser, R. O., & Smith, A. (2004). Which intention? Whose intention? Condom use and theories of individual decision making. *Psychology, Health and Medicine, 9*(2), 193–204.

De Vries, H., Engels, R., Kremers, S., Wetzels, J. & Mudde, A. (2003). Parents' and friends' smoking status as predictors of smoking onset: Findings from six European countries. *Health Education Research, 18*(5), 627–636.

DeLongis, A., Coyne, J. C., Dakof, G., Folkman, S., & Lazarus, R. S. (1982). Relationship of daily hassles, uplifts, and major life events to health status. *Health Psychology, 1*(2), 119–136.

Denman, S., Dwyer, D. M., Israel, E., & Vacek, P. (1993). Handwashing and glove use in a long-term care facility – Maryland. *JAMA, 270*, 1678.

Denscombe, M. (2001). Peer group pressure, young people and smoking: New developments and policy implications. *Drugs: Education, Prevention, and Policy, 8*(1), 7–32.

Department of Health (1992). *The health of the nation: A strategy for health in England.* London: HMSO.

Department of Health (1998a). *Our healthier nation: A contract for health.* London: HMSO.

Department of Health (1998b). *Smoking kills: A white paper on tobacco.* London: HMSO.

Department of Health (1999). *Saving lives: Our healthier nation.* London: HMSO.

Department of Health (2001a). *Better services, better sexual health: The national strategy for sexual health and HIV.* London: HMSO.

Department of Health (2001b). *National Service Framework for older people.* London: Department of Health.

Department of Health (2002). *Getting ahead of the curve: A strategy for combating infectious diseases.* London: HMSO.

Department of Health (2003). *5 A DAY: Just eat more (fruit and veg).* London: HMSO.

References

Department of Health (2004a). *Choosing health: Making healthy choices easier*. London: HMSO.

Department of Health (2004b). *At least 5 a week: Evidence on the impact of physical activity and its relationship to health*. London: HMSO.

Department of Health (2005). *Choosing a better diet*. London: HMSO.

Department of Health (2007). *Immunisation against infectious disease: 'The Green Book' – 2006 updated edition*. London: HMSO.

Department of Health (2011). *The Eatwell Plate*. Retrieved 2 April 2013 from https://www.gov.uk/government/news/about-the-eatwell-plate

Department of Transport (2011). *THINK! Seat belts*. London: Department for Transport.

Des Jarlais, D. C., Lyles, C., Crepaz, N., & the TREND group (2004). Improving the reporting quality of nonrandomized evaluations of behavioral and public health interventions: The TREND statement. *American Journal of Public Health, 94*(3), 361–366.

Di Noia, J., Schinke, S. P., Prochaska, J. O., & Contento, I. R. (2006). Application of the transtheoretical model to fruit and vegetable consumption among economically disadvantaged African-American adolescents: Preliminary findings. *American Journal of Health Promotion, 20*(5), 342–348.

DiCenso, A., Guyatt, G., Willan, A., & Griffith, L. (2002). Interventions to reduce unintended pregnancies among adolescents: Systematic review of randomised controlled trials. *British Medical Journal, 324*(7351), 1426. doi: 10.1136/bmj.324.7351.1426

DiClemente, C. C. V. (1997). The transtheoretical model of health behaviour change. *American Journal of Health Promotion, 12*, 11–12.

DiClemente, C. C., Prochaska, J. O., Fairhurst, S. K., Velicer, W. F., Velasquez, M. M., & Rossi, J. S. (1991). The process of smoking cessation: An analysis of precontemplation, contemplation, and preparation stages of change. *Journal of Consulting and Clinical Psychology, 59*(2), 295–304.

Diener, E., Oishi, S., & Lucas, R. E. (2003). Personality, culture, and subjective well-being: Emotional and cognitive evaluations of life. *Annual Review of Psychology, 54*(1), 403–425.

DiMatteo, M. R., Giordani, P. J., Lepper, H. S., & Croghan, T. W. (2002). Patient adherence and medical treatment outcomes: A meta-analysis. *Medical Care, 40*(9), 794–811.

Dockray, S. (2011). *Cortisol, daily hassles and overweight status in adolescence*. Cambridge: Proquest, UMI Dissertation Publishing.

Doll, R., & Hill, A. B. (1952). Study of the aetiology of carcinoma of the lung. *British Medical Journal, 2*(4797), 1271–1286.

Dombrowski, S. U., Sniehotta, F. F., Avenell, A., Johnston, M., MacLennan, G., & Araújo-Soares, V. (2012). Identifying active ingredients in complex behavioural interventions for obese adults with obesity-related co-morbidities or additional risk factors for co-morbidities: A systematic review. *Health Psychology Review, 6*(1), 7–32.

Donaldson, L. J., Rutter, P. D., Ellis, B. M., Greaves, F. E., Mytton, O. T., Pebody, R. G., & Yardley, I. E. (2009). Mortality from pandemic A/H1N1 2009 influenza in England: Public health surveillance study. *British Medical Journal, 339*, b5213.

Dovey, T. M. (2010). *Eating behaviour*. Maidenhead: Open University Press.

Doweiko, H. E. (2006). *Concepts of chemical dependency* (6th ed.). Belmont, CA: Thomson Brooks/Cole.

Downing-Matibag, T. M., & Geisinger, B. (2009). Hooking up and sexual risk taking among college students: A health belief model perspective. *Qualitative Health Research, 19*(9), 1196–1209.

Dragan, A., & Akhtar-Danesh, N. (2007). Relation between body mass index and depression: A structural equation modelling approach. *BMC Medical Research Methodology, 10*, 7–17.

Drayton, V. L. C., Montgomery, S. B., Modeste, N. N., & Frye-Anderson, B. A. (2002). The health belief model as a predictor of repeat pregnancies among Jamaican teenage mothers. *International Quarterly of Communicating Health Education, 21*, 67–81.

Drobes, D. J., Saladin, M. E., & Tiffany, S. T. (2001). Classical conditioning mechanisms in alcohol dependence. In N. Heather, T. J. Peters, & T. Stockwell. *International handbook of alcohol dependence and problems* (pp. 281–297). New York: John Wiley & Sons.

Dulmen, S., Sluijs, E., Dijk, L., Ridder, D., Heerdink, R., & Bensing, J. (2007). Patient adherence to medical treatment: A review of reviews. *BMC Health Services Research*, *7*, 55.

Durrani, S., Hussain, M., & Ugwu, C. (2007). Depression in older people. *Clinical Focus Primary Care*, *2*(3), 112.

Dymek-Valentine, M., Rienecke-Hoste, R., & Engelberg, M. J. (2005). Psychosocial assessment in bariatric surgery candidates. In J. E. Mitchell & M. Zwaan (Eds.), *Bariatric surgery: A guide for mental health professionals* (pp. 15–38). New York: Taylor & Francis.

Dyson, J., Lawton, R., Jackson, C., & Cheater, F. (2010). Does the use of a theoretical approach tell us more about hand hygiene behaviour? The barriers and levers to hand hygiene. *Journal of Infection Prevention*, *12*, 17–24.

Edmonds, B. M. T., Coleman, J., Armstrong, K., & Shea, J. A. (2011). Risk perceptions, worry, or distrust: What drives pregnant women's decisions to accept the H1N1 vaccine? *Maternal and Child Health Journal*, *15*(8), 1203–1209.

Egger, G., & Swinburn, B. (1997). An 'ecological' approach to the obesity pandemic. *British Medical Journal*, *315*, 477–480.

Eggertson, L. (2010). Lancet retracts 12-year-old article linking autism to MMR vaccines. *Canadian Medical Association Journal*, *182*(4), E199–E200.

Ekeland, E., Heian, F., Hagen, K., & Coren, E. (2005). Can exercise improve self esteem in children and young people? A systematic review of randomized controlled trials. *British Journal of Sports Medicine*, *39*(11), 792–798.

Elgert, K. D. (2009). *Immunology: Understanding the immune system*. Hoboken, NJ: Wiley Blackwell.

Elwyn, G., Edwards, A., Kinnersley, P., & Grol, R. (2000). Shared decision making and the concept of equipoise: The competencies of involving patients in healthcare choices. *British Journal of General Practice*, *50*, 892–899.

Engel, G. L. (1977). The need for a new medical model: A challenge for biomedicine. *Science*, *196*, 129–135.

Engel, G. L. (1980). The clinical application of the biopsychosocial model. *American Journal of Psychiatry*, *137*, 535–544.

Engels, R. C., Wiers, R., Lemmers, L., & Overbeek, G. (2005). Drinking motives, alcohol expectancies, self-efficacy, and drinking patterns. *Journal of Drug Education*, *35*(2), 147–166.

Epstein, R. M., Franks, P., Fiscella, K., Shields, C. G., Meldrum, S., Kravitz, R. L., & Duberstein, P. R. (2005). Measuring patient-centred communication in patient–physician consultations: Theoretical and practical issues. *Social Science and Medicine*, *61*(7), 1516–1528.

Erasmus, V., Daha, T. J., Brug, H., Richardus, J. H., Behrendt, M. D., Vos, M. C., & van Beeck, E. F. (2010). Systematic review of studies on compliance with hand hygiene guidelines in hospital care. *Infection Control and Hospital Epidemiology*, *31*, 283–294.

Evans, D. W. (2006). How social marketing works in health care. *British Medical Journal*, *332*, 1207–1210.

Evers, K. E., Paiva, A. L., Johnson, J. L., Cummins, C. O., Prochaska, J. O., Prochaska, J. M., … Gökbayrak, N. S. (2012). Results of a transtheoretical model-based alcohol, tobacco and other drug intervention in middle schools. *Addictive Behaviors*, *37*(9), 1009–1018.

Faculty of Dental Surgery (1997). *National clinical guidelines: The Royal College of Surgeons of England*. London: Faculty of Dental Surgery.

Fagan, P., Eisenberg, M., Frazier, L., Stoddard, A. M., Avrunin, J. S., & Sorensen, G. (2003). Employed adolescents and beliefs about self-efficacy to avoid smoking. *Addictive Behaviors*, *28*(4), 613–626.

Farooqi, I. S., Jebb, S. A., Langmack, G., Lawrence, E., Cheetham, C. H., Prentice, A. M., … O'Rahilly, S. (1999). Effects of recombinant leptin therapy in a child with congenital leptin deficiency. *New England Journal of Medicine*, *341*(12), 879–884.

Ferri, M., Amato, L., & Davoli, M. (2006). Alcoholics Anonymous and other 12-step programmes for alcohol dependence. *Cochrane Database of Systematic Reviews*, *3*(2).

References

Fillenbaum, G. G., Pieper, C. F., Cohen, H. J., Cornoni-Huntley, J. C., & Guralnik, J. M. (2000). Comorbidity of five chronic health conditions in elderly community residents: Determinants and impact on mortality. *Journal of Gerontology and Biological Science*, *55*(2), M84–89.

Finer, N. (2006). Medical consequences of obesity. *Journal of Medicine*, *34*, 510–514.

Fishbein, M., & Ajzen, I. (1975). *Belief, attitude, intention and behavior: An introduction to theory and research*. Reading, MA: Addison-Wesley.

Fleming, M., Mihic, S. J. & Harris, R. A. (2001). Ethanol. In J. G. Hardman, L. E. Limbird, & A. G. Gilman (Eds.), *The pharmacological basis of therapeutics* (pp. 429–445). New York: McGraw-Hill.

Floyd, D. L., Prentice-Dunn, S., & Rogers, R. W. (2000). A meta-analysis of protection motivation theory. *Journal of Applied Social Psychology*, *30*, 407–429.

Folkman, S., & Lazarus, R. S. (1988). Coping as a mediator of emotion. *Journal of Personality and Social Psychology*, *54*(3), 466–475.

Ford, S., Schofield, T., & Hope, T. (2003). What are the ingredients for a successful evidence-based patient choice consultation? A qualitative study. *Social Science and Medicine*, *56*, 589–602.

Forsén, A. (2010). Psychosocial stress as a risk for breast cancer. *Psychotherapy and Psychosomatics*, *55*(2–4), 176–185.

Forshaw, M. (2002). *Essential health psychology*. London: Oxford University Press.

Forster, A. S., Marlow, L. A., Wardle, J., Stephenson, J., & Waller, J. (2010). Understanding adolescents' intentions to have the HPV vaccine. *Vaccine*, *28*(7), 1673–1676.

Forster, A., Wardle, J., Stephenson, J., & Waller, J. (2010). Passport to promiscuity or lifesaver: Press coverage of HPV vaccination and risky sexual behavior. *Journal of Health Communication*, *15*(2), 205–217.

Foster, C., Hillsdon, M., Thorogood, M., Kaur, A., & Wedatilake, T. (2005). *Interventions for promoting physical activity*, CD003180. Cochrane Database of Systematic Reviews.

Foster, C. D., Wadden, T. A., Makris, A. P., Davidson, D., Sanderson, R. S., Allison, D. B., & Kessle, A. (2003). Primary care physicians' attitudes about obesity and its treatment. *Obesity Research*, *11*(10), 1168–1171.

Fountoulakis, K. N., Fotiou, F., Iacovides, A., & Kaprinis, G. (2005). Is there a dysfunction in the visual system of depressed patients? *Annals of Psychiatry*, *4*(7), 1–10.

Fox, S. A., Heritage, J., Stockdale, S. E., Asch, S. M., Duan, N., & Reise, S. P. (2009). Cancer screen adherence: Does physician–patient communication matter? *Patient Education and Counselling*, *75*(2), 178–184.

Francis, J. J., O'Connor, D., & Curran, J. (2012). Theories of behaviour change synthesised into a set of theoretical groupings: Introducing a thematic series on the theoretical domains framework. *Implementation Science*, *7*(1), 1–9.

French, D. S., Green, S. E., O'Connor, D. A., McKenzie, J. E., Francis, J. J., Michie, S., … Grimshaw, J. M. (2012). Developing theory-informed behaviour change interventions to implement evidence into practice: A systematic approach using the theoretical domains framework. *Implementation Science*, *7*(1), 38.

French, D., Vedhara, K., Kaptein, A. A., & Weinman, J. (2010). *Health psychology* (2nd ed.). Oxford: BPS Blackwell.

Freund, K. M., Belanger, A. J., D'Agostino, R. B., & Kannel, W. B. (1993). The health risks of smoking the Framingham study: 34 years of follow-up. *Annals of Epidemiology*, *3*(4), 417–424.

Garcia-Retamero, R., & Cokely, E. T. (2011). Effective communication of risks to young adults: Using message framing and visual aids to increase condom use and STD screening. *Journal of Experimental Psychology: Applied*, *17*(3), 270–287.

Geliebter, A., & Aversa, A. (2003). Emotional eating in overweight, normal weight and underweight individuals. *Journal of Eating Behaviors*, *4*, 341–347.

Gibbons, F. X., & Gerrard, M. (1995). Predicting young adults' health risk behaviour. *Journal of Personality and Social Psychology*, *69*, 505–517.

Giles, M., & Cairns, E. (1995). Blood donation and Ajzen's theory of planned behaviour: An examination of perceived behavioural control. *British Journal of Social Psychology*, *34*, 173–188.

Gilvarry, C. (2005). Children of alcoholics: The UK's largest survey. *Addiction Today*, Sept./Oct., 23–25.

Ginzburg, K., Wrensch, M., Rice, T., Farren, G., & Spiegel, D. (2008). Breast cancer and psychosocial factors: Early stressful life events, social support, and well-being. *Psychosomatics*, *49*(5), 407–412.

Glanz, K., Rimmer, B. K., & Lewis, F. M. (2002). *Health behavior and health education*. San Francisco: Jossey-Bass.

Glaser, R., & Kiecolt-Glaser, J. (1994). *Handbook of human stress and immunity*. London: Academic Press.

Glaser, R., & Kiecolt-Glaser, J. (1997). Chronic stress modulates the virus-specific immune response to latent herpes simplex virus Type 1. *Annals of Behavioral Medicine*, *19*(2), 78–82.

Glynn, L., Emmett, P., & Rogers, I. (2005). Food and nutrient intakes of a population sample of 7-year-old children in the south-west of England in 1999/2000: What difference does gender make? *Journal of Human Nutrition and Dietetics*, *18*(1), 7–19.

Goddard, E., & Green, H. (2004). *General household survey 2004*. London: Office for National Statistics.

Gold, M. S., & Miller, N. S. (1997). Intoxication and withdrawal from alcohol. In N. S. Miller, M. S. Gold & D. E. Smith (Eds.), *Manual of therapeutics of addictions* (pp. 13–40). New York: Wiley-Liss.

Goldmeier, D., Garvey, L., & Barton, S. (2008). Does chronic stress lead to increased rates of recurrences of genital herpes? A review of the psychoneuroimmunological evidence. *International Journal of STD and AIDS*, *19*(6), 359–362.

Gollwitzer, P. M. (1990). Action phases and mind-sets. In E. T. Higgins & J. R. M. Sorrentino (Eds.), *The handbook of motivation and cognition: Foundations of social behavior* (Vol. 2, pp. 53–92). New York: Guilford.

Gollwitzer, P. M. (1993). Goal achievement: The role of intentions. In W. Stroebe & M. Hewstone (Eds.), *European review of social psychology* (Vol. 4, pp.141–185). New York: Wiley.

Gollwitzer, P. M. (1999). Implementation-intentions: Strong effects of simple plans. *American Psychologist*, *54*, 493–504.

Gollwitzer, P. M., & Sheeran, P. (2006). Implementation-intentions and goal achievement: A meta analysis of effects and processes. *Advances in Experimental Social Psychology*, *38*, 69–119.

Gomez, C. R., Boehmer, E. D., & Kovacs, E. J. (2005). The aging innate immune system. *Current Opinion in Immunology*, *17*, 457–462.

Gore, S. A., Foster, J. A., DiLillo, V. G., Kirk, K., & Smith West, D. (2003). Television viewing and snacking. *Eating Behaviors*, *4*(4), 399–405.

Gould, D. (1996). Can ward-based learning improve infection control? *Nursing Times*, *92*, 42–43.

Graham, J. E., Christian, L. M., & Kiecolt-Glaser, J. (2006). Stress, age, and immune function: Toward a lifespan approach. *Journal of Behavioral Medicine*, *29*(4), 389–400.

Grant, B. F., Stinson, F. S., Dawson, D. A., Chou, S. P., Dufour, M. C., Compton, W., Pickering, R. P., & Kaplan, K. (2004). Prevalence and co-occurrence of substance use disorders and independent mood and anxiety disorders: Results from the National Epidemiologic Survey on Alcohol and Related Conditions. *Archives of General Psychiatry*, *61*(8), 807–816.

Green, G., MacIntyre, S., West, P., & Ecob, R. (1991). Like parent like child? Associations between drinking and smoking behaviour of parents and their children. *British Journal of Addiction*, *86*(6), 745–759.

Green, L. W., & Kreuter, M. W. (1999). *Health promotion and planning: An educational and ecological approach* (3rd ed.) Mountain View, CA: Mayfield.

Greene, M. G., Adelman, R. D., Friedmann, E., & Charon, R. (1994). Older patient satisfaction during an initial medical encounter. *Social Science and Medicine*, *38*(9), 1279–1288.

Gregory, J., Lowe, S., Bates, C. J., & Britain, G. (2000). *National diet and nutrition survey: Young people aged 4 to 18 years. Report of the diet and nutrition survey* (Vol. 1). London: HMSO.

Grilo, C. M., Masheb, R. M., & Salan, S. L. (2005). Cognitive behavioural therapy guided self-help and orlistat for the treatment of binge eating disorder: A randomised double-blind placebo-controlled trial. *Biological Psychiatry, 57*, 1193–1201.

Guglielmi, R. S., & Tatrow, K. (1998). Occupational stress, burnout, and health in teachers: A methodological and theoretical analysis. *Review of Educational Research, 68*(1), 61–99.

Guo, B., Aveyard, P., Fielding, A., & Sutton, S. (2009). Do the transtheoretical model processes of change, decisional balance and temptation predict stage movement? Evidence from smoking cessation in adolescents. *Addiction, 104*(5), 828–838.

Gutierrez, J.-P., McPherson, S., Fakoya, A., Matheou, A., & Bertozzi, S. (2010). Community-based prevention leads to an increase in condom use and a reduction in sexually transmitted infections (STIs) among men who have sex with men (MSM) and female sex workers (FSW): the Frontiers Prevention Project (FPP) evaluation results. *BMC Public Health, 10*(1), 497.

Haddow, J. E., Palomaki, G. E., Knight, G. J., Williams, J., Pulkkinen, A., Canick, J. A., … Bowers, G. B. (1992). Prenatal screening for Down's syndrome with use of maternal serum markers. *New England Journal of Medicine, 327*(9), 588–593.

Hagger, M. S., Chatzisarantis, N. L. D., & Biddle, S. J. H. (2002). A meta-analytic review of the theories of reasoned action and planned behaviour in physical activity: Predictive validity and the contribution of additional variables. *Journal of Sport and Exercise Psychology, 24*, 3–32.

Hall, J. A., & Roter, D. L. (2002). Do patients talk differently to male and female physicians? A meta-analytic review. *Patient Education and Counseling, 48*, 217–224.

Hall, J., Roter, D., & Katz, N. (1988). Meta-analysis of correlates of provider behaviour in medical encounters. *Medical Care, 26*(7), 657–675.

Hall, M., Baum, A., Buysse, D. J., Prigerson, H. G., Kupfer, D. J., & Reynolds, C. F. (1998). Sleep as a mediator of the stress–immune relationship. *Psychosomatic Medicine, 60*(1), 48–51.

Halm, E. A., Mora, P., & Leventhal, H. (2006). No symptoms, no asthma: The acute episodic disease belief is associated with poor self-management among inner-city adults with persistent asthma. *Chest, 129*(3), 573–580.

Hamilton-West, K. (2006). Factors influencing MMR vaccination decisions following a mumps outbreak on a university campus. *Vaccine, 24*(24), 5183–5197.

Hammond, J. S., Eckles, J. M., Gomez, G. A., & Cunningham, D. N. (1990). HIV, trauma, and infection control: Universal precautions are universally ignored. *Journal of Trauma, 30*, 555–558.

Handwashing Liaison Group (1999). Hand washing: A modest measure – with big effects. *British Medical Journal, 318*, 686.

Hardman, A. E. (2001). Physical activity and cancer risk. *Proceedings of the Nutrition Society, 60*(1), 107–113.

Harlan, L. C., Bernstein, A. B., & Kessler, L. G. (1991). Cervical cancer screeing: Who is not screened and why? *American Journal of Public Health, 81*(7), 885–890.

Hart, C. L., Davey Smith, G., Hole, D. J. & Hawthorne, V. M. (1999). Alcohol consumption and mortality from all causes, coronary heart disease and stroke: Results from a prospective cohort study of Scottish men with 21 years of follow up. *British Medical Journal, 318*, 1725–1729.

Hatch, S., & Dohrenwend, B. (2007). Distribution of traumatic and other stressful life events by race/ethnicity, gender, SES and age: A review of the research. *American Journal of Community Psychology, 40*(3–4), 313–332.

Hatherall, B., Ingham, R., Stone, N., & McEachran, J. (2007). How, not just if, condoms are used: The timing of condom application and removal during vaginal sex among young people in England. *Sexually Transmitted Infections, 83*(1), 68–70.

Haynes, R. B. (1982). Improving patient compliance: an empirical review. In R. B. Stuart (Ed.), *Adherence, compliance and generalisation in behavioural medicine* (pp. 56–78). New York: Brunner/Mazel Inc.

Haynes, R. B., Akloo, E., Sahota, N., McDonald, H. P., & Yao, X. (2008). Interventions for enhancing medication adherence. *Cochrane Database of Systematic Reviews*(2). doi: 10.1002/14651858.CD000011.pub3.

Haynes, R. B., Sackett, D. L., & Taylor, D. W. (1979). *Compliance in health care*. Baltimore, MD: John Hopkins University Press.

Hazenberg, M. D., Stuart, J. W. T. C., Otto, S. A., Borleffs, J. C. C., Boucher, C. A. B., de Boer, R. J., … Hamann, D. (2000). T-cell division in human immunodeficiency virus (HIV)-1 infection is mainly due to immune activation: A longitudinal analysis in patients before and during highly active antiretroviral therapy (HAART). *Blood, 95*(1), 249–255.

Health Protection Agency (2003). Cover programme: January to March 2003. *CDR Weekly, 91*, 465–468.

Health Protection Agency (2007). July to September 2007. *Health Protection Report, 1*, 15.

Health Protection Agency (2012). *HIV in the United Kingdom: 2011 Report*. London: HPA.

Heaney, L. G., & Horne, R. (2012). Non-adherence in difficult asthma: Time to take it seriously. *Thorax, 67*, 268–270.

Heath, A. C., Madden, P. A., Slutske, W. S., & Martin, N. G. (1995). Personality and the inheritance of smoking behaviour: A genetic perspective. *Behavior Genetics, 25*(2), 103–117.

Heatherton, T. F., & Baumeister, R. F. (1991). Binge eating as an escape from self awareness. *Psychological Bulletin, 110*, 86–108.

Heatherton, T. F., Kozlowski, L. T., Frecker, R. C., & Fagerström, K. O. (1991). The Fagerström test for nicotine dependence: A revision of the Fagerström Tolerance Questionnaire. *British Journal of Addiction, 86*(9), 1119–1127.

Heckhausen, H., & Gollwitzer, P. M. (1987). Thought contents and cognitive functioning in motivational versus volitional states of mind. *Motivation and Emotion, 11*(2), 101–120.

Heikkilä, K., Nyberg, S. T., Theorell, T., Fransson, E. I., Alfredsson, L., Bjorner, J. B., & Kivimäki, M. (2013). Work stress and risk of cancer: Meta-analysis of 5700 incident cancer events in 116 000 European men and women. *British Medical Journal, 346*, 1–10.

Henderson, N. J., & Huon, G. F. (2002). Negative affect and binge eating in overweight women. *British Journal of Health Psychology, 7*, 77–87.

Henningfield, J. E. (1995). Nicotine medications for smoking cessation. *New England Journal of Medicine, 333*, 1196–1203.

Herbert, T. B., & Cohen, S. (1993). Stress and immunity in humans: A meta-analytic review. *Psychosomatic Medicine, 55*(4), 364–379.

Herman, C. P., & Mack, D. (1975). Restrained and unrestrained eating. *Journal of Personality, 43*, 647–660.

Hill, A. J. (1993). Pre-adolescent dieting: Implications for eating disorders. *International Review of Psychiatry, 5*(1), 87–99.

Hill, A., & Silver, E. (1995). Fat, friendless and unhealthy: 9-year-old children's perception of body shape stereotypes. *International Journal of Obesity and Related Metabolic Disorders, 19*(6), 423–430.

Hill, A., Draper, E., & Stack, J. (1994). A weight on children's minds: Body shape dissatisfactions at 9 years old. *International Journal of Obesity, 18*(6), 383–389.

Hillsdon, M., & Thorogood, M. (1996). A systematic review of physical activity promotion strategies. *British Journal of Sports Medicine, 30*(2), 84–89.

Hillsdon, M., Thorogood, M., White, I., & Foster, C. (2002). Advising people to take more exercise is ineffective: A randomized controlled trial of physical activity promotion in primary care. *International Journal of Epidemiology, 31*(4), 808–815.

Hochbaum, G. M. (1956). Why people seek diagnostic x-rays. *Public Health Reports, 71*(4), 377–380.

Hoehn, M. M., & Yahr, M. D. (1998). Parkinsonism: onset, progression, and mortality. *Neurology, 50*(2), 318–318.

Hoeppner, B. B., Redding, C. A., Rossi, J. S., Pallonen, U. E., Prochaska, J. O., & Velicer, W. F. (2012). Factor structure of decisional balance and temptations scales for smoking: Cross-validation in urban female African-American adolescents. *International Journal of Behavioral Medicine, 19*(2), 217–227.

Hollis, J., Connett, J., Stevens, V., & Greenlick, M. (1990). Stressful life events, Type A behavior, and the prediction of cardiovascular and total mortality over six years. *Journal of Behavioral Medicine, 13*(3), 263–280.

Holmes, T. H., & Rahe, R. H. (1967). The social readjustment rating scale. *Journal of Psychosomatic Research*, *11*, 213–218.

Honey, K., Morgan, M., & Bennett, P. (2003). A stress-coping transactional model of low mood following childbirth. *Journal of Reproductive and Infant Psychology*, *21*(2), 129–143.

Horne, R. (1997). Representations of medication and treatment: Advances in theory and measurement. In K. J. Petrie, & J. A. Weinman (Eds.), *Perceptions of health and illness: Current research and applications* (pp. 155–188). London: Harwood Academic Press.

Horne, R. 2000. Nonadherence to medication: Causes and implications for care. In: Gard, P. (ed.) *Personal and Social Factors in Pharmacy Practice*. Oxford: Blackwell Science 111–30.

Horne, R. (2001). Compliance, adherence and concordance. In K. Taylor & G. Harding (Eds.), *Pharmacy practice* (pp. 148–168). London: Taylor & Francis.

Horne, R. (2006). Compliance, adherence, and concordance: Implications for asthma treatment. *CHEST*, *130*(1), 65–72.

Horne, R., & Weinman, J. (1999). Patients' beliefs about prescribed medicines and their role in adherence to treatment in chronic physical illness. *Journal of Psychosomatic Research*, *47*(6), 555–567.

Horne, R., & Weinman, J. (2002). Self-regulation and self-management in asthma: Exploring the role of illness perceptions and treatment beliefs in explaining non-adherence to preventer medication. *Psychology and Health*, *17*(1), 17–32.

Horne, R. & Weinman, J. 2004. The theoretical basis of concordance and issues for research. In: Bond, C. (ed.). *Concordance: A Partnership in Medicine-taking.*, London: Pharmaceutical Press.

Horne, R., Cooper, V., & Gellaitry, G. (2007). Patients' perceptions of highly active antiretroviral therapy in relation to treatment uptake and adherence: the utility of the necessity–concerns framework. *Journal of Acquired Immune Deficiency Syndromes*, *45*(3), 334–341.

Horne, R., Weinman, J., & Hankins, M. (1999). The Beliefs About Medicines Questionnaire: The development and evaluation of a new method for assessing the cognitive representation of medication. *Psychology and Health*, *14*(1), 1–24.

Horne, R., Weinman, J., Barber, N., Elliott, R., Morgan, M., & Cribb, A. (2005). Concordance, adherence and compliance in medicine taking. London: NCCSDO.

House of Lords (2011). *Behaviour change: Report from the House of Lords Science and Technology Select Committee*. London: HMSO.

Hsu, L., Mulliken, B., McDonagh, B., Krupa Das, S., Rand, W., Fairburn, C., ... Shikora, S. (2002). Binge eating disorder in extreme obesity. *International Journal of Obesity*, *26*(10), 1398–1403.

Hu, G. J., Tuomilehto, J., Silventoinen, K., Barengo, N. C., Peltonen, P., & Jousilahti, P. (2005). The effects of physical activity and body mass index on cardiovascular, cancer and all-cause mortality among 47,212 middle-aged Finnish men and women. *International Journal of Obesity*, *29*, 894–902.

Hudson, J. I., Hiripi, E., Pope Jr, H. G., & Kessler, R. C. (2007). The prevalence and correlates of eating disorders in the National Comorbidity Survey Replication. *Biological Psychiatry*, *61*(3), 348–358.

Ichikawa, M., Nakahara, S., & Wakai, S. (2002). Mortality of front-seat occupants attributable to unbelted rear-seat passengers in car crashes. *Lancet*, *359*(9300), 43–44.

Ingham, R., Woodcock, A., & Stenner, K. (1991). Getting to know you ... Young people's knowledge of their partners at first intercourse. *Journal of Community and Applied Social Psychology*, *1*, 117–132.

Isozaki, M., Kuno-Sakai, H., Hoshi, N., Takesue, R., Takakura, I., Kimura, M., ... Mitsuda, M. (1982). Effects and side effects of a new trivalent combined measles–mumps–rubella (MMR) vaccine. *Tokai Journal of Experimental and Clinical Medicine*, *7*(5), 547–550.

Jacka, F., Pasco, J., Williams, L., Leslie, E., Dodd, S., Nicholson, G., ... Berk, M. (2011). Lower levels of physical activity in childhood associated with adult depression. *Journal of Science and Medicine in Sport*, *14*(3), 222–226.

Jackson, L. D. (1992). Information complexity and medical communication: The effects of technical language and the amount of information in a medical message. *Health Communication*, *4*(3), 197–210.

Janssen, I., Katzmarzyk, P. T., & Ross, R. (2004). Waist circumference and not body mass index explains obesity-related health risk. *American Journal of Clinical Nutrition*, *79*(3), 379–384.

Jarvis, M. J. (2004). ABC of smoking cessation: Why people smoke. *British Medical Journal*, *328*(7434), 277–279.

Jennison, K. M. (2004). The short-term effects and unintended long-term consequences of binge drinking in college: A 10-year follow-up study. *American Journal of Drug and Alcohol Abuse*, *30*(3), 659–684.

Johannson, G., Aronsson, G., & Lindstrom, B. O. (1978). Social psychological and neuroendocrine stress reactions in highly mechanised work. *Ergonomics*, *21*, 583–599.

Johnson, A. M., Wadsworth, J., Wellings, K., & Field, J. (1994). *Sexual attitudes and lifestyles*. London: Blackwell Scientific Publications.

Johnson, J. V., & Hall, E. M. (1988). Job strain, work place social support, and cardiovascular disease: A cross-sectional study of a random sample of the Swedish working population. *American Journal of Public Health*, *78*(10), 1336–1342.

Johnson, R. L., Roter, D., Powe, N. R., & Cooper, L. A. (2004). Patient race/ethnicity and quality of patient–physician communication during medical visits. *American Journal of Public Health*, *94*(12), 2084–2090.

Johnson, S. S., Paiva, A. L., Cummins, C. O., Johnson, J. L., Dyment, S. J., Wright, J. A., … Sherman, K. (2008). Transtheoretical model-based multiple behavior intervention for weight management: Effectiveness on a population basis. *Preventive Medicine*, *46*(3), 238–246.

Johnston, M., Weinman, J., & Chater, A. (2011). A quarter century of health psychology. *The Psychologist*, *24*(12), 890–902.

Jorenby, D. E., Leischow, S. J., Nides, M. A., Rennard, S. I., Johnston, J. A., Hughes, A. R., … Baker, T. B. (1999). A controlled trial of sustained-release bupropion, a nicotine patch, or both for smoking cessation. *New England Journal of Medicine*, *340*(9), 685–691.

Jotangia, D., Moody, A., Stamakakis, E., & Wardle, H. (2005). *Obesity among children under 11*. London: National Centre for Social Research.

Julien, R. M. (1996). *A primer of drug action: A concise, nontechnical guide to the actions, uses and side effects of psychoactive drugs* (7th ed.). New York: W. H. Freeman.

Kadden, R., Carbonari, J., Litt, M., Tonigan, S., & Zweben, A. (1998). Matching alcoholism treatments to client heterogeneity: Project MATCH three-year drinking outcomes. *Alcoholism: Clinical and Experimental Research*, *22*(6), 1300–1311.

Kanjirath, P. P., Kim, S. E., & Inglehart, M. R. (2011). Diabetes and oral health: The importance of oral health related behavior. *Journal of Dental Hygiene*, *85*(4), 264–272.

Kanner, A., Coyne, J., Schaefer, C., & Lazarus, R. (1981). Comparison of two modes of stress measurement: Daily hassles and uplifts versus major life events. *Journal of Behavioral Medicine*, *4*(1), 1–39.

Kaplan, S. H., Greenfield, S., & Ware, J. E. (1989). Assessing the effects of physician–patient interactions on the outcomes of chronic disease. *Medical Care*, *27*(7), 679.

Karasek, R. A. (1979). Job demands, job decision latitude, and mental strain: Implications for job redesign. *Administrative Science Quarterly*, *24*(2), 285–308.

Karsan, H. A., Rojter, S. E., & Saab, S. (2004). Primary prevention of cirrhosis. *Postgraduate Medicine*, *115*, 25–30.

Kashani, J. H., Hodges, K. K., Simonds, J. F., & Hilderbrand, E. (1981). Life events and hospitalization in children: A comparison with a general population. *British Journal of Psychiatry*, *139*(3), 221–225.

Kellar, I., & Abraham, C. (2005). Randomized controlled trial of a brief research-based intervention promoting fruit and vegetable consumption. *British Journal of Health Psychology*, *10*(4), 543–558.

References

Kelly, M., Steele, J., & Nuttall, N. (2000). *Adult dental health survey 1998: Oral health in the United Kingdom*. London: HMSO.

Kendall, P. C., & Hammen, C. (1998). *Abnormal psychology: Understanding human problems* (2nd ed.). Boston: New York: Houghton Mifflin.

Kenfield, S. A., Wei, E. K., Rosner, B. A., Glynn, R. J., Stampfer, M. J., & Colditz, G. A. (2010). Burden of smoking on cause-specific mortality: Application to the Nurses' Health Study. *Tobacco Control, 19*(3), 248–254.

Kennedy, G. C. (1953). The role of depot fat in the hypothalamic control of food intake in the rat. *Proceedings of the Royal Society of London, 140*, 578–592.

Keski-Rahkonen, A., Kaprio, J., Rissanen, A., Virkkunen, M., & Rose, R. J. (2003). Breakfast skipping and health-compromising behaviors in adolescents and adults. *European Journal of Clinical Nutrition, 57*(7), 842–853.

Keys, A., Brozek, J., Henschel, A., Mickelson, O., & Taylor, H. L. (1950). *The biology of human starvation* (Vols. 1 and 2). Minneapolis: University of Minnesota Press.

Kiecolt-Glaser, J. K., Glaser, R., Shuttleworth, E. C., Dyer, C. S., Ogrocki, P., & Speicher, C. E. (1987). Chronic stress and immunity in family caregivers of Alzheimer's disease victims. *Psychosomatic Medicine, 49*(5), 523–535.

Kiecolt-Glaser, J. K., Marucha, P. T., Mercado, A., Malarkey, W., & Glaser, R. (1995). Slowing of wound healing by psychological stress. *The Lancet, 346*(8984), 1194–1196.

Kiecolt-Glaser, J. K., Robles, T. F., Heffner, K. L., Loving, T. J., & Glaser, R. (2002). Psycho-oncology and cancer: psychoneuroimmunology and cancer. *Annals of Oncology, 13*(4), 165–170.

Kiellman, A., Akre, O., Norming, U., Tomblom, M., & Gustafsson, O. (2009). 15-year followup of a population based prostate cancer screening study. *Journal of Urology, 181*(4), 1615–1621.

Kimm, S. Y., Glynn, N. W., Obarzanek, E., Kriska, A. M., Daniels, S. R., Barton, B. A., & Liu, K. (2005). Relation between the changes in physical activity and body-mass index during adolescence: A multicentre longitudinal study. *The Lancet, 366*(9482), 301–307.

Kirby, J. B. (2002). The influence of parental separation on smoking initiation in adolescents. *Journal of Health and Social Behavior, 43*, 56–71.

Kirk, S. F., Penney, T. L., & McHugh, T. L. (2010). Characterizing the obesogenic environment: The state of the evidence with directions for future research. *Obesity Reviews, 11*(2), 109–117.

Knowles, J., Walter, L., & Buckle, G. (2008). *Mobile phone and seat belt usage rates in London 2008*. TRL Project Report PPR 364. Wokingham: TRL Ltd.

Kok, G., Schaalma, H., Ruiter, R. A., Van Empelen, P., & Brug, J. (2004). Intervention mapping: Protocol for applying health psychology theory to prevention programmes. *Journal of Health Psychology, 9*(1), 85–98.

Kopelman, P. G. (2000). Obesity as a medical problem. *Nature, 404*(6778), 635–643.

Kordoutis, P. S., Loumakou, M., & Sarafidou, J. O. (2000). Heterosexual relationship characteristics, condom use and safe sex practices. *AIDS Care, 12*(6), 767–782.

Kouvonen, A., Kivimäki, M., Virtanen, M., Pentti, J., & Vahtera, J. (2005). Work stress, smoking status, and smoking intensity: An observational study of 46 190 employees. *Journal of Epidemiology and Community Health, 59*(1), 63–69.

Kreibig, S. D. (2010). Autonomic nervous system activity in emotion: A review. *Biological Psychology, 84*, 394–421.

Kremers, S. P., Mesters, I., Pladdet, I. E., van den Borne, B., & Stockbrügger, R. W. (2000). Participation in a sigmoidoscopic colorectal cancer screening program: A pilot study. *Cancer Epidemiology Biomarkers and Prevention, 9*(10), 1127–1130.

Kristofferzon, M. L., Lindqvist, R., & Nilsson, A. (2011). Relationships between coping, coping resources and quality of life in patients with chronic illness: A pilot study. *Scandinavian Journal of Caring Sciences, 25*(3), 476–483.

Kumanyika, S. K., Horn, L. V., Bowen, D., Perri, M. G., Rolls, B. J., Czajkowski, S. M., & Schron, E. (2000). Maintenance of dietary behaviour change. *Health Psychology, 19*(1), 42–56.

Kuntsche, E., Knibbe, R., Gmel, G., & Engels, R. (2005). Why do young people drink? A review of drinking motives. *Clinical Psychology Review, 25*(7), 841–861.

Kurtz, Z., & Thornes, R. (2000). *Health needs of school age children: The views of children, parents and teachers linked to local and national information*. London: HMSO.

Kushner, M. G., Abrams, K., & Borchardt, C. (2000). The relationship between anxiety disorders and alcohol use disorders: A review of major perspectives and findings. *Clinical Psychology Review, 20*(2), 149–171.

La-Forge, R. (1995). Exercise associated mood alterations: A review of interactive neurobiological mechanisms, medicine, exercise. *Nutrition and Health, 4*, 17–32.

Lamerz, A., Kuepper-Nybelen, J., Wehle, C., Bruning, N., Trost-Brinkhues, G., Brenner, H., … Herpertz-Dahlmann, B. (2005). Social class, parental education, and obesity prevalence in a study of six-year-old children in Germany. *International Journal of Obesity, 29*(4), 373–380.

Lancucki, L., Sasieni, P., Patnick, J., Day, T., & Vessey, M. (2012). The impact of Jade Goody's diagnosis and death on the NHS Cervical Screening Programme. *Journal of Medical Screening, 19*(2), 89–93.

Landrine, H., & Klonoff, E. (1994). Cultural diversity in causal attributions for illness: The role of the supernatural. *Journal of Behavioral Medicine, 17*(2), 181–193.

Lang, A., & Froelicher, E. S. (2006). Management of overweight and obesity in adults: Behavioural intervention for long-term weight loss and maintenance. *European Journal of Cardiovascular Nursing, 5*, 102–114.

Langer, E. J., & Rodin, J. (1976). The effects of choice and enhanced personal responsibility for the aged: A field experiment in an institutional setting. *Journal of Personality and Social Psychology, 134*, 191–198.

Lapierre, S., Erlangsen, A., Waern, M., De Leo, D., Oyama, H., Scocco, P., … Quinnett, P. (2011). A systematic review of elderly suicide prevention programs. *Crisis: The Journal of Crisis Intervention and Suicide Prevention, 32*(2), 88–98.

Larson, E. (1988). A causal link between handwashing and risk of infection? Examination of the evidence. *Infection Control and Hospital Epidemiology, 9*(1), 28–36.

Lau, R. R. (1982). Origins of health locus of control beliefs. *Journal of Personality and Social Psychology, 42*, 322–334.

Lazarus, R. (1995). Vexing research problems inherent in cognitive-mediational theories of emotion and some solutions. *Psychological Inquiry, 6*, 183–265.

Lazarus, R. (1998). *Fifty years of the research and theory of R. S. Lazarus: An analysis of historical and perennial issues*. Hillsdale, NJ: Lawrence Erlbaum Associates.

Lazarus, R. S. (1999). *Stress and emotion: A new synthesis*. New York: springer.

Lazarus, R., & Folkman, S. (1984). *Stress, appraisal, and coping*. New York: Springer.

Lee, C., Dobson, A. J., Brown, W. J., Bryson, L., Byles, J., Warner-Smith, P., & Young, A. F. (2005). Cohort profile: The Australian longitudinal study on women's health. *International Journal of Epidemiology, 34*(5), 987–991.

Lee, S., Back, A., Block, S., & Stewart, S. (2002). Enhancing physician–patient communication. *Hematology, 46*(1), 464–483.

Lehrer, P. M., Isenberg, S., & Hochron, S. M. (1993). Asthma and emotion: A review. *Journal of Asthma, 30*(1), 5–21.

Leventhal, H. (1984). A perceptual-motor theory of emotion. In L. Berkowitz (Ed.), *Advances in experimental psychology* (Vol. 17, pp. 117–182). Orlando, FL: Academic Press.

Leventhal, H., & Mora, P. A. (2008). Predicting outcomes or modeling process? Commentary on the health action process approach. *Applied Psychology, 57*(1), 51–65.

Leventhal, H., Diefenbach, M., & Leventhal, E. A. (1992). Illness cognition: Using common sense to understand treatment adherence and affect cognition interactions. *Cognitive Therapy and Research, 16*(2), 143–163.

Leventhal, H., Meyer, D., & Nerenz, D. (1980). The common sense representation of illness danger. *Medical Psychology, 2*, 7–30.

Ley, P. (1988). *Communicating with patients*. London: Croom Helm.

Ley, P. (1989). Improving patients' understanding, recall, satisfaction and compliance. In A. Broome (Ed.), *Health psychology* (pp. 74–102). London: Chapman & Hall.

References

Ley, P., & Morris, L. A. (1984). Psychological aspects of written information for patients. In S. Rachman (Ed.), *Contributions to medical psychology* (pp. 117–149). Oxford: Pergamon Press.

Li, C., Pentz, M. A. & Chou, C. P. (2002). Parental substance use as a modifier of adolescent substance use risk. *Addiction, 97*, 1537–1550.

Li, C., Unger, J. B., Schuster, D., Rohrbach, L. A., Howard-Pitney, B., & Norman, G. (2003). Youths' exposure to environmental tobacco smoke (ETS) associations with health beliefs and social pressure. *Addictive Behaviours, 28*, 39–53.

Liew, P.-L., Lee, W.-J., Wang, W., Lee, Y.-C., Chen, W.-Y., Fang, C.-L., & Huang, M.-T. (2008). Fatty liver disease: Predictors of nonalcoholic steatohepatitis and gallbladder disease in morbid obesity. *Obesity Surgery, 18*(7), 847–853.

Lowe, C., Horne, P. J., Tapper, K., Bowdery, M., & Egerton, C. (2004). Effects of a peer modelling and rewards-based intervention to increase fruit and vegetable consumption in children. *European Journal of Clinical Nutrition, 58*(3), 510–522.

Lu, B., Kumar, A., Castellsagué, X., & Giuliano, A. (2011). Efficacy and safety of prophylactic vaccines against cervical HPV infection and diseases among women: A systematic review and meta-analysis. *BMC Infectious Diseases, 11*(1), 13. doi: 10.1186/1471-2334-11-13

Luszczynska, A. (2006). An implementation intentions intervention, the use of a planning strategy, and physical activity after myocardial infarction. *Social Science and Medicine, 62*(4), 900–908.

Luszczynska, A., & Schwarzer, R. (2003). Planning and self-efficacy in the adoption and maintenance of breast self-examination: A longitudinal study on self-regulatory cognitions. *Psychology and Health, 18*, 93–108.

Luszczynska, A., & Schwarzer, R. (2005). Social cognitive theory. In M. Conner & P. Norman (Eds.), *Predicting health behaviour* (2nd ed.). Maidenhead: Open University Press.

Luszczynska, A., Scholz, U., & Schwarzer, R. (2005). The General Self-Efficacy Scale: Multicultural validation studies. *Journal of Psychology, 139*(5), 439–457.

Lydyard, P. M., & Porakishvili, N. (2012). Cells, tissues and organs of the immune system. In D. Male, J. Brostoff, D. B. Roth, & I. M. Roitt (Eds.), *Immunology* (8th ed., pp. 17–51). London: Elsevier.

Lyons, A. C., & Chamberlain, K. (2006). *Health psychology: A critical introduction.* Cambridge: Cambridge University Press.

Ma, Y., Bertone-Johnson, E. R., Stanek III, E. J., Reed, G. W., Herbert, J. R., Cohen, N. L., … Ockene, I. S. (2005). Eating patterns in a free-living healthy US adult population. *Ecology of Food and Nutrition, 44*(1), 37–56.

Macdonald, E. (Ed.). (2004). *Difficult conversations in medicine.* Oxford: Oxford University Press.

Maisto, S. A., Galizio, M., & Connors, G. J. (2004). *Drug use and abuse* (4th ed.). Belmont, CA: Wadsworth/Thomson.

Mancuso, C. A., Sayles, W., Robbins, C., Phillips, E. G., Ravenell, K., Duffy, C., … Charlson, M. (2006). Barriers and facilitators to healthy physical activity in asthma patients. *Journal of Asthma, 43*, 137–143.

Marcos, A., Nova, E., & Montero, A. (2003). Changes in the immune system are conditioned by nutrition. *European Journal of Clinical Nutrition, 57*(S1), S66–S69.

Marino, R., & Gonzales-Portillo, M. (2000). Preconquest Peruvian neurosurgeons: A study of Inca and pre-Columbian trephination and the art of medicine in ancient Peru. *Neurosurgery, 47*, 940–950.

Marks, D. F. (1994). Psychology's role in The Health of the Nation. *The Psychologist*, March, 119–121.

Marks, D. F., Murray, M. P., Evans, B., & Estacio, E. V. (2011). *Health psychology: Theory, research and practice* (3rd ed.) London: Sage.

Marlatt, G. A., & Donovan, D. D. M. (Eds.). (2005). *Relapse prevention: Maintenance strategies in the treatment of addictive behaviours.* New York: Guilford Press.

Marlatt, G. A., & Gordon, J. R. (1985). *Relapse prevention: Maintenance strategies in addictive behaviour change.* New York: Guilford.

Marlow, L. A., Waller, J., & Wardle, J. (2007). Parental attitudes to pre-pubertal HPV vaccination. *Vaccine, 25*(11), 1945–1952.

Marmot, M. G., Bosma, H., Hemmingway, H., Brunner, E., & Stansfield, S. (1997). Contribution of job control and other risk factors to social variations in coronary heart disease incidence. *Epidemiology and Public Health*, *350*, 235–239.

Marteau, T. M., & Croyle, R. T. (1998). The new genetics: Psychological responses to genetic testing. *British Medical Journal*, *316*(7132), 693–696.

Martin, C. K., Coulon, S. M., Markward, N., Greenway, F. L., & Anton, S. D. (2009). Association between energy intake and viewing television, distractibility, and memory for advertisements. *American Journal of Clinical Nutrition*, *89*(1), 37–44.

Martin, J., Chater, A., & Lorencatto, F. (2013). Effective behaviour change techniques in the prevention and management of childhood obesity. *International Journal of Obesity*, *37*(10), 1287–94.

Martins., Y. (2002). Try it, you'll like it! Early dietary experiences and food acceptance patterns. *Journal of Pediatric Nutrition and Development*, *98*, 12–20.

Marucha, P. T., Kiecolt-Glaser, J. K., & Favagehi, M. (1998). Mucosal wound healing is impaired by examination stress. *Psychosomatic Medicine*, *60*(3), 362–365.

Marx, J. (2002). Unraveling the causes of diabetes. *Science*, *296*(5568), 686–689.

Matarazzo, J. D. (1980). Behavioral health and behavioral medicine: Frontiers for a new health psychology. *American Psychologist*, *35*, 807–817.

Matarazzo, J. D. (1984). Behavioural health: A 1990 challenge for the health sciences professions. In J. D. Matarazzo, N. E. Miller, S. M. Weiss, J. A. Herd, & S. M. Weiss (Eds.), *Behavioural health: A handbook of health enhancement and disease prevention* (pp. 3–40). New York: Wiley.

Mattick, R. P., & Hall, W. (1996). Are detoxification programmes effective? *Lancet*, *347*(8994), 97–100.

Maunsell, E., Brisson, J., Mondor, M., Verreault, R., & Deschênes, L. (2001). Stressful life events and survival after breast cancer. *Psychosomatic Medicine*, *63*(2), 306–315.

Mayer, J. (1953). Glucostatic metabolism of regulation of food intake. *New England Journal of Medicine*, *249*, 13–16.

McAteer, J., Stone, S., Fuller, C., Charlett, A., Cookson, B., Slade, R., & Michie, S. (2008). Development of an observational measure of healthcare worker hand-hygiene behaviour: The hand-hygiene observation tool (HHOT). *Journal of Hospital Infection*, *68*(3), 222–229.

McEachan, R., Conner, M., Taylor, N. J., & Lawton, R. (2011). Prospective prediction of health-related behaviours with the theory of planned behaviour: A meta-analysis. *Health Psychology Review*, *5*(2), 97–144.

McEwen, A., Hajek, P., McRobbie, H., & West, R. (2008). *Manual of smoking cessation: A guide for counsellors and practitioners*. Oxford: Blackwell publishing.

McEwen, A., West, R., & McRobbie, H. (2008). Motives for smoking and their correlates in clients attending Stop Smoking treatment services. *Nicotine and Tobacco Research*, *10*(5), 843–850.

McGuire, W. J. (1964). Inducing resistance to persuasion: Some contemporary approaches. In L. Berkowitz (ed.), *Advances in experimental psychology* (Vol. 1, pp. 191–229). New York: Academic Press.

McKenzie, J. F., & Smeltzer, J. L. (2000). *Planning, implementing, and evaluating health promotion programs: A primer* (2nd ed.). Boston: Allyn & Bacon.

McKeown, T. (1979). *The role of medicine*. Oxford: Blackwell.

McLaren, E. H. (2009). Is screening cost effective? *British Medical Journal*, *339*, 3040.

McMillan, B., & Conner, M. (2003). Applying an extended version of the theory of planned behaviour to illicit drug use among students. *Journal of Applied Social Psychology*, *33*, 1662–1683.

McMillan, B., Higgins, A. R., & Conner, M. (2005). Using an extended theory of planned behaviour to understand smoking amongst schoolchildren. *Addiction Research and Theory*, *13*(3), 293–306.

Mellinkoff, S. M., Frankland, M., Boyle, D., & Greipel, M. (1956). Relationship between serum amino acid concentration and fluctuations in appetite. *Journal of Applied Physiology*, *8*(5), 535–538.

Mercken, L., Candel, M., Willems, P., & De Vries, H. (2007). Disentangling social selection and social influence effects on adolescent smoking: The importance of reciprocity in friendships. *Addiction*, *102*(9), 1483–1492.

References

Meyer, I. H., Sternfels, P., Fagan, J. K., Copeland, L., & Ford, J. G. (2001). Characteristics and correlates of asthma knowledge among emergency department users in Harlem. *Journal of Asthma, 38*(7), 531–539.

Michie, S., & Abraham, C. (2004). Interventions to change health behaviours: Evidence-based or evidence inspired? *Psychology and Health, 19,* 29–49.

Michie, S., Abraham, C., & Johnston, M. (2004). Health psychology training: The UK model. In S. Michie & C. Abraham (Eds.), *Health psychology in practice* (pp. 7–45). London: British Psychological Society and Blackwell.

Michie, S., Abraham, C., Eccles, M. P., Francis, J. J., Hardeman, W., & Johnston, M. (2011). Strengthening evaluation and implementation by specifying components of behaviour change interventions: A study protocol. *Implementation Science, 6,* 10. doi: 10.1186 1748-5908-6-10.

Michie, S., Ashford, S., Sniehotta, F. F., Dombrowski, S. U., Bishop, A., & French, D. P. (2011). A refined taxonomy of behaviour change techniques to help people change their physical activity and healthy eating behaviours: The CALO-RE taxonomy. *Psychology and Health, 26*(11), 1479–1498.

Michie, S., Fixen, D., Grimshaw, J. M., & Eccles, M. P. (2009). Specifying and reporting complex behaviour change interventions: The need for a scientific method. *Implementation Science, 4*(40), 1–6.

Michie, S., Hyder, N., Walia, A., & West, R. (2011). Development of a taxonomy of behaviour change techniques used in individual behavioural support for smoking cessation. *Addictive Behaviors, 36*(4), 315–319.

Michie, S., Johnston, M., Abraham, C., Francis, J., & Eccles, M. P. (2013). The behavior change technique taxonomy (v1) of 93 hierarchically clustered techniques: Building an international consensus for the reporting of behavior change interventions. *Annals of Behavioral Medicine,* 1–15.

Michie, S., Johnston, M., Abraham, C., Lawton, R., Parker, D., & Walker, A. (2005). Making psychological theory useful for implementing evidence based practice: A consensus approach. *Quality and Safety in Health Care, 14*(1), 26–33.

Michie, S., Rothman, A. J., & Sheeran, P. (2007). Advancing the science of behaviour change. *Psychology and Health, 22*(3), 249–253.

Michie, S., Rumsey, N., Fussell, A., Hardeman, W., Johnston, M., Newman, S., & Yardley, L. (2004). *Improving health: Changing behaviour. NHS health trainer handbook.* London: Department of Health/British Psychological Society.

Michie, S., van Stralen, M. M., & West, R. (2011). The behaviour change wheel: A new method for characterising and designing behaviour change interventions. *Implementation Science, 6*(1), 42.

Michie, S., Whittington, C., Hamoudi, Z., Zarnani, F., Tober, G., & West, R. (2012). Identification of behaviour change techniques to reduce excessive alcohol consumption. *Addiction, 107*(8), 1431–1440.

Milkman, K. L., Beshears, J., Choi, J. J., Laibson, D., & Madrian, B. C. (2011). Using implementation intentions prompts to enhance influenza vaccination rates. *Proceedings of the National Academy of Sciences, 108*(26), 10415–10420.

Miller, G. E., & Cohen, S. (2001). Psychological interventions and the immune system: A meta-analytic review and critique. *Health Psychology, 20*(1), 47–63.

Miller, J. W., Naimi, T. S., Brewer, R. D., & Jones, S. E. (2007). Binge drinking and associated health risk behaviors among high school students. *Pediatrics, 119*(1), 76–85.

Miller, L. G., Liu, H., Hays, R. D., Golin, C. E., Ye, Z., Beck, C. K., ... Wenger, N. S. (2003). Knowledge of antiretroviral regimen dosing and adherence: A longitudinal study. *Clinical Infectious Diseases, 6*(4), 514–518.

Miller, W. R., & Wilbourne, P. L. (2002). Mesa Grande: A methodological analysis of clinical trials of treatments for alcohol use disorders. *Addiction, 97*(3), 265–277.

Milne, S., Orbell, S., & Sheeran, P. (2002). Combining motivational and volitional interventions to promote exercise participation: Protection motivation theory and implementation intentions. *British Journal of Health Psychology, 7*(2), 163–184.

Milne, S., Sheeran, P., & Orbell, S. (2000). Prediction and intervention in health-related behaviour: A meta-analytic review of protection motivation theory. *Journal of Applied Social Psychology*, *30*, 106–143.

Minichiello, V., Browne, J., & Kendig, H. (2000). Perceptions and consequences of ageism: Views of older people. *Ageing and Society*, *20*(3), 253–278.

Moher, D., Hopewell, S., Schulz, K. F., Montori, V., Gøtzsche, P. C., Devereaux, P.J., ... Altman, D. G. (2010). CONSORT 2010 explanation and elaboration: Updated guidelines for reporting parallel group randomised trial. *British Medical Journal*, *340*, 869.

Mond, J. M., & Calogero, R. M. (2009). Excessive exercise in eating disorder patients and in healthy women. *Australasian Psychiatry*, *43*(3), 227–234.

Moore, L., Paisley, C. M., & Dennehy, A. (2000). Are fruit tuck shops in primary schools effective in increasing pupils' fruit consumption? A randomised controlled trial. *Nutrition and Food Science*, *30*(1), 35–39.

Moore, L., Smith, C., & Catford, J. (1994). Binge drinking: Prevalence, patterns and policy. *Health Education Research*, *9*(4), 497–505.

Morel, O., Luca, F., Grunebaum, L., Jesel, L., Meyer, N., Desprez, D., ... Simon, C. (2011). Short-term very low-calorie diet in obese females improves the haemostatic balance through the reduction of leptin levels, PAI-1 concentrations and a diminished release of platelet and leukocyte-derived microparticles. *International Journal of Obesity*, *35*(12), 1479–1486.

Morrison, D. S., Petticrew, M., & Thomson, H. (2003). What are the most effecive ways of improving population health through transport interventions? Evidence from systematic reviews. *Journal of Epidemiology and Community Health*, *57*(5), 327–333.

Morrison, V., & Bennett, P. (2009). *An introduction to health psychology* (2nd ed.). Harlow: Pearson Education.

Morrison, V., & Bennett, P. (2012). *An introduction to health psychology* (3rd ed.). Harlow: Pearson Education.

Moss-Morris, R., Weinman, J., Petrie, K., Horne, R., Cameron, L., & Buick, D. (2002). The Revised Illness Perception Questionnaire (IPQ-R). *Psychology and Health*, *17*(1), 1–16.

Mota, J., Fidalgo, F., Silva, R., Ribeiro, J. C., Santos, R., Carvalho, J., & Santos, M. P. (2008). Relationships between physical activity, obesity and meal frequency in adolescents. *Annals of Human Biology*, *35*(1), 1–10.

Moyer, A. E. (1977). Robert Hooke's ambiguous presentation of 'Hooke's Law'. *Isis*, *68*(2), 266–275.

Mundy-Bosse, B. L., Thornton, L. M., Yang, H.-C., Andersen, B. L., & Carson, W. E. (2011). Psychological stress is associated with altered levels of myeloid-derived suppressor cells in breast cancer patients. *Cellular Immunology*, *270*(1), 80–87.

Murasko, D. M., Weiner, P., & Kaye, D. (1987). Decline in mitogen induced proliferation of lymphocytes with increasing age. *Clinical and Experimental Immunology*, *70*, 440–448.

Murray, C. J. L., Richards, M. A., Newton, J. N., Fenton, K. A., Anderson, H. R., Atkinson, C., ... Davis, A. (2013). UK health performance: Findings of the Global Burden of Disease Study 2010. *The Lancet Online*.

Murray, M., & McMillan, C. (1993). Health beliefs, locus of control, emotional control and women's cancer screening behaviour. *British Journal of Clinical Psychology*, *32*, 87–100.

Murray, R. P., Connett, J. E., Tyas, S. L., Bond, R., Ekuma, O., Silversides, C. K., & Barnes, G. E. (2002). Alcohol volume, drinking pattern and cardiovascular disease morbidity and mortality: Is there a U-shaped function? *American Journal of Epidemiology*, *155*, 242–248.

Mytton, O., Rutter, P., Mak, M., Stanton, E., Sachedina, N., & Donaldson, L. (2012). Mortality due to pandemic (H1N1) 2009 influenza in England: A comparison of the first and second waves. *Epidemiology and Infection*, *140*(09), 1533–1541.

Naidoo, J., & Willis, J. (2005). *Public health and health promotion: Developing practice* (2nd ed.). London: Baillière Tindall.

National Cooperative Highway Research Program (2007). *Public information and education in the promotion of highway safety*. Washington, DC: Transportation Research Board.

Neame, R., & Hammond, A. (2005). Beliefs about medications: A questionnaire survey of people with rheumatoid arthritis. *Rheumatology*, *44*, 762–767.

References

NHS (2013). NHS cervical screening programme: About cervical screening. Retrieved 11 February 2013, from http://www.cancerscreening.nhs.uk/cervical/about-cervical-screening.html

NHS Choices (2012). *Cold sore (herpes simplex virus)* [online]. NHS Choices. Available at http://www.nhs.uk/conditions/Cold-sore/Pages/Introduction.aspx (accessed 11 February 2013).

NHS Executive (1996). *Patient partnership: Building a collaborative strategy.* Leeds: NHS Executive.

NHS Health and Social Care Information Centre (2006). *Statistics on obesity, physical activity and diet.* London: HMSO.

NHS Health and Social Care Information Centre (2008). *Health survey for England: 2007. Latest trends.* London: NHS.

NHS Health and Social Care Information Centre (2011). *Statistics on alcohol: England, 2011.* London: NHS.

NHS Health and Social Care Information Centre (2012a). *Statistics on alcohol: England, 2012.* London: NHS Health and Social Care Information Centre.

NHS Health and Social Care Information Centre (2012b). *Statistics on smoking: England, 2012.* London: NHS.

NHS Health and Social Care Information Centre (2013). *Statistics on obesity, physical activity and diet: England, 2013.* London: HMSO.

NICE (2006). *Obesity: Guidance on the prevention, identification, assessment and management of overweight and obesity in adults and children.* London: HMSO.

NICE (2007). *Behaviour change at population, community and individual levels: NICE public health guidance 6.* London: National Institute for Health and Clinical Excellence.

NICE (2009). *Costing statement: Medicines adherence; involving patients in decisions about prescribed medicines and supporting adherence.* London: NICE.

NICE (2011). *Tuberculosis: Clinical diagnosis and management of tuberculsosis, and measures for its prevention and control: NICE Clinical Guidelines.* London: NICE.

Nichol, K. L., Margolis, K. L., Lind, A., Murdoch, M., McFadden, R., Hauge, M., ... Drake, M. (1996). Side effects associated with influenza vaccination in healthy working adults: A randomized, placebo-controlled trial. *Archives of Internal Medicine, 156*(14), 1546–1550.

Nichols, K. (1993). *Psychological care in physical illness.* London: Nelson Thornes.

Nieminen, P., Vuorma, S., Viikki, M., Hakama, M., & Anttila, A. (2004). Comparison of HPV test versus conventional and automation-assisted Pap screening as potential screening tools for preventing cervical cancer. *BJOG: An International Journal of Obstetrics and Gynaecology, 111*(8), 842–848.

Nogueras, M., Marinsalta, N., Roussell, M., & Notario, R. (2001). Importance of hand germ contamination in health-care workers as possible carriers of nosocomial infections. *Revista do Instituto de Medicina Tropical de São Paulo, 43,* 149–152.

Norman, P., & Brain, K. (2005). An application of an extended health belief model to the prediction of breast self-examination among women with a family history of breast cancer. *British Journal of Health Psychology, 10*(1), 1–16.

Norman, P., Bennett, P., Smith, C., & Murphy, S. (1997). Health locus of control and leisure time exercise. *Personality and Individual Differences, 23,* 769–774.

Norman, P., Boer, H., & Seydel, E. R. (2005). Protection motivation theory. In M. Conner & P. Norman (Eds.), *Predicting health behaviour* (2nd ed.). Maidenhead: Open University Press.

Northouse, L. L., & Northouse, P. G. (1998). An introduction to health communication. In L. L. Northouse & P. G. Northouse (Eds.), *Health communication: Strategies for health professionals* (pp. 1–11). Norwalk, CT: Appleton and Lange.

Northouse, P. G., & Northouse, L. L. (1985). *Health communication: A handbook for health professionals.* Englewood Cliffs, NJ: Prentice Hall.

Nutbeam, D. (1998). Evaluating health promotion-progress, problems and solutions. *Health Promotion International, 13*(1), 27–44.

Nutbeam, D., Smith, C., & Catford, J. (1990). Evaluation in health education: A review of progress, possibilties, and problems. *Journal of Epidemiology and Community Health, 44,* 83–89.

O'Connor, D. B., Hendrickx, H., Dadd, T., Elliman, T. D., Willis, T. A., Talbot, D., ... Dye, L. (2009). Cortisol awakening rise in middle-aged women in relation to psychological stress. *Psychoneuroendocrinology, 34*(10), 1486–1494.

O'Connor, D. B., Jones, F., Conner, M., McMillan, B., & Ferguson, E. (2008). Effects of daily hassles and eating style on eating behavior. *Health Psychology, 27*(1, Suppl), S20–S31.

O'Dea, J. A. (2003). Why do kids eat healthful food? Perceived benefits of and barriers to healthful eating and physical activity among children and adolescents. *Journal of the American Dietetic Association, 103*(4), 497.

O'Donovan, G., Blazevich, A. J., Boreham, C., Cooper, A. R., Crank, H., Ekelund, U., ... Gill, J. M. (2010). The ABC of physical activity for health: A consensus statement from the British Association of Sport and Exercise Sciences. *Journal of Sports Sciences, 28*(6), 573–591.

Office of National Statistics (2008). *Three years on: A survey of the emotional development and wellbeing of children and young people.* London: Department of Health.

Ogden, J. (2000). *Health psychology: A textbook* (2nd ed.). Buckingham: Open University Press.

Ogden, J. (2003). Some problems with social cognition models: A pragmatic and conceptual analysis. *Health Psychology, 22*, 424–428.

Ogden, J. (2004). *Health psychology: A textbook* (3rd ed.). Maidenhead: Open University Press.

Ogden, J. (2005). Exploring the impact of obesity surgery on patients' health status: A quantitative and qualitative study. *Obesity Surgery, 15*(2), 266–272.

Ogden, J. (2010). *The psychology of eating: From healthy to disordered behaviour* (2nd ed.). Oxford: Blackwell.

Ogden, J. (2012). *Health psychology: A textbook* (5th ed.). Maidenhead: Open University Press.

Ogden, J., & Sidhu, S. (2006). Adherence, behavior change, and visualization: A qualitative study of the experiences of taking an obesity medication. *Journal of Psychosomatic Research, 61*(4), 545–552.

Ogden, J., Ambrose, L., Khadra, A., Manthri, S., Symons, L., Vass, A., & Williams, M. (2001). A questionnaire study of GPs' and patients' beliefs about the different components of patient centredness. *Patient Education and Counseling, 47*(3), 223–227.

Park, E. W. (2010). Medical jargon used in health care communication of family physician. *Korean Journal of Family Medicine, 31*(6), 453–460.

Pearce, A., Law, C., Elliman, D., Cole, T. J., & Bedford, H. (2008). Factors associated with uptake of measles, mumps, and rubella vaccine (MMR) and use of single antigen vaccines in a contemporary UK cohort: Prospective cohort study. *British Medical Journal, 336*(7647), 754–757.

Pearson, N., Atkin, A. J., Biddle, S. J. H., Gorely, T., & Edwardson, C. (2009). Patterns of adolescent physical activity and dietary behaviours. *International Journal of Behavioural Nutrition and Physical Activity, 6*(45), 1–7.

Peltola, H., Patja, A., & Leinikkii, P. (1998). No evidence for measles, mumps and rubella vaccine associated inflammatory bowel disease or autism in a 14-year prospective study. *The Lancet, 351*, 1327–1328.

Pennebaker, J. W. (1993). Putting stress into words: health, linguistic, and therapeutic implication. *Behavioral Research Therapy*, 31, pp. 539–48.

Pennebaker, J. W. (1997). Writing about emotional experiences as a therapeutic process. *Psychological Science, 8*(3), 162–166.

Peto, R. (1994). Smoking and death: The past 40 years and the next 40. *British Medical Journal, 309*(6959), 937–939.

Petrie, K. J., Booth, R. J., Pennebaker, J. W., Davison, K. P., & Thomas, M. G. (1995). Disclosure of trauma and immune response to a hepatitis B vaccination program. *Journal of Consulting and Clinical Psychology, 63*(5), 787–792.

Petrie, K. J., Fontanilla, I., Thomas, M. G., Booth, R. J., & Pennebaker, J. W. (2004). Effect of written emotional expression on immune function in patient with human immunodeficiency virus infection: A randomized trial. *Psychosomatic Medicine, 66*(2), 272–275.

Petticrew, M., Fraser, J. M., & Regan, M. F. (1999). Adverse life-events and risk of breast cancer: A meta-analysis. *British Journal of Health Psychology, 4*(1), 1–17.

References

Petty, R., & Cacioppo, J. (1986). The elaboration likelihood model of persuasion. In L. Berkowitz (Ed.), *Advances in experimental social psychology* (Vol. 19). New York: Academic Press.

Phillips, K. A., Osborne, R. H., & Giles, G. G. (2008). Psychosocial factors and survival of young women with breast cancer: A population-based prospective cohort study. *Journal of Clinical Oncology, 26,* 4666–4671.

Pinquart, M., & Sörensen, S. (2001). Gender differences in self-concept and psychological well-being in old age: A meta-analysis. *Journals of Gerontology Series B: Psychological Sciences and Social Sciences, 56*(4), P195–P213.

Plotnikoff, R. C., & Higginbotham, N. (2002). Protection motivation theory and exercise behaviour change for the prevention of coronary heart disease in a high risk, Australian representative community sample of adults. *Psychology, Health and Medicine, 7*(1), 87–98.

Polivy, J., & Herman, C. P. (1985). Dieting and binging: A causal analysis. *American Psychologist, 40,* 193–201.

Polivy, J., & Herman, C. P. (1999). Distress and eating: Why do dieters overeat? *International Journal of Eating Disorders, 26,* 153–164.

Pongracic, J. A., O'Connor, G. T., Muilenberg, M. L., Vaughn, B., Gold, D. R., Kattan, M., ... Mitchell, H. E. (2010). Differential effects of outdoor versus indoor fungal spores on asthma morbidity in inner-city children. *Journal of Allergy Clinical Immunology, 125*(3), 593–599.

Povey, R., Conner, M., Sparks, P., James, R., & Shepherd, R. (2000). The theory of planned behaviour and healthy eating: Examining additive and moderating effects of social influence variables. *Psychology and Health, 14,* 991–1006.

Prelog, M. (2006). Aging of the immune system: A risk factor for autoimmunity? *Autoimmunity Reviews, 5*(2), 136–139.

Pressman, S. D., Cohen, S., Miller, G. E., Barkin, A., Rabin, B. S., & Treanor, J. J. (2005). Loneliness, social network size, and immune response to influenza vaccination in college freshman. *Health Psychology, 24*(3), 297–306.

Prestwich, A., Lawton, R., & Conner, M. (2003). The use of implementation intentions and the decision balance sheet in promoting exercise behaviour. *Psychology and Health, 18*(6), 707–721.

Prichard, I., & Tiggeman, M. (2008). Relations among exercise type, self-objection, and body image in the fitness centre environment: The role of reasons for exercise. *Psychology of Sport and Exercise, 9*(6), 855–866.

Prochaska, J. O., & DiClemente, C. C. (1983). Stages and processes of self-change of smoking: Toward an integrative model of change. *Journal of Consulting and Clinical Psychology, 51,* 390–395.

Prochaska, J. O., Velicer, W. F., DiClemente, C. C., & Fava, J. L. (1988). Measuring processes of change: Applications to the cessation of smoking. *Journal of Consulting and Clinical Psychology, 56*(1), 520–528.

Puhl, R., & Brownell, K. D. (2001). Bias, discrimination, and obesity. *Obesity Research, 9*(12), 788–805.

Puhl, R. M., & Schwartz, M. B. (2003). If you are good you can have a cookie: How memories of childhood food rules link to adult eating behaviors. *Eating Behaviors, 4*(3), 283–293.

QAA (2010).

Rabinowitz, S., Melamed, S., Weisberg, E., Tal, D., & Ribak, J. (1992). Personal determinants of leisure-time exercise activities. *Perceptual and Motor Skills, 75,* 779–784.

Rasmussen, A. F., Marsh, J. T., & Brill, N. Q. (1957). Increased susceptibility to herpes simplex in mice subjected to avoidance-learning stress or restraint. *Experimental Biology and Medicine, 96,* 183–189.

Reed, G. M., Kemeny, M. E., Taylor, S. E., Wang, H. Y. J., & Visscher, B. R. (1994). Realistic acceptance as a predictor of decreased survival time in gay men with AIDS. *Health Psychology, 13,* 299–307.

Reichert, F. F., Barros, A. J., Domingues, M. R., & Hallal, P. C. (2007). The role of perceived personal barriers to engagement in leisure-time physical activity. *American Journal of Public Health, 97*(3), 515–519.

Reid, A. E., & Aiken, L. S. (2011). Integration of five health behaviour models: Common strengths and unique contributions to understanding condom use. *Psychology and Health*, *26*(11), 1499–1520.

Riazi, A., Pickup, J., & Bradley, C. (2004). Daily stress and glycaemic control in Type 1 diabetes: Individual differences in magnitude, direction, and timing of stress-reactivity. *Diabetes Research and Clinical Practice*, *66*(3), 237–244.

Rice, D. P. (1993). The economic cost of alcohol abuse and alcohol dependence: 1990. *Alcohol Health and Research World*, *17*(1), 10–11.

Rivis, A., Sheeran, P., & Armitage, C. J. (2006). Augmenting the theory of planned behaviour with the prototype/willingness model: Predictive validity of actor versus abstainer prototypes for adolescents' health-protective and health-risk intentions. *British Journal of Health Psychology*, *11*(3), 483–500.

Roberts, K. J. (2002). Physician–patient relationships, patient satisfaction, and antiretroviral medication adherence among HIV-infected adults attending a public health clinic. *AIDS Patient Care and STDs*, *16*(1), 43–50.

Robinson, F. P., Mathews, H. L., & Witek-Janusek, L. (2000). Stress reduction and HIV disease: A review of intervention studies using a psychoneuroimmunology framework. *Journal of the Association of Nurses in AIDS Care*, *11*(2), 87–96.

Robinson, S., & Harris, H. (2011). *Smoking and drinking among adults, 2009*. Newport: Office for National Statistics.

Rodgers, R. F., Paxton, S. J., Massey, R., Campbell, K. J., Wertheim, E. H., Skouteris, H., & Gibbons, K. (2013). Maternal feeding practices predict weight gain and obesogenic eating behaviors in young children: A prospective study. *International Journal of Behavioral Nutrition and Physical Activity*, *10*(1), 24.

Rogers, R. W. (1975). A protection motivation theory of fear appeals and attitude change. *Journal of Psychology*, *91*, 93–114.

Rolland, K., Farnhill, D., & Griffiths, R. A. (1996). Children's perceptions of their current and ideal body sizes and body mass index. *Perceptual and Motor Skills*, *82*, 651–656.

Rose, G. (1993). *The strategy of preventive medicine*. Oxford: Oxford University Press.

Rose, J. E. (1991). Transdermal nicotine and nasal nicotine administration as smoking cessation treatments. In J. A. Cocores (ed.). *The clinical management of nicotine dependence* (pp. 196–207). New York: Springer-Verlag.

Rosengren, A., Hawken, S., Ounpuu, S., Sliwa, K., Zubaid, M., & Almahmeed, W. A. (2004). Association of psychosocial risk factors with risk of acute myocardial infarction in 11,119 cases and 13,648 controls from 52 countries (the INTERHEART study): Case-control study. *The Lancet*, *364*, 953–962.

Rosengren, A., Orth-Gomer, K., Wedel, H., & Wilhelmsen, L. (1993). Stress life events, social support, and mortality in men born in 1933. *British Medical Journal*, *307*, 1102–1105.

Rosenstock, I. M. (1966). Why people use health services. *Milbank Memorial Fund Quarterly*, *44*, 94–124.

Rosenstock, I. M. (2005). Why people use health services. *Milbank Quarterly*, *83*(4), 1–32.

Ross, C. E., & Duff, R. S. (1982). Returning to the doctor: The effect of client characteristics, type of practice, and experiences with care. *Journal of Health and Social Behavior*, *23*, 119–131.

Roter, D., & Hall, J. A. (Eds.) (2006). *Doctors talking with patients/patients talking with doctors: Improving communication in medical visits* (2nd ed.). Westport, CT: Praeger.

Rotter, J. B. (1954). *Social learning and clinical psychology*. New York: Prentice-Hall.

Rotter, M. L. (1997). 150 years of hand disinfection: Semmelweis' heritage. *Hygiene and Medicine*, *22*, 332–339.

Rovio, S., Kåreholt, I., Helkala, E.-L., Viitanen, M., Winblad, B., Tuomilehto, J., ... Kivipelto, M. (2005). Leisure-time physical activity at midlife and the risk of dementia and Alzheimer's disease. *The Lancet Neurology*, *4*(11), 705–711.

Royal College of Physicians (2013). *Action on obesity: Comprehensive care for all. Report of a working party*. London: RCP.

References

Rubak, S., Sandbæk, A., Lauritzen, T., & Christensen, B. (2005). Motivational interviewing: A systematic review and meta-analysis. *British Journal of General Practice, 55*(513), 305–312.

Rubin, R. S. (2002). Will the real SMART goals please stand up. *The Industrial-Organizational Psychologist, 39*(4), 26–27.

Rucker, D., Padwal, R., Li, S. K., Curioni, C., & Lau, D. C. (2007). Long term pharmacotherapy for obesity and overweight: Updated meta-analysis. *British Medical Journal, 335*(7631), 1194–1199.

Sala, F., Krupat, E., & Rother, D. (2002). Satisfaction and the use of humour by physicians and patients. *Psychology and Health, 17,* 269–280.

Sandberg, S., Järvenpää, S., Penttinen, A., Paton, J. Y., & McCann, D. C. (2004). Asthma exacerbations in children immediately following stressful life events: A Cox's hierarchical regression. *Thorax, 59*(12), 1046–1051.

Sapolsky, R. M. (2004). *Why zebras don't get ulcers* (3rd ed.). New York: Holt Paperbacks.

Sarkar, N. N. (2008). Barriers to condom use. *European Journal of Contraception and Reproductive Health Care, 13*(2), 114–122.

Saunders, J. B., Aasland, O. G., Babor, T. F., & Grant, M. (1993). Development of the alcohol use disorders identification test (AUDIT): WHO collaborative project on early detection of persons with harmful alcohol consumption-II. *Addiction, 88*(6), 791–804.

Schillo, B. A., & Reischl, T. M. (1993). HIV-related knowledge and precautions among Michigan nurses. *American Journal of Public Health, 83,* 1438–1442.

Schnall, P. L., Landsbergis, P. A., & Baker, D. (1994). Job strain and cardiovascular disease. *Annual Review of Public Health, 15*(1), 381–411.

Schwartz, M. B., Chamblis, H. O., Brownell, K. D., Blair, S. N., & Billington, C. (2003). Weight bias among health professionals specialising in obesity. *Obesity Research, 11*(9), 1033–1039.

Schwarzer, R. (1992). *Self-efficacy: Thought control of action.* Washington, DC: Hemisphere Publishing Corporation.

Schwarzer, R. (2008). Modelling health behaviour change: How to predict and modify the adoption and maintenance of health behaviours. *Applied Psychology: An International Review, 57,* 1–29.

Schwarzer, R. (2011). The Health Action Process Approach (HAPA) retrieved 18 August 2011, from http://www.hapa-model.de/

Schwarzer, R., & Fuchs, R. (1995). Self-efficacy and health behaviours. In M. Conner & P. Norman (Eds.), *Predicting health behaviour.* Buckingham: Open University Press.

Schwarzer, R., & Luszczynska, A. (2008). How to overcome health-compromising behaviors. *European Psychologist, 13*(2), 141–151.

Schwarzer, R., Schuz, B., Ziegelmann, J. P., Lippke, S., Luszczynska, A., & Scholz, U. (2007). Adoption and maintenance of four health behaviours: Theory-guided longitudinal studies on dental flossing, seat belt use, dietary behaviour, and physical activity. *Annals of Behaviour Medicine, 33,* 156–166.

Schwarzer, R., Sniehotta, F. F., Lippke, S., Luszczynska, A., Scholz, U., Schüz, B., ... Ziegelmann, J. P. (2003). On the assessment and analysis of variables in the health action process approach: Conducting an investigation. Berlin: Freie Universeitat Berlin.

Segerstrom, S. C., & Miller, G. E. (2004). Psychological stress and the human immune system: A meta-analytic study of 30 years of inquiry. *Psychological Bulletin, 130*(4), 601–630.

Selye, H. (1936). A syndrome produced by diverse nocuous agents. *Nature, 138,* 32–33.

Selye, H. (1976). The stress concept. *Journal of Canadian Medical Association, 115*(8), 718–723.

Sheeran, P. (2002). Intention–behaviour relations: A conceptual and empirical review. In W. Strobe & M. Hewstone (Eds.), *European review of social psychology* (Vol. 12, pp. 1–36). Chichester: Wiley.

Sheeran, P., Abraham, C., & Orbell, S. (1999). Psychosocial correlates of heterosexual condom use: a meta-analysis. *Psychological Bulletin, 125*(1), 90–132.

Sheeran, P., Milne, S., Webb, T., & Gollwitzer, P. (2005). Implementation intentions and health behaviour. In M. Conner & P. Norman. (Eds.), *Predicting health behaviour* (2nd ed., pp. 276–323). Maidenhead: Open University Press.

Simon, G. E., Von Korff, M., Saunders, K., Miglioretti, D. L., Crane, P. K., van Belle, G., & Kessler, R. C. (2006). Association between obesity and psychiatric disorders in the US adult population. *Archives of General Psychiatry, 63*(7), 824–830.

Simpson, M., Buckman, R., Stewart, M., Maguire, P., Lipkin, M., Novack, D., & Till, J. (1991). Doctor–patient communication: The Toronto consensus statement. *British Medical Journal, 303*(6814), 1385–1387.

Simpson, S. H., Eurich, D. T., & Majumdar, S. R. (2006). A meta-analysis of the association between adherence to drug therapy and mortality. *British Medical Journal, 333*, 15–18.

Simsekoglu, O., & Lajunen, T. (2008). Social psychology of seat belt use: A comparison of theory of planned behavior and health belief model. *Transportation Research Part F, 11*, 181–191.

Sjöberg, L., Holm, L. E., Ullén, H., & Brandberg, Y. (2004). Tanning and risk perception in adolescents. *Health, Risk and Society, 6*(1), 81–94.

Smailbegovic, M. S., Laing, G. J., & Bedford, H. (2003). Why do parents decide against immunization? The effect of health beliefs and health professionals. *Child: Care, Health and Development, 29*(4), 303–311.

Sniehotta, F., Scholz, U., & Schwarzer, R. (2005). Bridging the intention–behaviour gap: Planning, self-efficacy, and action control in the adoption and maintenance of physical exercise. *Psychology and Health, 20*(2), 143–160.

Snow, S. J. (2002). Commentary: Sutherland, Snow and water: The transmission of cholera in the nineteenth century. *International Journal of Epidemiology, 31*(5), 908–911.

Soames-Job, R. F. (1988). Effective and ineffective use of fear in health promotion campaigns. *American Journal of Public Health, 78*(2), 163–165.

Soltani-Arabshahi, R., Wong, B., Feng, B.-J., Goldgar, D. E., Duffin, K. C., & Krueger, G. G. (2010). Obesity in early adulthood as a risk factor for psoriatic arthritis. *Archives of Dermatology, 146*(7), 721–726.

Speisman, J. C., Lazarus, R. S., Mordkoff, A., & Davison, L. (1964). Experimental reduction of stress based on ego-defense theory. *Journal of Abnormal and Social Psychology, 68*(4), 367–380.

Spencer, L., Adams, T. B., Malone, S., Roy, L., & Yost, E. (2006). Applying the transtheoretical model to exercise: A systematic and comprehensive review of the literature. *Health Promotion Practice, 7*(4), 428–443.

Spitzer, R. L., Devlin, M., Walsh, B. T., Hasin, D., Wing, R., Marcus, M., … Agras, S. (1992). Binge eating disorder: A multisite field trial of the diagnostic criteria. *International Journal of Eating Disorders, 11*(3), 191–203.

Stapleton, M., Howard-Thompson, A., George, C., Hoover, R. M., & Self, T. H. (2011). Smoking and asthma. *Journal of the American Board of Family Medicine, 24*(3), 313–322.

Stead, L. F., Perera, R., Bullen, C., Mant, D., & Lancaster, T. (2008). Nicotine replacement therapy for smoking cessation. *Cochrane Database of Systematic Reviews, 1*(1).

Steadman, L., & Quine, L. (2004). Encouraging young males to perform testicular self-examination: A simple, but effective, implementation intentions intervention. *British Journal of Health Psychology, 9*(4), 479–487.

Steadman, L., & Quine, L. (2006). An implementation intentions intervention to increase uptake of mammography. *Annals of Behavioral Medicine, 32*(2), 127–134.

Stein, M., & Miller, A. H. (1993). Stress, the immune system, and health and illness. In L. G. S. Breznitz (Ed.), *Handbook of stress: Theoretical and clinical aspects* (2nd ed., pp. 127–141). New York: Free Press.

Steptoe, A., & Wardle, J. (2001). Locus of control and health behaviour revisited: A multivariate analysis of young adults from 18 countries. *British Journal of Psychology, 92*(4), 659–672.

Steptoe, A., Wardle, J., Fuller, R., Davidsdottir, S., Davou, B., & Justo, J. (2002). Seatbelt use, attitudes, and changes in legisation: An international study. *American Journal of Preventive Medicine, 23*(4), 254–259.

Stice, E. (2001). A prospective test of the dual-pathway model of bulimic pathology: Mediating effects of dieting and negative affect. *Journal of Abnormal Psychology, 110*, 124–135.

Stirling, A. M., Wilson, P., & McConnachie, A. (2001). Deprivation, psychological distress, and consultation length in general practice. *British Journal of General Practice, 51*, 456–460.

Stocking, B. (1991). Patient's charter. *British Medical Journal, 303*(6811), 1148–1149.

Stolte, I. G., Dukers, N. H., Geskus, R. B., Coutinho, R. A., & Wit, J. B. (2004). Homosexual men change to risky sex when perceiving less threat of HIV/AIDS since availability of highly active antiretroviral therapy: A longitudinal study. *AIDS, 18*(2), 303–309.

Stone, E. G., Morton, S. C., Hulscher, M. E., Maglione, M. A., Roth, E. A., Grimshaw, J. M., … Shekelle, P. G. (2002). Interventions that increase use of adult immunization and cancer screening services: A meta-analysis. *Annals of Internal Medicine, 136*(9), 641–651.

Stroebe, W. (2011). *Social psychology and health*. Maidenhead: Open University Press.

Stroebe, W., & Stroebe, M. S. (1995). *Social psychology and health*. Buckingham: Open University Press.

Ströhle, A. (2009). Physical activity, exercise, depression and anxiety disorders. *Journal of Neural Transmission, 116*(6), 777–784.

Stunkard, A. J., Harris, J. R., Pedersen, N. L., & McClearn, G. E. (1990). The body-mass index of twins who have been reared apart. *New England Journal of Medicine, 322*(21), 1483–1487.

Sugiyama, T., Healy, G. N., Dunstan, D. W., Salmon, J., & Owen, N. (2008). Joint associations of multiple leisure-time sedentary behaviours and physical activity with obesity in Australian adults. *International Journal of Behavioral Nutrition and Physical Activity, 5*(1), 35.

Sutton, S. (2001). Back to the drawing board? A review of applications of the transtheoretical model to substance use. *Addiction, 96*(1), 175–186.

Sutton, S. (2008). How does the health action process approach (HAPA) bridge the intention–behavior gap? An examination of the model's causal structure. *Applied Psychology, 57*(1), 66–74.

Sutton, S., Wardle, J., Taylor, T., McCaffery, K., Williamson, S., Edwards, R., … Atkin, W. (2000). Predictors of attendance in the United Kingdom flexible sigmoidoscopy screening trial. *Journal of Medical Screening, 7*, 99–104.

Syrjälä, A. M. H., Niskanen, M. C., & Knuuttila, M. L. (2002). The theory of reasoned action in describing tooth brushing, dental caries and diabetes adherence among diabetic patients. *Journal of Clinical Periodontology, 29*(5), 427–432.

Tamres, L. K., Janicki, D., & Helgeson, V. S. (2002). Sex differences in coping behavior: A meta-analytic review and an examination of relative coping. *Personality and Social Psychology Review, 6*(1), 2–30.

Tataranni, P., Harper, I., Snitker, S., Del Parigi, A., Vozarova, B., Bunt, J., … Ravussin, E. (2003). Body weight gain in free-living Pima Indians: Effect of energy intake vs expenditure. *International Journal of Obesity, 27*(12), 1578–1583.

Tayafian, S. S., Aghamolaei, T., Gregory, D., & Madani, A. (2011). Prediction of seat belt use among Iranian automobile drivers: Application of the theory of planned behaviour and the health belief model. *Traffic Injury Prevention, 12*(1), 48–53.

Taylor, S. E. (2006). *Health psychology* (6th ed.). New York: McGraw-Hill.

Taylor, S. E., & Seeman, T. E. (1999). Psychosocial resources and the SES–health relationship. *Annals of the New York Academy of Science, 896*, 210–225.

Taylor, S. E., Kemeny, M. E., Reed, G. H., Bower, J. E., & Gruenewald, T. L. (2000). Psychological resources, positive illusions and health. *American Psychologist, 55*(1), 99–109.

Teesson, M., Hall, W., Proudfoot, H., & Degenhardt, L. (2012). *Addictions* (2nd ed.). Hove: Psychology Press.

Teh, W. T., Teede, H., Paul, E., Harrison, C. L., Wallace, E. M., & Allan, C. (2011). Risk factors for gestational diabetes mellitus: Implications for the application of screening guidelines. *Australian and New Zealand Journal of Obsterics and Gynaecology, 51*(1), 26–30.

Telama, R., Yang, X., Viikari, J., Välimäki, I., Wanne, O., & Raitakari, O. (2005). Physical activity from childhood to adulthood: A 21-year tracking study. *American Journal of Preventive Medicine, 28*(3), 267–273.

Thirlaway, K., & Upton, D. (2009). *The psychology of lifestyle: Promoting health behaviour*. Abingdon: Routledge.

Thomas, D. B., Gao, D. L., Ray, R. M., Wang, W. W., Allison, C. J., Chen, F. L., ... Self, S. G. (2002). Randomized trial of breast self-examination in Shanghai: Final results. *Journal of the National Cancer Institute, 94*(19), 1445–1457.

Thompson, M. A., & Gray, J. J. (1995). Development and validation of a new body-image assessment scale. *Journal of Personality Assessment, 64*(2), 258–269.

Todd, J., Currie, C., & Smith, R. (2000). *Health behaviours of Scottish schoolchildren: Technical report 3. Eating patterns and physical activity in the 1990s.* Edinburgh: RUHBC and HEBS.

Tolar, A. (1978). Some antecedents and personality correlates of health locus of control. *Psychological Reports, 43*, 1159–1165.

Tolvanen, M., Lahti, S., Miettunen, J., & Hausen, H. (2012). Relationship between oral health-related knowledge, attitudes and behavior among 15–16-year-old adolescents: A structural equation modelling approach. *Acta Odontologica Scandinavia, 70*(2), 169–176.

Torgerson, J., & Sjöström, L. (2001). The Swedish Obese Subjects (SOS) study: Rationale and results. *International Journal of Obesity. Supplement, 25*(1), S2–S4.

Toschke, A. M., Küchenhoff, H., Koletzko, B., & Kries, R. (2005). Meal frequency and childhood obesity. *Obesity Research, 13*(11), 1932–1938.

Towle, A., & Godolphin, W. (1999). Framework for teaching and learning informed shared decision making. *British Medical Journal, 319*(7212), 766–771.

Trost, S. G., Owen, N., Bauman, A. E., Sallis, J. F., & Brown, W. (2002). Correlates of adults' participation in physical activity: Review and update. *Medicine and Science in Sports and Exercise, 34*, 1996–2001.

Tsutsumi, A., Kayaba, K., & Ishikawa, S. (2011). Impact of occupational stress on stroke across occupational classes and genders. *Social Science and Medicine, 72*(10), 1652–1658.

Tuckett, D., Boulton, M., Olson, C., & Williams, A. (1985). *Meetings between experts.* London: Tavistock.

Tuldrà, A., Fumaz, C. R., Ferrer, M. J., Bayés, R., Arnó, A., Balagué, M., ... Clotet, B. (2000). Prospective randomized two-arm controlled study to determine the efficacy of a specific intervention to improve long-term adherence to highly active antiretroviral therapy. *JAIDS: Journal of Acquired Immune Deficiency Syndromes, 25*(3), 221–228.

Tuthill, A., Slawik, H., O'Rahilly, S., & Finer, N. (2006). Psychiatric co-morbidities in patients attending specialist obesity services in the UK. *Quarterly Journal of Medicine, 10*, 1–9.

United States Department of Agriculture (1992). *The Food Guide Pyramid.* Washington DC: USDA.

Van den Eijnden, R. J. J. M., Spikerman, R., & Engels, R. C. M. E. (2006). Relative contribution of smoker prototypes in predicting smoking among adolescents: A comparison with factors from the theory of planned behaviour. *European Addiction Research, 12*(3), 113–120.

van Sluijs, E. M., McMinn, A. M., & Griffin, S. J. (2007). Effectiveness of interventions to promote physical activity in children and adolescents: Systematic review of controlled trials. *British Medical Journal, 335*:703.

Vedhara, K., Bennett, P. D., Clark, S., Lightman, S.L., Shaw, S., Perks, P., Hunt, M.A., Philip, J.M., Tallon, D., Murphy, P.J., Jones, R.W., Wilcock, G.K., Shanks, N.M. Enhancement of antibody responses to influenza vaccination in the elderly following a cognitive-behavioural stress management intervention. *Psychotherapy and Psychosomatics, , 72*(5), pp. 245–252.

Vedhara, K. (2003). Enhancement of antibody responses to influenza in the elderly following a cognitive-behavioural stress management intervention. *Psychotherapy Psychosomatic, 72*, 245–252.

Vedhara, K., & Irwin, M. E. (2005). *Human psychoneuroimmunology.* Oxford: Oxford University Press.

Vermeire, E., Hearnshaw, H., Rätsep, A., Levasseur, G., Petek, D., van Dam, H., ... Dale, J. (2007). Obstacles to adherence in living with type-2 diabetes: An international qualitative study using meta-ethnography (EUROBSTACLE). *Primary Care Diabetes, 1*(1), 25–33.

References

Vögele, C. (2005). Etiology of obesity. In S. Munsch & C. Beglinger (Eds.), *Obesity and binge eating disorder* (pp. 62–73). Basel, Karger: Bibl Psychiatr.

Vögele, C., & Woodward, H. (2005). Körperbild, Diätverhalten und körperliche Aktivität bei 9–10 jährigen Kindern [Body image, dietary behaviour and physical activity in 9–10-year-old children]. *Kindheit und Entwicklung (Themenheft Essstörungen bei Kindern und Jugendlichen), 14,* 229–236.

Voils, C. I., Steffens, D. C., Flint, E. P., & Bosworth, H. B. (2005). Social support and locus of control as predictors of adherence to antidepressant medication in an elderly population. *American Journal of Geriatric Psychology, 13*(2), 157–165.

Waggoner, S. E. (2003). Cervical cancer. *The Lancet, 361*(9376), 2217–2225.

Wakefield, A. J., Murch, S. H., Anthony, A., Linnell, J., Casson, D. M., Malik, M., … Walker-Smith, J. A. (1998). Ileal-lymphoid-nodular hyperplasia, non-specific colitis, and pervasive developmental disorder in children. *The Lancet, 351*(9103), 637–641.

Walboomers, J. M., Jacobs, M. V., Manos, M. M., Bosch, F. X., Kummer, J. A., Shah, K. V., … Munoz, N. (1999). Human papillomavirus is a necessary cause of invasive cervical cancer worldwide. *Journal of Pathology, 189*(1), 12–19.

Walburn, J., Vedhara, K., Hankins, M., Rixon, L., & Weinman, J. (2009). Psychological stress and wound healing in humans: A systematic review and meta-analysis. *Journal of Psychosomatic Research, 67*(3), 253–271.

Wald, N. J., & Hackshaw, A. K. (1996). Cigarette smoking: An epidemiological overview. *British Medical Bulletin, 52*(1), 3–11.

Walker, J. (2001). *Control and the psychology of health.* Buckingham: Open University Press.

Wallace, L. S. (2002). Osteoporosis prevention in college women: Application of the expanded health belief model. *American Journal of Health Behaviour, 26,* 163–172.

Waller, J., McCaffery, K. J., Forrest, S., & Wardle, J. (2004). Human papillomavirus and cervical cancer: Issues for biobehavioral and psychosocial research. *Annals of Behavioral Medicine, 27*(1), 68–79.

Wallston, K. A. (1992). Hocus-pocus, the focus isn't strictly on locus: Rotter's social learning theory modified for health. *Cognitive Therapy and Research, 16,* 183–199.

Wallston, K. A., Wallston, B. S., & DeVellis, R. (1978). Development of multidimensional health locus of control (MHLC) scales. *Health Education Monographs, 6,* 160–170.

Walsh, K., & Alexander, G. (2000). Alcoholic liver disease. *Postgraduate Medicine, 76,* 280–286.

Walter, L., Broughton, J., & Buckle, G. (2007). *Mobile phone and seat belt usage rates in London 2007.* Wokingham: TRL Ltd.

Wang, F., Orpana, H. M., Morrison, H., de Groh, M., Dai, S., & Luo, W. (2012). Long-term association between leisure-time physical activity and changes in happiness: Analysis of the Prospective National Population Health Survey. *American Journal of Epidemiology, 176*(12), 1095–1100.

Warburton, D. E., Nicol, C. W., & Bredin, S. S. (2006). Health benefits of physical activity: The evidence. *Canadian Medical Association Journal, 174*(6), 801–809.

Wardle, J., Cooke, L. J., Gibson, E. L., Sapochnik, M., Sheiham, A., & Lawson, M. (2003). Increasing children's acceptance of vegetables: A randomized trial of parent-led exposure. *Appetite, 40*(2), 155–162.

Webb, T. L., Sheeran, P., & Luszczynska, A. (2009). Planning to break unwanted habits: Habit strength moderates implementation intention effects on behaviour change. *British Journal of Social Psychology, 48*(3), 507–523.

Weinman, J., Petrie, K. J., Moss–Morris, R., & Horne, R. (1996). The Illness Perception Questionnaire: A new method for assessing the cognitive representation of illness. *Psychology and Health, 11*(3), 431–445.

Weinstein, N. (1984). Why it won't happen to me: Perceptions of risk factors and susceptibility. *Health Psychology, 3,* 431–457.

Weinstein, N. (1987). Unrealistic optimism about illness susceptibility: Conclusion from a community-wide sample. *Journal of Behavioural Medicine, 10,* 481–500.

Weinstein, N. D. (1982). Unrealistic optimism about susceptibility to health problems. *Journal of Behavioural Medicine, 5,* 441–460.

Weinstein, N. D., Marcus, S. E., & Moser, R. P. (2005). Smokers' unrealistic optimism about their risk. *Tobacco Control*, *14*(1), 55–59.

Weinstock, M. A., Rossi, J. S., Redding, C. A., & Maddock, J. E. (2002). Randomized controlled community trial of the efficacy of a multicomponent stage-matched intervention to increase sun protection among beachgoers. *Preventive Medicine*, *35*(6), 584–592.

Weiss, G. L., & Larson, D. L. (1990). Health value, health locus of control, and the prediction of health protective behaviours. *Social Behaviour and Personality*, *18*, 121–136.

West, R. (2004). ABC of smoking cessation: Assessment of dependence and motivation to stop smoking. *British Medical Journal*, *328*(7435), 338–339.

West, R. (2005). Time for a change: Putting the transtheoretical (stages of change) model to rest. *Addiction*, *100*(8), 1036–1039.

Whelton, S. P., Chin, A., Xin, X., & He, J. (2002). Effect of aerobic exercise on blood pressure: A meta-analysis of randomized, controlled trials. *Annals of Internal Medicine*, *136*(7), 493–503.

Wilkinson, D., & Abraham, C. (2004). Constructing an integrated model of the antecedents of adolescent smoking. *British Journal of Health Psychology*, *9*(3), 315–333.

Williams, E. S., Lawrence, E. R., Campbell, K. S., & Spiehler, S. (2009). The effect of emotional exhaustion and depersonalization on physician–patient communication: A theoretical model, implications, and directions for future research. *Health Care Management*, *8*, 3–20.

Williamson, D. A., Lawson, O. J., Brooks, E. R., Wozniak, P. J., Ryan, D., Bray, G. A., & Duchmann, E. G. (1995). Association of body mass with dietary restraint and disinhibition. *Appetite*, *25*, 31–41.

Wind, M., Bourdeaudhuij, I., Velde, S. J., Sandvik, C., Due, P., Klepp, K. I., & Brug, J. (2006). Correlates of fruit and vegetable consumption among 11-year-old Belgian-Flemish and Dutch schoolchildren. *Journal of Nutrition Education and Behavior*, *38*(4), 211–221.

Witte, K., & Allen, M. (2000). A meta-analysis of fear appeals: Implications for effective public health campaigns. *Health Education and Behavior*, *27*(5), 591–615.

Wolden, S. L., Hancock, S. L., Carlson, R. W., Goffinet, D. R., Jeffrey, S. S., & Hoppe, R. T. (2000). Management of breast cancer after Hodgkin's disease. *Journal of Clinical Oncology*, *18*(4), 765–772.

Wong, C. L., & Mullan, B. A. (2009). Predicting breakfast consumption: An application of the theory of planned behaviour and the investigation of past behaviour and executive fuction. *British Journal of Health Psychology*, *14*, 489–504.

Woods, C., Mutrie, N., & Scott, M. (2002). Physical activity intervention: A transtheoretical model-based intervention designed to help sedentary young adults become active. *Health Education Research*, *17*(4), 451–460.

World Health Organisation (1948). *Constitution of the World Health Organisation*. Geneva: WHO Basic Documents.

World Health Organisation (1984). *Health promotion: A WHO discussion document on the concepts and principles*. Geneva: WHO.

World Health Organisation (1990). *Diet, nutrition, and the prevention of chronic diseases*. Geneva: WHO.

World Health Organisation (1999). *World health report 1998: Life in the 21st century. A vision for all*. Geneva: WHO.

World Health Organisation (2002). *The world health report: Reducing risks, promoting healthy life*. Geneva: WHO.

World Health Organisation (2011). *WHO report on the global tobacco epidemic, 2011: Warning about the dangers of tobacco*. Geneva: WHO.

Wrosch, C., Scheier, M. F., Miller, G. E., Schulz, R., & Carver, C. S. (2003). Adaptive self-regulation of unattainable goals: Goal disengagement, goal reengagement, and subjective well-being. *Personality and Social Psychology Bulletin*, *29*(12), 1494–1508.

Wyler, A. R., Masuda, M., & Holmes, T. H. (1971). Magnitude of life events and seriousness of illness. *Psychosomatic Medicine*, *33*, 112–115.

Yanovski, S. Z. (1995). The chicken or the egg: Binge eating disorder and dietary restraint. *Appetite*, *24*, 258.

References

Yarbrough, S. S., & Braden, C. J. (2001). Utility of health belief model as a guide for explaining or predicting breast cancer screening behaviours. *Journal of Advanced Nursing*, *33*(5), 677–688.

Zachariae, R., Pedersen, C. G., Jensen, A. B., Ehrnrooth, E., Rossen, P. B., & Maase, H. V. D. (2003). Association of perceived physician communication style with patient satisfaction, distress, cancer-related self efficacy, and perceived control over the disease. *British Journal of Cancer*, *88*, 658–665.

Zhu, M., Cummings, P., Chu, H., & Cook, L. J. (2007). Association of rear seat safety belt use with death in a traffic crash: A matched cohort study. *Injury Prevention*, *13*(3), 183–185.

Zoorob, R., Anderson, R., Cefalu, C., & Sidani, M. (2001). Cancer screening guidelines. *American Family Physician*, *63*(6), 1101–1112.

Zwerling, A., Behr, M. A., Verma, A., Brewer, T. F., Menzies, D., & Pai, M. (2011). The BCG World Atlas: A database of global BCG vaccination policies and practices. *PLoS Medicine*, *8*(3), e1001012.

Index

Emboldened entries refer to those appearing in the glossary.

operant conditioning 7, 74, 87, 184
opioids 73
opportunistic screening 119
optimistic bias 31–2, 36, 96, 184
oral hygiene *see* dental care
Orlistat 78
Orth-Gomer, K. 138
Our healthier nation (1998) 15–16
outcome expectancies 27, 42, 47,
    123, 184

panic attacks 9
parasympathetic nervous system 9, 184
Parcel, G. S. 50
Park, E. W. 157
pathogens 5, 6, 10, 177, 184
patient-centred approach 153–4, 158, 163
patient satisfaction 155, 160–1, 166
Pennebaker, J. W. 147
perceived behavioural control (PBC) 33,
    34, 35, 36
  definition of 184
  medical adherence 165
  smoking 96
  tooth brushing 112
perceptions and practicalities approach
    (PAPA) 163, 164–5, 169
peripheral nervous system (PNS) 9, 136
personality
  Freudian theory 7
  HIV progression 145
  humoral theory 5
  theory of planned behaviour 33
Petrie, K. J. 147, 165
Petticrew, M. 109
physical activity 3, 11, 12, 16, 36, 64
  behaviour change techniques 55
  exercise programmes 180
  health action process approach 43
  health belief model 23
  health locus of control 25
  health promotion 69–72
  implementation-intentions 48
  intention-behaviour gap 41
  social cognitive theory 28
  theory of planned behaviour 34
  transtheoretical model of change 46
physical inactivity 13, 14, 68, 76

Plotnikoff, R. C. 30
policy 14–15
population screening 119–20
postnatal depression 142–3
Potamianos, G. 112
poverty 15
PRECEDE/PROCEED model 50–2,
    53, 184
premature mortality 13–15, 36, 69,
    74, 95, 184
prevention 4, 12, 96, 185
prevention paradox 125
preventive health behaviours 101–16
  hand washing 57, 109, 110–11
  immunisation 4, 118, 124–30, 131
  screening 4, 23, 24, 41, 118, 119–24,
    130, 131, 158
  seat belt use 23, 25, 43, 108–9, 114
  sexual health 103–8
  tooth brushing 25, 34, 112–13
problem-focused coping 141, 142,
    148, 179, 185
processes of change 45
Prochaska, O. J. 188
Project MATCH 92, 93
Propert, K. 126
prostate cancer 123, 146
protection motivation theory (PMT)
    29–32, 47–8, 185
provider behaviour 155
psychoneuroimmunology (PNI) 7,
    144–6, 148–50, 185
psycho-social interventions 91–2, 185
psychosomatic medicine 7

Rahe, R. H. 137
randomised controlled trials (RCTs)
    52, 71, 167
recall 166
Reed, G. M. 145
Reid, A. E. 105
reinforcement 7, 25, 45, 57, 186
relapse prevention 45, 55, 78,
    97–8, 186
religion 5
respiratory disease 11–12, 13
respiratory system 9
response efficacy 30, 31